The Bright Pearls that the Compilers of the Six Books Agreed Upon

Madīnah Academic Center for Serving the Qur'an and Sunnah

Published by Tahdhīb Channel

Introduction

In the name of Allah, the Most Compassionate, the Most Merciful.

All praise is due to Allah; we praise Him and seek His help and forgiveness.

We seek refuge with Allah from the evil of our selves and from our bad deeds.

Whoever Allah guides, none can lead astray, and whoever He leads astray, none can guide.

I bear witness that none is worthy of worship but Allah, and I bear witness that Muhammad is His slave and messenger.

To proceed:

The Sunnah is the second source of legislation in Islam, and it is unanimously regarded by Muslims as an independent source.

The Sunnah and Qur'an are correlated and inseparable.

The Qur'an cannot be properly understood and cannot provide its ultimate benefit without the Sunnah.

The Sunnah is a guardian of the Qur'an; were it not for the Sunnah, anyone could say whatever he liked about the Qur'an.

Out of His favor upon this Ummah, Allah Almighty endowed it with distinguished figures and select elite, at its early stage, who devoted themselves to serving the pure Sunnah. They gathered it directly from those who heard it and collected it from those who memorized it. To this end, they expended their wealth and lifetime. Thanks to their great effort, we have many huge books that comprise the legacy of our Prophet (may Allah's peace and blessings be upon him). It is because of this that they merit the pleasure of Allah Almighty and deserve gratitude and honor.

Those widely renowned books include the following:

Al-Jāmi' Al-Sahīh by Al-Bukhāri

Al-Jāmi' Al-Sahīh by Muslim

Jāmi' Al-Tirmidhi

Sunan Abu Dāwūd

Sunan Al-Nasā'i

Sunan Ibn Mājah

Muslim scholars devoted attention to the books of Sunnah in general and to those Six Books in particular: Al-Bukhāri, Muslim, Abu Dāwūd, Al-Tirmidhi, Al-Nasā'i, and Ibn Mājah. They gave extraordinary attention to these books, in terms of their chains of transmission and texts. So, they memorized, verified, arranged, abridged, and commented on these important compilations.

As another manifestation of this interest, scholars compiled the Hadīths whose Takhrīj (verification and authentication) is subject to agreement among the compilers of the Six Books. The first to undertake such a great endeavor was Imam Ibn al-Athīr (d. 606 AH) (may Allah have mercy upon him)

in his book Jāmi' Al-Usūl fi Ahādīth Al-Rasūl. However, he counted Al-Muwatta' for Imam Mālik

among the Six Books, following the approach of the earlier scholars. Latter scholars of Hadīth, on the other hand, replaced Al-Muwatta' with Sunan Ibn Mājah, something which became common and traditional among scholars.

Scholars who wrote on this topic include Imam Al-Hāfizh 'Alā' al-Dīn Maghlatāy (d. 762 AH). He authored a book titled Al-Durar Al-Manzhūm min Kalām Al-Mustafa Al-Ma'sūm. However, he only cited the Hadīths on Islamic rulings and excluded other Hadīths.

Among the contemporary scholars is Dr. 'Awwād al-Khalaf, who penned a book titled Saḥīḥ Al-Huffāẓh mimma Ittafaqa 'alayhi Al-A'immah Al-Sittah. But he did not follow the traditional way of counting the Hadīths.

For example, if a Hadīth is reported by a certain Companion and narrated in only four of the Six Books, and another version of the Hadīth is reported by another Companion and narrated in two of the Six Books, in such a case the scholars of Hadīth do not consider this Hadīth one of the Hadīths whose Takhrīj is subject to agreement among the compilers of the Six Books; rather, they deem it two separate Hadīths. Dr. 'Awwād, on the other hand, regards the two Hadīths as one and counts it among the Hadīths whose Takhrīj is subject to agreement among the compilers of the Six Books.

Hence, there was still a need for compiling a book that comprises the Hadīths whose Takhrīj is agreed upon among the compilers of the Six Books, taking into consideration the methodology adopted by the scholars of Hadīth.

It is a favor from Allah that He enabled us to contribute to this great work under the auspices of Madīnah Academic Center for Serving the Qur'an and Sunnah by writing this book, which we called Al-La'āli' Al-Muḍī'ah fima Ittafaqa 'alayhi As-ḥāb Al-Kutub Al-Sittah.

The Book Methodology:

In this book, we have adopted the following methodology:

1. We include in this book the Hadīths for which the compilers of the Six Books made Takhrīj via one Companion. If there are two Companions, even if the Hadīth's wording is the same, we deem it as two Hadīths as per the rule established among the scholars of Hadīth.

An example is a Hadīth reported by Anas who said:

"The Prophet (may Allah's peace and blessings be upon him) forbade using animals as targets."

The Hadīth, as reported by Anas, is narrated in the Six Books, except for Al-Tirmidhi who narrated it through Abu al-Dardā'. Therefore, we did not include it in this book.

2. The Hadīths are arranged by topic in accordance with the order adopted in Saḥīḥ Muslim, for it is the best book in terms of arrangement.

3. The wordings included in the book are those narrated by Al-Bukhāri, given his great care in this regard.

4. We only mention the name of the Companion in a chain of transmission for the sake of brevity. And we may also mention the name of the succeeding Tābi'i (one who met a Companion and died as a Muslim),

if contextually needed.

We have greatly benefited from the book Al-Lu'lu' wa Al-Marjān by Shaykh Fu'ād 'Abd al-Bāqi, for he compiled therein the Hadīths on which both Al-Bukhāri and Muslim agreed on its Takhrīj.

Nonetheless, we corrected the author with regard to some Hadīths, which he did not include in his book.

Benefits of this book:

1. We compiled in this book the Hadīths whose original versions were subject to Takhrīj by the famous Six Compilers of Hadīth, namely Al-Bukhāri, Muslim, Abu Dāwūd, Al-Tirmidhi, Al-Nasā'i, and Ibn Mājah. Indeed, these are the most authentic among the Prophet's reported statements.

2. Undoubtedly, whoever wants to memorize the Six Books should first begin with the Hadīths agreed upon among those six scholars, and then memorize the Hadīths agreed upon between Al-Bukhāri and Muslim, then the Hadīths narrated by Al-Bukhāri alone, then the Hadīths narrated by Muslim alone, and then the additional Hadīths narrated by each of the four Imams and that agree with the conditions of both Al-Bukhāri and Muslim or one of them.

3. The book is short and easy to read, use, and benefit from.

This idea first originated thanks to a suggestion from brother Kamrān Malik, director of Tahdhīb Channel. May Allah accept this from him, reward him, and increase his keenness to serve and spread the Sunnah.

Finally, I would like to thank the researchers Shaykh Muhammad Sa'dullah Khān, Shaykh Hāfizh Ahmad, and Shaykh 'Abdullah Nūr for the great efforts they made in collecting the Hadīths, extracting them from the Six Books, and arranging them in accordance with the approach of the scholars of Hadīth. May Allah reward them abundantly for what they did for us and all Muslims.

In conclusion, I would like to note that the administration of Madīnah Academic Center for Serving the Qur'an and Sunnah played a big part in writing and publishing this book.

I implore Allah Almighty to enable those in charge of this center and all who support it and work in it to serve His religion and spread the Sunnah of His Prophet (may Allah's peace and blessings be upon him), and I ask Him to bless their efforts and guide them to what He likes and is pleased with.

May Allah accept this work from us, render it sincerely done for His sake, and record it among our good deeds to benefit us on a day when no wealth or children will be of any avail; indeed, He is All-Hearing, Responsive.

'Uthmān Safdar

Director of Madīnah Academic Center for Serving the Qur'an and Sunnah

Book of Faith

Chapter: The call to the two testimonies and Islamic teachings

Ibn 'Abbās (may Allah be pleased with him) reported that the Messenger of Allah (may Allah's peace and blessings be upon him) said to Mu'ādh ibn Jabal as he was sending him to Yemen: "You will come to a people of the Scripture. When you reach them, invite them to testify that there is no true god but Allah and that Muhammad is His Messenger. If they obey you in that, tell them that Allah has enjoined on them five prayers every day and night. If they obey you in that, tell them that Allah has enjoined Zakah on them, to be taken from the rich amongst them and given to the poor amongst them. If they obey you in that, beware of taking their best properties; and fear the invocation of an oppressed person, for there is no barrier between his invocation and Allah."

Sahīh Al-BukhāriBook of ZakahCapter: Taking Zakah from the rich and giving it to the poor, wherever they are; Hadīth no. 1496.Sahīh MuslimBook of FaithChapter: The call to the two testimonies and Islamic teachings; Hadīth no. 19.Sunan Abu DāwudBook of ZakahChapter: Zakah on grazing livestock; Hadīth no. 1584.Jāmi' At-TirmidhiBook of ZakahAs reported from the Prophet (may Allah's peace and blessings be upon him)Chapter: What is reported on the undesirability of taking the best property as Zakah; Hadīth no. 625.Sunan An-Nasā'iBook of ZakahChapter: The Obligation of Zakah; Hadīth no. 2435.Sunan Ibn MājahBook of ZakahChapter: Ordaining Zakah; Hadīth no. 1783.Chapter: The command to fight peopleuntil they say there is no true god but Allah, Muhammad is the Messenger of Allah.Abu Hurayrah (may Allah be pleased with him) reported: When the Messenger of Allah (may Allah's peace and blessings be upon him) passed away and Abu Bakr (may Allah be pleased with him) became Caliph, and some of the Arabs apostatized, 'Umar (may Allah be pleased with him) said: "How can you fight the people when the Messenger of Allah (may Allah's peace and blessings be upon him) said: 'I was commanded to fight people until they say 'there is no true god but Allah'; and whoever says it, their property and lives become safe from me, except when justified by law, and their reckoning will be with Allah'?" He replied: "By Allah, I will surely fight those who made a distinction between prayer and Zakah, for Zakah is the right in wealth. By Allah, if they withhold from me as much as a rope that they used to give to the Messenger of Allah (may Allah's peace and blessings be upon him), I will definitely fight them for withholding it!" 'Umar (may Allah be pleased with him) said: "By Allah, when Allah made Abu Bakr incline to this (approach), I knew it was the right thing."Sahīh Al-BukhāriBook of ZakahChapter: The obligation of Zakah; Hadīth no. 9931, 0041.Sahīh MuslimBook of FaithChapter:

The command to fight people until they say there is no true god but Allah, Muhammad is the Messenger of Allah; Hadīth no. 02.Sunan Abu DāwudBook of ZakahHadīth no. 6551.Jāmi' At-TirmidhiBook of Faith as reported from the prophet (PBUH)Chapter: What is reported on "I have been commanded to fight people until they say there is no true god but Allah"; Hadīth no. 7062.Sunan An-Nasā'iBook of ZakahChapter: The withholder of Zakah; Hadīth no. 3442.Sunan Ibn MājahBook of TribulationsChapter: Refraining from fighting the one who says there is no true god but Allah; Hadīth no. 7293.

Chapter: The branches of faith

Abu Hurayrah (may Allah be pleased with him) reported that the Prophet (may Allah's peace and blessings be upon him) said: "Faith consists of sixty-something branches; and modesty is a branch of faith."

Sahīh Al-BukhāriBook of FaithChapter: Matters of faith; Hadīth no. 9.

Sahīh Muslim

Book of Faith

Chapter: Branches of faith; Hadīth no. 53.

Sunan Abu Dāwud

Book of Sunnah

Chapter: Refutation of Irjā'; Hadīth no. 6764.

Jāmi' At-Tirmidhi

Book of Faith as reported from the prophet (PBUH)

Chapter: What is reported on completing faith and its increase and decrease; Hadīth no. 4162.

Sunan An-Nasā'i

Book of Faith and its Tenets

Chapter: Mention of the branches of faith; Hadīth no. 5005.

Sunan Ibn Mājah

Introduction of Ibn Mājah

Chapter: Regarding faith; Hadīth no. 75.

Ibn 'Umar (may Allah be pleased with him) reported that the Messenger of Allah (may Allah's peace and blessings be upon him) passed by an Ansāri man who was preaching to his brother about modesty. The Messenger of Allah (may Allah's peace and blessings be upon him) said: "Leave him, for indeed modesty is a part of faith."

Sahīh Al-Bukhāri

Book of Faith

Chapter: Modesty is a part of faith; Hadīth no. 24.

Sahīh MuslimBook of FaithChapter: Branches of faith; Hadīth no. 36.Sunan Abu DāwudBook of Good MannersChapter: Modesty; Hadīth no. 4795.Jāmi' At-TirmidhiBook of Faith reported from the Prophet (PBUH)Chapter: What is reported on modesty being a part of faith; Hadīth no. 2615.Sunan An-Nasā'iBook of Faithand its TeachingsChapter: Modesty; Hadīth no. 3305.Sunan Ibn MājahIntroduction of Ibn MājahChapter: Regarding faith; Hadīth no. 85.

Chapter: Clarifying that faith decreases by sin and that a sinner is deemed lacking in faith, meaning that his faith is incomplete

Abu Hurayrah (may Allah be pleased with him) reported that the Prophet (may Allah's peace and blessings be upon him) said: "The adulterer is not a believer while he is committing adultery. The drinker of wine is not a believer while he is drinking wine. The thief is not a believer while he is stealing. The plunderer is not a believer while he is plundering and the people are looking on."

Sahīh Al-BukhāriBook of Injustices and UsurpationChapter: Seizing what belongs to others without their permission; Hadīth no. 5742.Sahīh MuslimBook of FaithChapter: Clarifying that faith decreases by sin and that a sinner is deemed lacking in faith, meaning that his faith is incomplete; Hadīth no. 75.Sunan Abu DāwudBook of SunnahChapter: Proof of increase and decrease of faith; Hadīth no. 9864.Jāmi' At-TirmidhiBook of Faith reported from the Prophet (PBUH)Chapter: The Hadīth: An adulterer is not a believer while he is committing adultery; Hadīth no. 5262.Sunan An-Nasā'iBook of Amputation of Thief's HandChapter: Taking theft seriously; Hadīth no. 0784.Sunan Ibn MājahBook of TribulationsChapter: Forbidding looting; Hadīth no. 6393.

Chapter: Pointing out the strictness of the prohibition of letting the clothing hang below the ankles, reminding others of the favors one did to them, and promoting goods by swearing; and clarifying the three types of people whom Allah will not speak to on the Day of Judgment, nor will He look at them or purify them, and for them will be a painful punishment.

Abu Hurayrah (may Allah be pleased with him) reported that the Prophet (may Allah's peace and blessings be upon him) said: "There are three types of people whom Allah will not speak to on the Day of Judgment, nor will He purify them, and for them will be a painful punishment: a man who has superfluous water on a way and he withholds it from wayfarers; a man who pledges allegiance to a ruler merely for worldly purposes; if he gives him what he wants, he honors his pledge; otherwise, he does not honor it; and a man who sells a commodity to another after 'Asr and he swears by Allah that he was offered such and such price, and so he believes him and takes it, although he was not offered that price."

Sahīh Al-BukhāriBook of RulingsChapter: The one who pledges allegiance to a man merely for worldly purposes; Hadīth no. 7212.Sahīh MuslimBook of FaithChapter: Pointing out the strictness of the prohibition of letting clothing hang below the ankles, reminding others of one's favors on them, and promoting goods by swearing; and clarifying the three types of people whom Allah will not speak to on the Day of Judgment, nor will He look at them nor purify them, and for them will be a painful punishment; Hadīth no. 108.Sunan Abu DāwudBook of SalesChapters on leasing/hiringChapter: Withholding water; Hadīth no. 3474.Jāmi' At-TirmidhiBook of Biographies reported from the Prophet (PBUH)Chapter: What is reported on breaking the pledge of allegiance; Hadīth no. 1595.Sunan An-Nasā'iBook of SalesChapter: Deceptive swearing in sale transactions; Hadīth no. 4462.Sunan Ibn MājahBook of TradeChapter: What is reported on the dislike of swearing in buying and selling; Hadīth no. 2207.

Chapter: The strict prohibition of killing oneself, and that whoever kills himself with something will be punished with it in Hell-fire, and that only Muslims will enter Paradise

Abu Hurayrah (may Allah be pleased with him) reported that the Prophet (may Allah's peace and blessings be upon him) said: "Whoever throws himself from a mountain and kills himself will be in

Hellfire falling down into it and abiding therein eternally forever; whoever drinks poison and kills himself with it will be carrying his poison in his hand and drinking it in Hellfire wherein he will abide eternally forever; and whoever kills himself with an iron weapon will be carrying that weapon in his hand and stabbing his abdomen with it in Hellfire wherein he will abide eternally forever."

Sahīh Al-BukhāriBook of MedicineChapter: Drinking poison and getting treated with it and with dangerous and impure things; Hadīth no. 5778.Sahīh MuslimBook of FaithChapter: The strict prohibition of killing oneself, and that whoever kills himself with something will be punished with it in Hellfire, and that only Muslims will enter Paradise; Hadīth no. 109.Sunan Abu DāwudBook of MedicineChapter: Disliked medicines; Hadīth no. 3872.Jāmi' At-TirmidhiBook of Medicine reported from the Prophet (PBUH)Chapter: What is reported on the one who kills himself with poison or something else; Hadīth no. 2044.Sunan An-Nasā'iBook of FuneralsChapter: Abandoning funeral prayer for the one who kills himself; Hadīth no. 1965.Sunan Ibn MājahBook of MedicineChapter: Prohibition of taking impure medicine; Hadīth no. 3460.

Thābit ibn Ad-Dahhāk (may Allah be pleased with him) - one of the Companions who gave the pledge of allegiance underneath the tree - reported that the Prophet (may Allah's peace and blessings be upon him) said: "Whoever swears by a religion other than Islam is as he says; the son of Adam is not bound by a vow regarding something he does not possess; whoever kills himself with something in this world will be punished with it on the Day of Judgment; whoever curses a believer, it is like killing him; and whoever accuses a believer of disbelief, it is like killing him."

Sahīh Al-BukhāriBook of Good MannersChapter: The prohibited name-calling and cursing; Hadīth no. 6047.Sahīh MuslimBook of FaithChapter: The strict prohibition of killing oneself, and that whoever kills himself with something will be punished with it in Hell-fire, and that only Muslims will enter Paradise; Hadīth no. 110.Sunan Abu DāwudBook of Oaths and VowsChapter: What is reported on swearing by disavowal of Islam and by a religion other than Islam; Hadīth no. 3257.Jāmi' At-TirmidhiBook of Faith reported from the Prophet (PBUH)Chapter: What is reported on the one who accuses a fellow Muslim of disbelief; Hadīth no. 2636.Sunan An-Nasā'iBook of Oaths and VowsChapter: Making a vow regarding something one does not possess; Hadīth no. 3813.Sunan Ibn MājahBook of ExpiationsChapter: The one who swears by a religion other than Islam; Hadīth no. 2098.Chapter: Allah pardons self-whisperings and inner thoughtsas long as they are not deeply established

Abu Hurayrah (may Allah be pleased with him) reported that the Prophet (may Allah's peace and blessings be upon him) said: "Allah pardons my followers for what they whisper to themselves or what comes to their minds, as long as they do not act upon it or speak it out."

Sahīh Al-BukhāriBook of Oaths and VowsChapter: If someone forgetfully breaks his oath; Hadīth no. 6664.Sahīh MuslimBook of FaithChapter: Allah pardons self-whisperings and inner thoughts as long as they are not deeply established; Hadīth no. 127.Sunan Abu DāwudBook of DivorceChapter: Self-whisperings regarding divorce; Hadīth no. 2209.Jāmi' At-TirmidhiBook of Divorce and Oath of Condemnation as reported from the Prophet (PBUH)Chapter: What is reported on the one who whispers to himself about divorcing his wife; Hadīth no. 1183.Sunan An-Nasā'iBook of DivorceChapter: The one who divorces his wife without uttering it; Hadīth no. 3435.Sunan Ibn MājahBook of DivorceChapter: The one who divorces his wife without uttering it; Hadīth no. 2040.Chapter: The obligation to believe in the message of our Prophet Muhammad (PBUH)to all humankind and that his religion abrogated all other religions

Abu Mūsa (may Allah be pleased with him) reported that the Prophet (may Allah's peace and blessings be upon him) said: "Three people will have a double reward: a man from the people of the Scripture who believed in his prophet and believed in Muhammad; a slave who fulfills his duty to Allah, the Almighty, and his duty to his master; and a man who has a female slave whom he properly disciplines and educates and then manumits her and marries her; for him is a double reward." 'Āmir said: "Here I have given you this (Hadīth) in return for nothing, whereas people would travel to Madīnah for less than that."

Sahīh Al-BukhāriBook of KnowledgeChapter: A man teaching his female slave and his wife; Hadīth no. 97.Sahīh MuslimBook of FaithChapter: The obligation to believe in the message of our Prophet Muhammad (PBUH) to all mankind and that his religion abrogated all other religions; Hadīth no. 154.Sunan Abu DāwudBook of MarriageChapter: A man manumits his female slave and then marries her; Ḥadīth no. 2053.Jāmiʻ At-TirmidhiBook of Marriage as reported from the Prophet (PBUH)Chapter: What is reported on the merit of this; Ḥadīth no. 1116.Sunan An-Nasā'iBook of MarriageChapter: A man manumits his female slave and then marries her; Ḥadīth no. 3344.Sunan Ibn MājahBook of MarriageChapter: A man manumits his female slave and then marries her; Ḥadīth no. 1956.

Book of Purification

Chapter: Ablution of the Prophet (PBUH)

'Abdullāh ibn Zayd (may Allah be pleased with him) was asked about the Prophet's ablution, so he asked for a vessel of water and performed ablution like that of the Prophet (may Allah's peace and blessings be upon him) in front of them. He poured water from the vessel on his hands, washing them thrice. Then, he put his hand in the vessel and rinsed his mouth and washed his nose with three handfuls. He put his hand in the water again and washed his face thrice. Then, he washed his hands twice up to the elbows, after which he put his hand in the water and passed them over his head once, bringing them to the front and to the back of his head. Then, he washed his feet up to the ankles.

Saḥīḥ Al-BukhāriBook of AblutionChapter: Washing the feet up to the ankles; Ḥadīth no. 186.Saḥīḥ MuslimBook of PurificationChapter: Ablution of the Prophet (PBUH); Ḥadīth no. 235.Sunan Abu DāwudBook of PurificationChapter: Description of the Prophet's ablution; Ḥadīth no. 118.Jāmiʻ At-TirmidhiBook of Purification as reported from the Prophet (PBUH)Chapter: The one who performs parts of his ablution twice and other parts thrice; Ḥadīth no. 47.Sunan An-Nasā'iBook of PurificationChapter: The limits in ablution; Ḥadīth no. 97.Sunan Ibn MājahBook of Purification and its SunnahsChapter: What is reported on wiping over the head; Ḥadīth no. 434.

Chapter: The tooth-stick

Abu Hurayrah (may Allah be pleased with him) reported that the Prophet (may Allah's peace and blessings be upon him) said: "Were it not that I would be overburdening my followers, I would order them to use the tooth-stick for every prayer."

Saḥīḥ Al-BukhāriBook of FridayChapter: Using the tooth-stick on Friday; Ḥadīth no.887.Saḥīḥ MuslimBook of PurificationChapter: The tooth-stick; Ḥadīth no. 252.Sunan Abu DāwudBook of PurificationChapter: The tooth-stick; Ḥadīth no. 46.Jāmiʻ At-TirmidhiBook of Purification as reported from the Prophet (PBUH)Chapter: What is reported on the tooth-stick; Ḥadīth no. 22.Sunan An-Nasā'iBook of PurificationChapter: Concession for a fasting person to use the tooth-stick at night; Ḥadīth no. 7.Sunan Ibn MājahBook of Purification and Its SunnahsChapter: The tooth-stick; Ḥadīth no. 287.

Chapter: The characteristics of Fitrah

Abu Hurayrah (may Allah be pleased with him) reported that the Prophet (may Allah's peace and blessings be upon him) said: "There are five characteristics of Fitrah: circumcision, shaving the pubes, plucking out armpit hair, clipping the nails, and trimming the mustache."

Saḥīḥ Al-BukhāriBook of ClothingChapter: Trimming the mustache; Ḥadīth no. 5889.Saḥīḥ MuslimBook of PurificationChapter: Characteristics of Fitrah; Ḥadīth no. 257.Sunan Abu DāwudBook of Hair CombingChapter: Trimming the mustache; Ḥadīth no. 4198.Jāmiʻ At-TirmidhiBook of Good Manners as reported from the Prophet (PBUH)Chapter: What is reported on nail clipping; Ḥadīth no. 2756.Sunan An-Nasā'iBook of PurificationChapter: Mention of Fitrah: Circumcision; Ḥadīth no. 9.Sunan Ibn MājahBook of Purification and Its SunnahsChapter: Fitrah; Ḥadīth no. 292.

Book: Cleaning after relieving oneself

Abu Ayyūb al-Ansāri (may Allah be pleased with him) reported that the Prophet (may Allah's peace and blessings be upon him) said: "When you relieve yourselves, do not face the Qiblah or turn your backs towards it. Rather, turn to the east or the west." Abu Ayyūb said: "We came to the Levant and found lavatories built in the direction of the Qiblah. We would turn ourselves and ask forgiveness from Allah, the Almighty."

Sahīh Al-BukhāriBook of PrayerChapter: The Qiblah for the people of Madinah, the Levant, and the East; Hadīth no. 394.Sahīh MuslimBook of PurificationChapter: Cleaning after relieving oneself; Hadīth no. 264.

Sunan Abu Dāwud

Book of Purification

Chapter: The dislike of facing the Qiblah while relieving oneself; Hadīth no. 9.

Jāmi' At-TirmidhiBook of Purification as reported from the Prophet (PBUH)Chapter: The prohibition of facing the Qiblah while defecating or urinating; Hadīth no. 8.

Sunan An-Nasā'i

Book of Purification

Chapter: The prohibition of turning one's back towards the Qiblah while relieving oneself; Hadīth no. 21.

Sunan Ibn MājahBook of Purification and Its SunnahsChapter: The prohibition of facing the Qiblah while defecating or urinating; Hadīth no. 318.

'Abdullāh ibn 'Umar (may Allah be pleased with him) related: "I went atop Hafsa's house and saw the Prophet (may Allah's peace and blessings be upon him) answering the call of nature while facing the Levant with his back towards the Qiblah."

Sahīh Al-BukhāriBook of the Allocation of One FifthChapter: What is reported on the Prophet's households and the houses ascribed to his wives; Hadīth no. 3102.Sahīh MuslimBook of PurificationChapter: Cleaning after relieving oneself; Hadīth no. 266.Sunan Abu DāwudBook of PurificationChapter: The concession in this regard; Hadīth no. 12.Jāmi' At-TirmidhiBook of Purification as reported from the Prophet (PBUH)Chapter: What is reported on the concession in this regard; Hadīth no. 11.Sunan An-Nasā'iBook of PurificationChapter: The concession in this regard inside houses; Hadīth no. 23.Sunan Ibn MājahBook of Purification and Its SunnahsChapter: The concession in this regard and its permissibility in the lavatory but not in the desert; Hadīth no. 322.

Chapter: The prohibition of using the right hand in cleaning oneself after answering the call of nature

Abu Qatādah (may Allah be pleased with him) reported that the Prophet (may Allah's peace and blessings be upon him) said: "When any one of you drinks, let him not breathe into the vessel, and when he goes to the toilet, let him not touch his penis with his right hand, nor wipe himself with his right hand."

Sahīh Al-BukhāriBook of AblutionChapter: The prohibition of using the right hand in cleaning oneself after answering the call of nature; Hadīth no. 153.Sahīh MuslimBook of PurificationChapter: The prohibition of using the right hand in cleaning oneself after answering the call of nature; Hadīth no. 267.Sunan Abu DāwudBook of PurificationChapter: The dislike of touching one's penis with the right hand while cleaning traces of urine; Hadīth no. 31.Jāmi' At-TirmidhiBook of Purification as reported from the Prophet (PBUH)Chapter: The dislike of using the right hand in cleaning oneself after answering the call of nature; Hadīth no. 15.Sunan An-Nasā'iBook of PurificationChapter: The prohibition of using the right hand in cleaning oneself after answering the call of nature; Hadīth no. 47.Sunan Ibn MājahBook of Purification and Its SunnahsChapter: The dislike of touching one's penis with the right hand and of using the right hand in cleaning oneself after answering the call of nature; Hadīth no. 310.

Chapter: Starting with the right side in ablution and other things

'A'ishah, may Allah be pleased with her, reported: "The Prophet, may Allah's peace and blessings be upon him, liked to start with the right side when wearing his sandals, combing his hair, purifying himself, and in all his affairs."

Sahīh Al-BukhāriBook of AblutionChapter: Starting with the right side in ablution and washing up; Hadīth no. 168.Sahīh MuslimBook of PurificationChapter: Starting with the right side in purification and other things; Hadīth no. 268.

Sunan Abu Dāwud

Book of Clothing

Chapter: Putting on shoes; Hadīth no. 4140.

Jāmi' At-TirmidhiBook of Friday as reported from the Prophet (PBUH)Chapter: What is recommended in starting with the right side in purification; Hadīth no. 608.Sunan An-Nasā'iBook of Washing Up and Dry AblutionChapter: Starting with the right side in purification; Hadīth no. 421.Sunan Ibn MājahBook of Purification and Its SunnahsChapter: Starting with the right side in ablution; Hadīth no. 401.

Chapter: Wiping over leather socks

Hammām ibn al-Hārith reported: I saw Jarīr ibn 'Abdullāh (may Allah be pleased with him) urinating then performing ablution and wiping over his leather socks. He then stood for prayer and prayed. He was asked about that and he said: "I saw the Prophet (may Allah's peace and blessings be upon him) do the same."

Sahīh Al-BukhāriBook of PrayerChapter: Praying while wearing leather socks; Hadīth no. 387.Sahīh MuslimBook of PurificationChapter: Wiping over leather socks; Hadīth no. 272.Sunan Abu DāwudBook of PurificationChapter: Wiping over leather socks; Hadīth no. 154.Jāmi' At-TirmidhiBook of Purification as reported from the Prophet (PBUH)Chapter: Wiping over leather socks; Hadīth no. 93.Sunan An-Nasā'iBook of the QiblahChapter: Praying while wearing leather socks; Hadīth no. 774.Sunan Ibn MājahBook of Purification and Its SunnahsChapter: What is reported on wiping over leather socks; Hadīth no. 543.

Hudhayfah (may Allah be pleased with him) reported: "The Prophet (may Allah's peace and blessings be upon him) went to the dump of some people and passed urine while standing. Then he asked for water and I brought it to him, and he performed ablution."

Sahīh Al-BukhāriBook of AblutionChapter: Urination while standing or sitting; Hadīth no. 224.Sahīh MuslimBook of PurificationChapter: Wiping over leather socks; Hadīth no. 273.Sunan Abu DāwudBook of PurificationChapter: Urination while standing; Hadīth no. 23.Jāmi' At-TirmidhiBook of Purification as reported from the Prophet (PBUH)Chapter: What is reported on the concession in this regard; Hadīth no. 13.Sunan An-Nasā'iBook of PurificationChapter: The concession for abandoning this; Hadīth no. 18.Sunan Ibn MājahBook of Purification and Its SunnahsChapter: What is reported on urination while standing; Hadīth no. 305.

Al-Mughīrah (may Allah be pleased with him) reported: "One night, I was traveling with the Prophet (may Allah's peace and blessings be upon him). He asked me: 'Do you have any water with you?' I replied: 'Yes!' So, he got off his she-camel and walked away till he disappeared in the darkness of the night. Then, he came back and I poured water for him from the waterskin. He washed his face and hands while wearing a woolen cloak from which he could not take his arms out. So, he took them out from underneath the cloak. Then, he washed his forearms and wiped over his head. I got down to take off his leather socks, but he said: 'Leave them, for I have performed ablution before putting them on.' So he wiped over them."

Sahīh Al-BukhāriBook of ClothingChapter: Wearing a woolen cloak in battle; Hadīth no. 5799.Sahīh MuslimBook of PurificationChapter: Wiping over leather socks; Hadīth no. 274.Sunan Abu DāwudBook of PurificationChapter: Wiping over leather socks; Hadīth no. 151.Jāmi' At-TirmidhiBook of Purification as reported from the Prophet (PBUH)Chapter: Wiping over the upper part of leather socks; Hadīth no. 98.Sunan An-Nasā'iBook of PurificationChapter: Wiping over leather socks; Hadīth no. 125.Sunan Ibn

MājahBook of Purification and Its SunnahsChapter: A man seeking help with his ablution and having someone pour water for him; Hadīth no. 389.

Chapter: The ruling on dogs drinking from people's vessels

Abu Hurayrah (may Allah be pleased with him) reported that the Prophet (may Allah's peace and blessings be upon him) said: "If a dog drinks from your vessel, wash it seven times."

Sahīh Al-BukhāriBook of AblutionChapter: Water used for washing a person's hair; Hadīth no. 172.Sahīh MuslimBook of PurificationChapter: The ruling on dogs drinking from people's vessels; Hadīth no. 279.Sunan Abu DāwudBook of PurificationChapter: Performing ablution with leftover water of a dog; Hadīth no. 73.Jāmi' At-TirmidhiBook of Purification as reported from the Prophet (PBUH)Chapter: What is reported on the leftover water of a dog; Hadīth no. 91.Sunan An-Nasā'iBook of PurificationChapter: The leftover water of a dog; Hadīth no. 64.Sunan Ibn MājahBook of Purification and Its SunnahsChapter: Washing a vessel after a dog drinks from it; Hadīth no. 364.

Chapter: The prohibition of urinating in still water

Abu Hurayrah (may Allah be pleased with him) reported that the Prophet (may Allah's peace and blessings be upon him) said: "None amongst you should urinate in still water, which does not flow, and then wash in it."

Sahīh Al-BukhāriBook of AblutionChapter: Urinating in still water; Hadīth no. 239.Sahīh MuslimBook of PurificationChapter: The prohibition of urinating in still water; Hadīth no. 282.Sunan Abu DāwudBook of PurificationChapter: Urinating in still water; Hadīth no. 69.Jāmi' At-TirmidhiBook of Purification as reported from the Prophet (PBUH)Chapter: The dislike of urinating in still water; Hadīth no. 68.Sunan An-Nasā'iBook of PurificationChapter: Still water; Hadīth no. 58.Sunan Ibn MājahBook of Purification and Its SunnahsChapter: The prohibition of urinating in still water; Hadīth no. 344.

Chapter: The ruling on infant's urine and how to wash it

Umm Qays bint Mihsan (may Allah be pleased with her) reported that she brought a young son of hers who had not started eating food to the Messenger of Allah (may Allah's peace and blessings be upon him), who seated him in his lap. The child urinated on the Messenger's clothes so he asked for water and sprinkled it (on the affected area) and did not wash it.

Sahīh Al-BukhāriBook of AblutionChapter: Urine of male infants; Hadīth no. 223.Sahīh MuslimBook of PurificationChapter: The ruling on infant's urine and how to wash it; Hadīth no. 287.Sunan Abu DāwudBook of PurificationChapter: Male infant's urine touching clothes; Hadīth no. 374.

Jāmi' At-Tirmidhi

Book of Purification as reported from the Prophet (PBUH)

Chapter: What is reported on sprinkling water on urine of male infant who has not started eating solid food; Hadīth no. 71.

Sunan An-Nasā'i

Book of Purification

Chapter: Urine of male infant who has not started eating solid food; Hadīth no. 302.

Sunan Ibn MājahBook of Purification and Its SunnahsChapter: What is reported on urine of male infant who has not started eating solid food; Hadīth no. 524.

Chapter: The ruling on semen

'Ā'ishah (may Allah be pleased with her) reported: "I used to wash semen off the Prophet's garment, and he would go out for prayer with water stains on his garment."

Saḥīḥ Al-BukhāriBook of AblutionChapter: Washing semen and rubbing it off and washing discharge from women; Ḥadīth no. 229.Saḥīḥ MuslimBook of PurificationChapter: The ruling on semen; Ḥadīth no. 289.Sunan Abu DāwudBook of PurificationChapter: Semen touching clothes; Ḥadīth no. 373.Jāmi' At-TirmidhiBook of Purification as reported from the Prophet (PBUH)Chapter: Washing semen off clothes; Ḥadīth no. 117.Sunan An-Nasā'iBook of PurificationChapter: Washing semen off clothes; Ḥadīth no. 294.Sunan Ibn MājahBook of Purification and Its SunnahsChapter: Semen touching clothes; Ḥadīth no. 536.

Chapter: Impurity of blood and how to wash it

Asmā' (may Allah be pleased with her) reported: "A woman came to the Prophet (may Allah's peace and blessings be upon him) and said: 'If anyone of us gets menstrual blood on her garment, what should she do?' He replied: 'She should scrape it, rub it with water, sprinkle water on it, and then she may pray wearing it.' "

Saḥīḥ Al-BukhāriBook of AblutionChapter: Washing blood; Ḥadīth no. 227.Saḥīḥ MuslimBook of PurificationChapter: Impurity of blood and how to wash it; Ḥadīth no. 291.Sunan Abu DāwudBook of PurificationChapter: Woman washing garment she wore during menses; Ḥadīth no. 360.Jāmi' At-TirmidhiBook of Purification as reported from the Prophet (PBUH)Chapter: What is reported on washing menstrual blood off clothes; Ḥadīth no. 138.Sunan An-Nasā'iBook of PurificationChapter: Menstrual blood touching clothes; Ḥadīth no. 293.Sunan Ibn MājahBook of Purification and Its SunnahsChapter: What is reported on menstrual blood touching clothes; Ḥadīth no. 629.

Chapter: Proof of the impurity of urine and the obligation to shield oneself from it

Ibn 'Abbās (may Allah be pleased with him) reported: "The Prophet (may Allah's peace and blessings be upon him) passed by two graves and said: 'They are being tortured, and they are not being tortured for a major sin. One of them would not save himself from being soiled with his urine, while the other was going about with calumnies.' He then took a green leaf of a date-palm tree, split it into two, and planted one on each grave. The people said: 'O Messenger of Allah, why did you do that?' He replied: 'I hope that their torture may be lessened until these become dry.' "

Saḥīḥ Al-BukhāriBook of AblutionChapter: What is reported on washing urine; Ḥadīth no. 218.Saḥīḥ MuslimBook of PurificationChapter: Proof of the impurity of urine and the obligation to shield oneself from it; Ḥadīth no. 292.Sunan Abu DāwudBook of PurificationChapter: Shielding oneself from urine; Ḥadīth no. 20.Jāmi' At-TirmidhiBook of Purification as reported from the Prophet (PBUH)Chapter: Taking the issue of urine seriously; Ḥadīth no. 70.Sunan An-Nasā'iBook of PurificationChapter: Shielding oneself from urine; Ḥadīth no. 31.Sunan Ibn MājahBook of Purification and Its SunnahsChapter: Taking the issue of urine seriously; Ḥadīth no. 347.

Book of Menstruation

Chapter: Foreplay with a menstruating woman above the waist-wrapper.

'Ā'ishah (may Allah be pleased with her) reported: "Whenever one of us was in her menses and the Messenger of Allah (may Allah's peace and blessings be upon him) wished to fondle her, he would ask her to put on the waist-wrapper and then he would fondle her." She added: "And who amongst you can have control over his desires as the Prophet (may Allah's peace and blessings be upon him) had over his desires."

Saḥīḥ Al-BukhāriBook of MenstruationChapter: Foreplay with a menstruating woman; Ḥadīth no. 302.Saḥīḥ MuslimBook of MenstruationChapter: Foreplay with a menstruating woman above the waist-wrapper; Hadīth no. 293.Sunan Abu DāwudBook of PurificationChapter: Man having intimacy with her without copulation; Hadīth no. 273.Jāmi' At-TirmidhiBook of Purification as reported from the Prophet (PBUH)Chapter: What is reported on foreplay wiht a menstruating woman; Hadīth no. 132.Sunan An-Nasā'iBook of PurificationChapter: Foreplay with a menstruating woman; Hadīth no. 286.Sunan Ibn MājahBook of Purification and Its SunnahsChapter: What a man can enjoy in his menstruating wife; Hadīth no. 635.

Chapter: The recommended amount of water in ritual bath and man and wife taking ritual bath together from the same vessel while in the same state and with one using water left by the other

'Ā'ishah (may Allah be pleased with her) reported: "The Prophet (may Allah's peace and blessings be upon him) and I used to take a bath from one vessel called Faraq."

Sahīh Al-BukhāriBook of the Ritual BathChapter: Man and wife taking ritual bath together; Hadīth no. 250.Sahīh MuslimBook of MenstruationChapter: The recommended amount of water in ritual bath and man and wife taking ritual bath together from the same vessel while in the same state and with one using water left by the other; Hadīth no. 319.Sunan Abu DāwudBook of PurificationChapter: The sufficient amount of water in ritual bath; Hadīth no. 238.Jāmi' At-TirmidhiBook of Clothing as reported from the Prophet (PBUH)Chapter: What is reported on letting the hair grow below the ears; Hadīth no. 1755.Sunan An-Nasā'iBook of PurificationChapter: The amount of water sufficient for a man's ritual bath; Hadīth no. 228.Sunan Ibn MājahBook of Purification and Its SunnahsChapter: Man and wife washing up from one vessel; Hadīth no. 376.

Chapter: Menstruating woman may wash her husband's hair and comb it; her leftover water is pure; and he can recline in her lap and recite Qur'an therein

'Ā'ishah (may Allah be pleased with her) said: "The Prophet (may Allah's peace and blessings be upon him) would bring his head out as he observed I'tikāf in the mosque and I would comb his hair while I was menstruating."

Sahīh Al-BukhāriBook of I'tikāf (Retirement for worship in the mosque)Chapter: Menstruating woman combing the hair of her husband while he is observing I'tikāf; Hadīth no. 2028.Sahīh MuslimBook of MenstruationChapter: Menstruating woman may wash her husband's hair and comb it; her leftover water is pure; and he can recline in her lap and recite Qur'an therein; Hadith no. 297.Sunan Abu DāwudBook of FastingChapter: Man observing I'tikāf entering home for some need; Hadīth no. 2469.Jāmi' At-TirmidhiBook of Fasting as reported from the Prophet (PBUH)Chapter: A man observing I'tikāf may go out for some need or not?; Hadīth no. 804.Sunan An-Nasā'iBook of PurificationChapter: Menstruating woman washing her husband's hair; Hadīth no. 275.Sunan Ibn MājahBook of Purification and Its SunnahsChapter: Menstruating woman picking up something from the mosque; Hadīth no. 633.

Chapter on pre-seminal fluid

'Ali (may Allah be pleased with him) said: "I was a man of frequent flow of pre-seminal fluid, and I felt shy to ask the Messenger of Allah (may Allah's peace and blessings be upon him) about it, so I asked Al-Miqdād ibn al-Aswad (to ask him). He did, and the reply was: 'It entails ablution.' "

Sahīh Al-BukhāriBook of AblutionChapter: Those who hold that ablution can only be invalidated by what comes out of the frontal and anal passages; Hadīth no. 178.Sahīh MuslimBook of MenstruationChapter: Pre-seminal fluid; Hadīth no. 303.Sunan Abu DāwudBook of PurificationChapter: About pre-seminal fluid; Hadīth no. 207.Jāmi' At-TirmidhiBook of Purification as reported from the Prophet (PBUH)Chapter: What is reported on semen and pre-seminal fluid; Hadīth no. 114.Sunan An-Nasā'iBook of PurificationChapter: Pre-seminal fluid that invalidates ablution and that which does not invalidate it;

Hadīth no. 157.Sunan Ibn MājahBook of Purification and Its SunnahsChapter: Ablution after discharge of pre-seminal fluid; Hadīth no. 504.

Chapter: Ritually impure person may sleep and is recommended to make ablution and wash his private parts if he wants to eat, drink, sleep, or copulate

Ibn 'Umar (may Allah be pleased with him) reported: "'Umar ibn al-Khattāb (may Allah be pleased with him) asked the Messenger of Allah (may Allah's peace and blessings be upon him): 'May anyone of us sleep while in a state of ritual impurity?' He replied: 'Yes. If anyone of you made ablution, he may sleep while in a state of ritual impurity.' "

Sahīh Al-BukhāriBook of the Ritual BathChapter: Sleep of the ritually impure; Hadīth no. 287.Sahīh MuslimBook of MenstruationChapter: Ritually impure person may sleep and is recommended to make ablution and wash his private parts if he wants to eat, drink, sleep, or copulate; Hadīth no. 306.Sunan Abu DāwudBook of PurificationChapter: Ritually impure person may sleep; Hadīth no. 221.Jāmi' At-TirmidhiBook of Purification as reported from the Prophet (PBUH)Chapter: What is reported on ablution by a ritually impure person if he wants to sleep; Hadīth no. 120.Sunan An-Nasā'iBook of PurificationChapter: Ablution by a ritually impure person if he wants to sleep; Hadīth no. 259.Sunan Ibn MājahBook of Purification and Its SunnahsChapter: Those who held that a ritually impure person may not sleep before making ablution like that of prayer; Hadīth no. 585.

Anas ibn Mālik (may Allah be pleased with him) reported that the Prophet of Allah (may Allah's peace and blessings be upon him) used to go to all his wives one after another in one night (copulating with them), and he had nine wives at the time.

Sahīh Al-BukhāriBook of MarriageChapter: He who copulates with his wives one after another and takes one ritual bath; Hadīth no. 5215.Sahīh MuslimBook of MenstruationChapter: Ritually impure person may sleep and is recommended to make ablution and wash his private parts if he wants to eat, drink, sleep, or copulate; Hadīth no. 309.Sunan Abu DāwudBook of PurificationChapter: Ritually impure person copulating again; Hadīth no. 218.Jāmi' At-TirmidhiBook of Purification as reported from the Prophet (PBUH)Chapter: What is reported on man copulating with his wives one after another and taking one ritual bath; Hadīth no. 140.Sunan An-Nasā'iBook of MarriageChapter: Mentioning the command to the Prophet (PBUH) concerning marriage and his wives; Hadīth no. 3198.Sunan Ibn MājahBook of Purification and Its SunnahsChapter: What is reported on man taking one ritual bath after copulating with all his wives; Hadīth no. 588.

Chapter: Description of ritual bath

Ibn 'Abbās (may Allah be pleased with him) reported: "Maymūnah (may Allah be pleased with her) said: 'I placed water for the Prophet's ritual bath and screened him with a garment. He poured water over his hands and washed them. Then he poured water with his right hand over his left and washed his private parts, rubbed with his hand the earth and washed it, rinsed his mouth, washed his nose by sniffing water then blowing it out, and then washed his face and forearms. After that he poured water over his head and his whole body. Then he moved aside and washed his feet. I gave him a piece of cloth but he did not take it then he came out shaking water off his hands.' "

Sahīh Al-BukhāriBook of the Ritual BathChapter: Shaking water off one's hands after ritual bathSahīh MuslimBook of MenstruationChapter: Description of ritual bath; Hadīth no. 317.Sunan Abu DāwudBook of PurificationChapter: Ritual bath; Hadīth no. 245.Jāmi' At-TirmidhiBook of Purification as reported from the Prophet (PBUH)Chapter: What is reported on ritual bath; Hadīth no. 103.Sunan An-Nasā'iBook of PurificationChapter: Washing one's legs in a place other than where he takes a bath; Hadīth no. 253.Sunan Ibn MājahBook of Purification and Its SunnahsChapter: What is reported on ritual bath; Hadīth no. 573.

Chapter: Woman in Istihādah and her ritual bath and prayer

'Ā'ishah (may Allah be pleased with her) reported: "Fātimah bint Abi Hubaysh came to the Prophet (may Allah's peace and blessings be upon him) and said: 'O Messenger of Allah, I am a woman who suffers from Istihādah and I never become pure. Should I abandon prayer?' He said: 'No, that is only a vein, not menstruation. So, when your period comes, stop praying, and when it ends, wash the blood away and pray.'" He (sub-narrator) said: "My father reported: 'And make ablution for every prayer till the next period comes.'"

Sahīh Al-BukhāriBook of AblutionChapter: Washing blood; Hadīth no. 228.Sahīh MuslimBook of MenstruationChapter: Woman in Istihādah and her ritual bath and prayer; Hadīth no. 333.Sunan Abu DāwudBook of PurificationChapter: Those who reported that a woman should not abandon prayer after her period ends; Hadīth no. 282.Jāmi' At-TirmidhiBook of Purification as reported from the Prophet (PBUH)Chapter: Woman in Istihādah; Hadīth no. 125.Sunan An-Nasā'iBook of PurificationChapter: Mention of menses; Hadīth no. 212.Sunan Ibn MājahBook of Purification and Its SunnahsChapter: What is reported on woman who kept count of her period days before blood continued to flow from her; Hadīth no. 621.

'Ā'ishah (may Allah be pleased with her) reported that Umm Habībah suffered Istihādah for seven years, and she asked the Messenger of Allah (may Allah's peace and blessings be upon him) about that so he ordered her to take a ritual bath, saying: "This is a vein." She used to take a ritual bath for every prayer.

Sahīh Al-BukhāriBook of MenstruationChapter: Vein of Istihādah; Hadīth no. 327.Sahīh MuslimBook of MenstruationChapter: Woman in Istihādah and her ritual bath and prayer; Hadīth no. 334.Sunan Abu DāwudBook of PurificationChapter: Those who reported that a woman in Istihādah should take a ritual bath for every prayer; Hadīth no. 291.Jāmi' At-TirmidhiBook of Purification as reported from the Prophet (PBUH)Chapter: What is reported on a woman in Istihādah taking a bath for every prayer; Hadīth no. 129.Sunan An-Nasā'iBook of PurificationChapter: Mention of taking a ritual bath after menstrual period ends; Hadīth no. 203.Sunan Ibn MājahBook of Purification and Its SunnahsChapter: What is reported on a woman in Istihādah who gets confused about blood and cannot determine the days of her menses; Hadīth no. 626.

Chapter: Woman in Istihādah is required to make up for missed fasting, but not missed prayer

Mu'ādhah reported that a woman asked 'Ā'ishah (may Allah be pleased with her): "Should a menstruating woman make up for missed prayers when she becomes pure?" She said: "Are you a Harūri? We would get our menses during the lifetime of the Prophet (may Allah's peace and blessings be upon him) and he did not order us to do this." Or she said: "We would not do this."

Sahīh Al-BukhāriBook of MenstruationChapter: Menstruating woman does not make up for missed prayers; Hadīth no. 321.Sahīh MuslimBook of MenstruationChapter: Menstruating woman is required to make up for missed fasting but not for missed prayer; Hadīth no. 335.Sunan Abu DāwudBook of PurificationChapter: Menstruating woman does not make up for missed prayer; Hadīth no. 262.Jāmi' At-TirmidhiBook of Purification as reported from the Prophet (PBUH)Chapter: What is reported on menstruating woman not having to make up for missed prayers; Hadīth no. 130.Sunan An-Nasā'iBook of Menstruation and IstihādahChapter: Menstruating woman is exempt from prayer; Hadīth no. 382.Sunan Ibn MājahBook of Purification and Its SunnahsChapter: Menstruating woman does not make up for missed prayer; Hadīth no. 631.

Chapter: A person taking a bath should screen himself with a cloth or the like

Um Hāni' bint Abi Tālib (may Allah be pleased with her) reported: "I went to the Messenger of Allah (may Allah's peace and blessings be upon him) during the Year of the Conquest and found him taking a bath while his daughter Fātimah was screening him. When I greeted him, he asked: 'Who is this?' I said: 'I am Um Hāni' bint Abi Tālib.' He said: 'Welcome, Um Hāni'.' After he finished bathing, he prayed eight Rak'ahs while wrapped in one garment. When he finished, I said: 'O Messenger of Allah, the son of my mother claimed that he would kill a man to whom I have given protection; so-and-so, son of

Hubayrah.' Thereupon, the Messenger of Allah (may Allah's peace and blessings be upon him) said: 'We give protection to whom you have given protection Um Hāni'.' This was in the forenoon."

Sahīh Al-BukhāriBook of PrayerChapter: Praying wrapped up in one garment; Hadīth no. 357.Sahīh MuslimBook of MenstruationChapter: A person taking a bath should screen himself with a cloth or the like; Hadīth no. 336.Sunan Abu DāwudBook of PrayerChapter: Duha (Forenoon) prayer; Hadīth no. 1291.Jāmi' At-TirmidhiBook of WitrChapter: What is reported on Duha prayer; Hadīth no. 474.Sunan An-Nasā'iBook of PurificationChapter: Mention of screening oneself while bathing; Hadīth no. 225.Sunan Ibn MājahBook of Dry AblutionChapter: What is reported on screening oneself while bathing; Hadīth no. 614.

Chapter: Abrogation of making ablution after eating something touched by fire

Ibn 'Abbās (may Allah be pleased with him) reported that the Messenger of Allah (may Allah's peace and blessings be upon him) drank milk and rinsed his mouth, saying: "It has fat."

Sahīh Al-BukhāriBook of AblutionChapter: Should mouth be rinsed after drinking milk?; Hadīth no. 211.Sahīh MuslimBook of MenstruationChapter: Abrogation of making ablution after eating something touched by fire; Hadīth no. 358.Sunan Abu DāwudBook of PurificationChapter: Making ablution after drinking milk; Hadīth no. 196.Jāmi' At-TirmidhiBook of Purification as reported from the Prophet (PBUH)Chapter: Rinsing one's mouth after drinking milk; Hadīth no. 89.Sunan An-Nasā'iBook of PurificationChapter: Rinsing one's mouth after drinking milk; Hadīth no. 187.Sunan Ibn MājahBook of Purification and Its SunnahsChapter: Rinsing one's mouth after drinking milk; Hadīth no. 498.

Chapter: Hide of dead animals is rendered pure by tanning

Ibn 'Abbās (may Allah be pleased with him) reported: "The Prophet (may Allah's peace and blessings be upon him) saw a dead sheep that had been given in charity to a freed slave-girl of Maymūnah and he said: 'Why don't you benefit of its hide?' They said: 'It is a dead animal.' He said: 'Its eating is unlawful.'"

Sahīh Al-BukhāriBook of ZakahChapter: Giving charity to the freed slaves of the Prophet's wives; Hadīth no. 1492.Sahīh MuslimBook of MenstruationChapter: Hide of dead animals is rendered pure by tanning; Hadīth no. 363.Sunan Abu DāwudBook of ClothingChapter: Hide of dead animals; Hadīth no. 4120.Jāmi' At-TirmidhiBook of Clothing as reported from the Prophet (PBUH)Chapter: What is reported on tanned hide of dead animals; Hadīth no. 1727.Sunan An-Nasā'iBook of Fara' and 'AtīrahChapter: Hide of dead animals; Hadīth no. 4235.Sunan Ibn MājahBook of ClothingChapter: Wearing the tanned hide of dead animals; Hadīth no. 3610.

Chapter: Dry ablution

Sa'īd ibn 'Abdur-Rahmān ibn Abza reported from his father: "A man came to 'Umar ibn al-Khattāb and said: 'I became ritually impure but there was no water available.' So 'Ammār ibn Yāsir said to 'Umar: 'Do you remember when you and I were traveling together (and we became ritually impure)? You chose not to pray, but I rolled myself on the ground and prayed. Then, I mentioned that to the Prophet (may Allah's peace and blessings be upon him) and he said: "It would have been sufficient for you to do like this," striking the earth lightly with his palms then blowing off the dust and passing his hands over his face and hands.'"

Sahīh Al-BukhāriBook of Dry AblutionChapter: Should a performer of dry ablution blow into his hands?; Hadīth no. 338.Sahīh MuslimBook of MenstruationChapter: Dry ablution; Hadīth no. 368.Sunan Abu DāwudBook of PurificationChapter: Dry ablution; Hadīth no. 322.Jāmi' At-TirmidhiBook of Purification as reported from the Prophet (PBUH)Chapter: What is reported on dry ablution; Hadīth no. 144.Sunan An-Nasā'iBook of PurificationChapter: Dry ablution by a non-traveler; Hadīth no. 311.Sunan Ibn MājahBook of Purification and Its SunnahsChapter: What is reported on dry ablution in one strike; Hadīth no. 569.

Chapter: The proof that a Muslim does not become impure

Abu Hurayrah (may Allah be pleased with him) reported that the Prophet (may Allah's peace and blessings be upon him) met him on a road in Madīnah while he was ritually impure. He sneaked away from him and went to take a ritual bath. When he came back, the Prophet (may Allah's peace and blessings be upon him) asked: "Where were you Abu Hurayrah?" He said: "I was ritually impure and disliked to sit with you in this state." The Prophet (may Allah's peace and blessings be upon him) said:"Glory be to Allah! A Muslim does not become impure."Sahīh Al-BukhāriBook of the Ritual BathChapter: Sweat of the ritually impure person is pure and a Muslim does not become impure; Hadīth no. 283.Sahīh MuslimBook of MenstruationChapter: The proof that a Muslim does not become impure; Hadīth no. 371.Sunan Abu DāwudBook of PurificationChapter: The ritually impure may shake hands; Hadīth no. 231.Jāmi' At-TirmidhiBook of Purification as reported from the Prophet (PBUH)Chapter: What is reported on handshake by the ritually impure; Hadīth no. 121.Sunan An-Nasā'iBook of PurificationChapter: Touching and sitting with the ritually impure; Hadīth no. 269.Sunan Ibn MājahBook of Purification and Its SunnahsChapter: Shaking hands with the ritually impure; Hadīth no. 534.

Chapter: What to say before entering the bathroom

Anas (may Allah be pleased with him) reported: "The Prophet (may Allah's peace and blessings be upon him) used to say upon entering the bathroom: 'O Allah, I seek refuge with You from male and female devils.'"

Sahīh Al-BukhāriBook of InvocationsChapter: The invocation when entering the bathroom; Hadīth no. 6322.Sahīh MuslimBook of MenstruationChapter: What to say before entering the bathroom; Hadīth no. 375.Sunan Abu DāwudBook of PurificationChapter: What to say before entering the bathroom; Hadīth no. 4.Jāmi' At-TirmidhiBook of Purification as reported from the Prophet (PBUH)Chapter: What to say when entering the bathroom; Hadīth no. 6.Sunan An-Nasā'iBook of PurificationChapter: The invocation to be said upon entering the bathroom; Hadīth no. 19.Sunan Ibn MājahBook of Purification and Its SunnahsChapter: What to say before entering the bathroom; Hadīth no. 298.

Book of Prayer

Chapter: The command to recite wording of Adhān twice and wording of Iqāmah once

Anas (may Allah be pleased with him) reported: "They proposed the fire and the bell (for announcing the time of prayer), so they mentioned Jews and Christians. So Bilāl was ordered to recite the wording of Adhān twice and the wording of Iqāmah once."

Sahīh Al-BukhāriBook of AdhānChapter: Start of Adhān; Hadīth no. 603.Sahīh MuslimBook of PrayerChapter: The command to recite the wording of Adhān twice and the wording of Iqāmah once; Hadīth no. 378.Sunan Abu DāwudBook of PrayerChapter: The Iqāmah; Hadīth no. 508.Jāmi' At-TirmidhiBook of Prayer as reported from the Prophet (may Allah's peace and blessings be upon him)Chapter: What is reported on pronouncing the wording of Iqāmah once; Hadīth no. 193.Sunan An-Nasā'iBook of AdhānChapter: Pronouncing the wording of Adhān twice; Hadīth no. 627.Sunan Ibn MājahBook of Adhān and its SunnahChapter: Pronouncing the wording of Iqāmah once; Hadīth no. 729.Chapter: It is recommended that the one who hears the Adhān to repeat after itand then invoke Allah's peace and blessings upon the Prophet and ask Allah to grant him Al-Wasīlah.

Abu Sa'īd al-Khudri (may Allah be pleased with him) reported that the Messenger of Allah (may Allah's peace and blessings be upon him) said: "When you hear the Adhān, say as the Muezzin says."

Sahīh Al-BukhāriBook of AdhānChapter: What to say upon hearing the Adhān; Hadīth no. 611.Sahīh MuslimBook of PrayerChapter: It is recommended that the one who hears the Adhān to repeat after it and then invoke Allah's peace and blessings upon the Prophet and ask Allah to grant him Wasīlah; Hadīth no. 383.Sunan Abu DāwudBook of PrayerChapter: What to say upon hearing the Adhān; Hadīth no. 522.Jāmi' At-TirmidhiBook of Prayer as reported from the Prophet (PBUH)Chapter: What to say upon hearing the Adhān; Hadīth no. 208.Sunan An-Nasā'iBook of AdhānChapter: Repeating after the Muezzin; Hadīth no. 673.Sunan Ibn MājahBook of Adhān and its SunnahChapter: What to say upon hearing the Adhān; Hadīth no. 720.Chapter: It is recommended to raise hands to the level of shouldersin the Takbīr of Ihrām and Rukū' (bowing) and in rising from Rukū'and that it is not done when rising from prostration

'Abdullāh ibn 'Umar (may Allah be pleased with him) reported: "I saw that whenever the Messenger of Allah (may Allah's peace and blessings be upon him) stood for prayer, he would raise his hands to the level of shoulders. He also used to do this in the Takbīr for Rukū' and as he raised his head from Rukū' and said: Allah hears whoever praises Him. He would not do that in prostration."

Sahīh Al-BukhāriBook of AdhānChapter: Raising the hands in Takbīr, Rukū', and rising; Hadīth no. 736.Sahīh MuslimBook of PrayerChapter: It is recommended to raise hands to the level of shoulders in the Takbīr of Ihrām and Rukū' and in rising from Rukū' and not in rising from prostration; Hadīth no. 390.Sunan Abu DāwudBook of PrayerChapters on the commencement of prayerChapter: Raising the hands in prayer; Hadīth no. 721.Jāmi' At-TirmidhiBook of Prayer as reported from the Prophet (PBUH)Chapter: Raising the hands before Rukū'; Hadīth no. 255.Sunan An-Nasā'iBook of Prayer CommencementChapter: What to do in prayer commencement; Hadīth no. 876.Sunan Ibn MājahBook of Performance of Prayer and its SunnahChapter: Raising the hands before Rukū' and upon rising from it; Hadīth no. 858.

Chapter: The obligation of reciting Al-Fātihah in each Rak'ah, and if one cannot recite it properly or learn it, he may recite other verses that are easy for him; Hadīth no. 723.

'Ubādah ibn as-Sāmit (may Allah be pleased with him) reported that the Messenger of Allah (may Allah's peace and blessings be upon him) said: "He who does not recite Al-Fātihah, his prayer is invalid."

Sahīh Al-BukhāriBook of AdhānChapter: The obligation of reciting (Al-Fātihah) in all prayers by the Imām and those led in prayer, by travelers and non-travelers, and in audible and inaudible prayers; Hadīth no. 756.Sahīh MuslimBook of PrayerChapter: The obligation of reciting Al-Fātihah in each Rak'ah, and if a person cannot recite it properly or learn it, he may recite other verses that are easy for him; Hadīth no. 394.Sunan Abu DāwudBook of PrayerChapter: He who does not recite Al-Fātihah in his prayer; Hadīth no. 822.Jāmi' At-TirmidhiBook of Prayer as reported from the Prophet (PBUH)Chapter: What is reported on the invalidity of prayer without the recitation of Al-Fātihah; Hadīth no. 247.Sunan An-Nasā'iBook of Prayer CommencementChapter: The obligation of reciting Al-Fātihah in prayer; Hadīth no. 910.Sunan Ibn MājahBook of Performing Prayer and its SunnahChapter: Reciting after the Imām; Hadīth no. 837.

Abu Hurayrah (may Allah be pleased with him) reported: A man entered the mosque and started praying while the Messenger of Allah (may Allah's peace and blessings be upon him) was sitting somewhere in the mosque. Thereafter, the man came and greeted him, so he said to him: "Go back and pray, for you have not prayed." The man went back and prayed then greeted him. After returning the greeting, he said: "Go back and pray, for you have not prayed." In the third time, the man said: "Teach me." Then he said: "When you rise for prayer, perform ablution properly, face the Qiblah, and say Takbīr. Then, recite some verses of what you know of the Qur'an. Then, bow and remain in this position till you feel settled in bowing. Then, raise your head and stand straight, and then prostrate yourself till you feel settled in prostration. Then, sit up till you feel settled in sitting. Then, prostrate yourself again till you feel settled in prostration, and then get up and stand straight. Do this in your whole prayer."

Sahīh Al-BukhāriBook of Oaths and VowsChapter: If a person forgetfully breaks his oath; Hadīth no. 6664.Sahīh MuslimBook of PrayerChapter: The obligation of reciting Al-Fātihah in each Rak'ah, and if a person cannot recite it properly or learn it, he may recite other verses that are easy for him; Hadīth no. 397.Sunan Abu DāwudBook of PrayerChapter: He who prays without making his back straight in Rukū' and prostration; Hadīth no. 856.Jāmi' At-TirmidhiBook of Prayer as reported from the Prophet (PBUH)Chapter: What is reported on the description of prayer; Hadīth no. 303.Sunan An-Nasā'iBook of Prayer CommencementChapter: Obligation of the first Takbīr; Hadīth no. 884.Sunan Ibn MājahBook of Performing Prayer and its SunnahChapter: Completing the prayer; Hadīth no. 1060.Chapter: The argument of those who held that Basmalah should not be pronounced audibly.Anas (may Allah be pleased with him) reported that the Prophet (may Allah's peace and blessings be upon him) and Abu Bakr and 'Umar (may Allah be pleased with both of them) used to start recitation in (audible) prayer with (Praise be to Allah, Lord of the worlds).Sahīh Al-BukhāriBook of AdhānChapter: What to say after Takbīr; Hadīth no. 743.Sahīh MuslimBook of PrayerChapter: The argument of those who held that Basmalah should not be pronounced audibly; Hadīth no. 399.Sunan Abu DāwudBook of PrayerChapter: Those who held that (In the name of Allah, the Most Compassionate, the Most Merciful) should be pronounced inaudibly; Hadīth no. 782.Jāmi' At-TirmidhiBook of Prayer as reported from the Prophet (PBUH)Chapter: Commencing recitation with (Praise be to Allah, Lord of the worlds); Hadīth no. 246.Sunan An-Nasā'iBook of Prayer CommencementChapter: Commencing with Al-Fātihah before other verses; Hadīth no. 903.Sunan Ibn MājahBook of Performing Prayer and its SunnahChapter: Commencing recitation; Hadīth no. 813.

Chapter: Tashahhud in prayer

'Abdullāh ibn Mas'ūd (may Allah be pleased with him) reported: Whenever we prayed with the Prophet (may Allah's peace and blessings be upon him), we used to say: "Peace be upon Allah before His servants; peace be upon Jibrīl; peace be upon Mikā'īl; and peace be upon so-and-so and so-and-so!" When the Prophet (may Allah's peace and blessings be upon him) finished the prayer, he turned toward us and said: "Indeed, Allah is Peace. So, when anyone of you sits in the prayer, let him say: 'All greetings, prayers, and good things are due to Allah; peace be upon you, O Prophet, and the mercy and blessings of Allah; peace be upon us and upon the righteous servants of Allah.' If he says that, it will include every righteous servant in the heavens and earth. 'I bear witness that there is no true god but Allah, and I bear witness that Muhammad is His servant and Messenger.' After that, he can say anything he wishes."

Sahīh Al-BukhāriBook of Seeking PermissionChapter: 'Peace' is one of the names of Allah Almighty; Hadīth no. 6230.Sahīh MuslimBook of PrayerChapter: Tashahhud in prayer; Hadīth no. 402.Sunan Abu DāwudBook of PrayerChapter: Tashahhud; Hadīth no. 968.Jāmi' At-TirmidhiBook of Prayer as reported from the Prophet (PBUH)Chapter: What is reported on Tashahhud; Hadīth no. 289.Sunan An-Nasā'iBook of Putting Hands TogetherChapter: How to make the first Tashahhud; Hadīth no. 1168.Sunan Ibn MājahBook of Performance of Prayerand its SunnahChapter: What is reported on Tashahhud; Hadīth no. 899.

Chapter: Invoking Allah's peace and blessings upon the Prophet after Tashahhud.

'Abdur-Rahmān ibn Abi Layla reported: I met Ka'b ibn 'Ujrah and he said to me: "Shall I give you a gift which I heard from the Prophet (may Allah's peace and blessings be upon him)?" I said: "Yes, indeed. Give it to me." He said: "We asked the Prophet (may Allah's peace and blessings be upon him), saying: 'O Messenger of Allah, how can we invoke blessings upon you, O people of the (Prophet's) house, for Allah has taught us how to invoke peace upon you?' He said: 'Say: O Allah, bestow Your prayers on Muhammad and the family of Muhammad as You bestowed Your prayers on Ibrahīm and the family of Ibrahīm; verily, You are Praiseworthy, Most Glorious! O Allah, bestow Your blessings on Muhammad and the family of Muhammad as You bestowed Your blessings on Ibrahīm and the family of Ibrahīm; verily, You are Praiseworthy, Most Glorious!'"

Sahīh Al-BukhāriBook of the Hadīths on the ProphetsChapter: Hadīth no. 3370.Sahīh MuslimBook of PrayerChapter: Invoking Allah's peace and blessings upon the Prophet after Tashahhud; Hadīth no. 406.Sunan Abu DāwudBook of PrayerChapter: Invoking Allah's peace and blessings upon the Prophet after Tashahhud; Hadīth no. 976.Jāmi' At-TirmidhiBook of Prayer as reported from the Prophet (PBUH)Chapter: What is reported on the description of invoking Allah's peace and blessings upon the Prophet; Hadīth no. 483.Sunan An-Nasā'iBook of ForgetfulnessChapter: Another type; Hadīth no. 1288.Sunan Ibn MājahBook of Performing Prayer and its SunnahChapter: Invoking Allah's peace and blessings upon the Prophet; Hadīth no. 904.

Chapter: Saying "Allah hears whoever praises Him", "Praise be to You, our Lord", and "Amen".

Abu Hurayrah (may Allah be pleased with him) reported that the Prophet (may Allah's peace and blessings be upon him) said: "When the Imām says 'Amen', say 'Amen', for if someone's 'Amen' coincides with that of the angels, his past sins will be forgiven."

Sahīh Al-BukhāriBook of AdhānChapter: The Imām saying 'Amen' audibly; Hadīth no. 780.Sahīh MuslimBook of PrayerChapter: Saying "Allah hears whoever praises Him", "Praise be to You, our Lord", and "Amen"; Hadīth no. 410.Sunan Abu DāwudBook of PrayerChapter: Repeating 'Amen' after the Imām; Hadīth no. 936.Jāmi' At-TirmidhiBook of Prayer as reported from the Prophet (PBUH)Chapter: What is reported on the merit of saying 'Amen'; Hadīth no. 250.Sunan An-Nasā'iBook of Prayer CommencementChapter: The Imām saying 'Amen' audibly; Hadīth no. 928.Sunan Ibn MājahBook of Establishing the Prayerand the Sunnah Acts Related to itChapter: The Imām saying 'Amen' audibly; Hadīth no. 851.

Chapter: Those led in prayer follow the Imām

Anas ibn Mālik (may Allah be pleased with him) reported: Once the Messenger of Allah (may Allah's peace and blessings be upon him) rode a horse and he fell off it and his right side got scraped. He offered one of the prayers while sitting and we also prayed behind him sitting. When he completed the prayer, he said: "The Imām is appointed to be followed. Pray standing if he prays standing, bow when he bows, and rise when he rises; and if he says: 'Allah hears whoever praises Him,' say: 'Praise be to You, our Lord.' Pray standing if he prays standing and pray sitting, all of you, if he prays sitting." Abu 'Abdullah said that Al-Humaydi said: "His statement: 'Pray sitting if he prays sitting' was made during his past illness, but later the Prophet (may Allah's peace and blessings be upon him) prayed sitting and the people prayed standing behind him, and he did not order them to sit. We should follow the latest actions of the Prophet (may Allah's peace and blessings be upon him)."

Sahīh Al-BukhāriBook of AdhānChapter: The Imām is appointed to be followed; Hadīth no. 689.Sahīh MuslimBook of PrayerChapter: Those led in prayer follow the Imām; Hadīth no. 411.Sunan Abu DāwudBook of PrayerChapter: The Imām praying while sitting; Hadīth no. 601.Jāmi' At-TirmidhiBook of Prayer as reported from the Prophet (PBUH)Chapter: The Hadīth: If the Imām prays sitting, then pray sitting; Hadīth no. 361.Sunan An-Nasā'iBook of Leading People in PrayerChapter: Following the Imām if he prays sitting; Hadīth no. 832.Sunan Ibn MājahBook of Establishing the Prayerand the Sunnah Acts Related to itChapter: What is reported on the appointment of the Imām to be followed; Hadīth no. 1238.Chapter: Men glorify Allah (say "Subhān Allah")and women clap to alert others to something during prayer.

Abu Hurayrah (may Allah be pleased with him) reported that the Prophet (may Allah's peace and blessings be upon him) said: "Men glorify Allah (say "Subhān Allah") and women clap."

Sahīh Al-BukhāriBook of Actionin PrayerChapter: Clapping for women; Hadīth no.1203.Sahīh MuslimBook of PrayerChapter: Men glorify Allah (say "Subhān Allah") and women clap to alert others to something during prayer; Hadīth no. 422.Sunan Abu DāwudBook of PrayerChapter: Clapping in prayer; Hadīth no. 939.Jāmi' At-TirmidhiBook of Prayer as reported from the Prophet (PBUH)Chapter: What is reported on glorifying Allah (saying "Subhān Allah") for men and clapping for women; Hadīth no. 369.Sunan An-Nasā'iBook of ForgetfulnessChapter: Clapping in prayer; Hadīth no. 1208.Sunan Ibn MājahBook of Establishing the Prayerand the Sunnah Acts Related to itChapter: Glorifying Allah (saying "Subhān Allah") for men and clapping for women in prayer; Hadīth no. 1034.

Chapter: The prohibition to get ahead of the Imām in Rukū', prostration, and the like

Abu Hurayrah (may Allah be pleased with him) reported that the Prophet (may Allah's peace and blessings be upon him) said: "Does he who raises his head before the Imām not fear that Allah may transform his head into that of a donkey or his figure into that of a donkey?"

Sahīh Al-BukhāriBook of AdhānChapter: The sin of raising one's head before the Imām; Hadīth no. 691.Sahīh MuslimBook of PrayerChapter: The prohibition to get ahead of the Imām in Rukū', prostration, and the like; Hadīth no. 427.Sunan Abu DāwudBook of PrayerChapter: Stressing the sinfulness of rising, bowing, or prostrating before the Imām; Hadīth no. 623.Jāmi' At-TirmidhiBook of Friday as reported from the Prophet (PBUH)Chapter: What is reported on stressing the sinfulness of raising one's head before the Imām; Hadīth no. 582.Sunan An-Nasā'iBook of Leading People in PrayerChapter: Getting ahead of the Imām; Hadīth no. 828.Sunan Ibn MājahBook of Performance of Prayer and its SunnahChapter: The prohibition to bow or prostrate before the Imām; Hadīth no. 961.

Chapter: Straightening the rows and the merit of the first one and then the next and the next; competing over the first row; and letting virtuous people be in the front and close to the Imām.

An-Nu'mān ibn Bashīr (may Allah be pleased with him) reported that the Prophet (may Allah's peace and blessings be upon him) said: "Straighten your rows or Allah will create dissension amongst you."

Sahīh Al-BukhāriBook of AdhānChapter: Straightening the rows upon Iqāmah and after it; Hadīth no. 717.Sahīh MuslimBook of PrayerChapter: Straightening the rows and the merit of the first one and then the next and the next; competing over the first row; and letting virtuous people be in the front and close to the Imām; Hadīth no. 436.Sunan Abu DāwudBook of Prayer - Chapters on the rowsChapter: Straightening the rows; Hadīth no. 663.Jāmi' At-TirmidhiBook of Prayer as reported from the Prophet (PBUH)Chapter: What is reported on establishing the rows; Hadīth no. 227.Sunan An-Nasā'iBook of Leading People in PrayerChapter: How the Imam straightens the rows; Hadīth no. 810.Sunan Ibn MājahBook of Establishing the Prayerand the Sunnah Acts Related to itChapter: Establishing the rows; Hadīth no. 994.Chapter: Women going out to mosques provided this does notlead to temptations and they do not apply perfume

Ibn 'Umar (may Allah be pleased with him) reported that the Prophet (may Allah's peace and blessings be upon him) said: "If the wife of anyone of you asks permission to go to the mosque, he should not prevent her."

Sahīh Al-BukhāriBook of MarriageChapter: Woman seeking her husband's permission to go to the mosque or elsewhere; Hadīth no. 5238.Sahīh MuslimBook of PrayerChapter: Women going out to mosques provided this does not lead to temptations and they do not apply perfume; Hadīth no. 442.Sunan Abu DāwudBook of PrayerChapter: What is reported on women going out to the mosque; Hadīth no. 566.Jāmi' At-TirmidhiBook of Friday as reported from the Prophet (PBUH)Chapter: What is reported on women going out to the mosque; Hadīth no. 570.Sunan An-Nasā'iBook of MosquesChapter: The prohibition of preventing women from going to mosques; Hadīth no. 706.Sunan Ibn MājahIntroduction of Ibn MājahChapter: Revering the Prophet's speech and the stern warning to those who oppose it; Hadīth no. 16.

Chapter: Recitation in Fajr prayer

Ibn 'Abbās (may Allah be pleased with him) reported that 'Umm Al-Fadl heard him reciting Surat al-Mursalāt and said: "By Allah, O son, you have reminded me, with your recitation of this Sūrah, that it was the last thing I heard from the Messenger of Allah (may Allah's peace and blessings be upon him), reciting it in Maghrib prayer."

Sahīh Al-BukhāriBook of AdhānChapter: The recitation in Maghrib prayer; Hadīth no. 763.Sahīh MuslimBook of PrayerChapter: The recitation in Fajr prayer; Hadīth no. 462.Sunan Abu DāwudBook of PrayerChapter: The amount of recitation in Maghrib prayer; Hadīth no. 810.Jāmi' At-TirmidhiBook of Prayer as reported from the Prophet (PBUH)Chapter: The recitation in Maghrib prayer; Hadīth no. 308.Sunan An-Nasā'iBook of Prayer CommencementChapter: Reciting Surat Al-Mursalāt in Maghrib prayer; Hadīth no. 986.Sunan Ibn MājahBook of Performance of Prayer and its SunnahChapter: The recitation in Maghrib prayer; Hadīth no. 831.

Chapter: The recitation in 'Ishā' prayer

Al-Barā (may Allah be pleased with him) reported: "I heard the Prophet (may Allah's peace and blessings be upon him) recite Surat At-Tīn in 'Ishā' prayer, and I have never heard anyone with a more pleasant voice or better recitation than him."

Sahīh Al-BukhāriBook of AdhānChapter: The recitation in 'Ishā' prayer; Hadīth no. 769.Sahīh MuslimBook of PrayerChapter: The recitation in 'Ishā' prayer; Hadīth no. 464.Sunan Abu DāwudBook of Prayer - Chapter on prayer during travelChapter: Shortening the recitation in prayer during travel; Hadīth no. 1221.Jāmi' At-TirmidhiBook of Prayer as reported from the Prophet (PBUH)Chapter: What is reported on the recitation in 'Ishā' prayer; Hadīth no. 310.Sunan An-Nasā'iBook of Prayer CommencementChapter: Recitation in the first Rak'ah of 'Ishā' prayer; Hadīth no. 1001.Sunan Ibn MājahBook of Performance of Prayer and its SunnahChapter: The recitation in 'Ishā' prayer; Hadīth no. 834.

Jābir ibn 'Abdullāh reported that Mu'ādh ibn Jabal (may Allah be pleased with him) used to pray with the Prophet (may Allah's peace and blessings be upon him) and then go to lead his people in prayer. Once he led the people in prayer and recited Sūrat Al-Baqarah. A man left the congregational prayer and prayed separately in a light manner. When Mu'ādh knew about it, he said: "He is a hypocrite." Upon earing this, the man went to the Prophet (may Allah's peace and blessings be upon him) and said: "O Messenger of Allah, we are people who work with our own hands and irrigate with our camels. Last night Mu'ādh led us in prayer and recited Sūrat Al-Baqarah; so I offered my prayer separately, and because of that, he claimed that I was a hypocrite." The Prophet (may Allah's peace and blessings be upon him) called Mu'ādh and said: "O Mu'ādh! Are you putting people to trial? - saying it three times - Recite Sūrat Ash-Shams, Sūrat Al-A'la, and the like."

Sahīh Al-BukhāriBook of Good MannersChapter: Those who hold that he who says that is not a disbeliever, based on personal interpretation or out of ignorance; Hadīth no. 6106.Sahīh MuslimBook of PrayerChapter: The recitation in 'Ishā' prayer; Hadīth no. 465.Sunan Abu DāwudBook of PrayerChapter: Offering brief prayer; Hadīth no. 790.Jāmi' At-TirmidhiBook of Friday as reported from the Prophet (PBUH)Chapter: What is reported on a man who offers obligatory prayer and then leads people in prayer; Hadīth no. 583.Sunan An-Nasā'iBook of Leading People in PrayerChapter: Difference between the intention of the Imām and the intention of those led in prayer; Hadīth no. 835.Sunan Ibn MājahBook of Performance of Prayer and its SunnahChapter: The recitation in 'Ishā' prayer; Hadīth no. 836.Chapter: Body parts that touch the ground in prostration and the prohibition of tuckingone's hair and garment and braiding one's hair while praying.

Ibn 'Abbās (may Allah be pleased with him) reported that the Prophet (may Allah's peace and blessings be upon him) said: "I have been commanded to prostrate myself on seven bones: the forehead - and he pointed to his - nose, hands, knees, and the ends of feet, and not to tuck the clothes or hair."

Sahīh Al-BukhāriBook of AdhānChapter: Prostration on the nose; Hadīth no. 812.Sahīh MuslimBook of PrayerChapter: Body parts that touch the ground in prostration and the prostration of tucking one's hair and garment and braiding one's hair while praying; Hadīth no. 490.Sunan Abu DāwudBook of PrayerChapter: Body parts that touch the ground in prostration; Hadīth no. 889.Jāmi' At-TirmidhiBook of Prayer as reported from the Prophet (PBUH)Chapter: What is reported on prostrating on seven body parts; Hadīth no. 273.Sunan An-Nasā'iBook of Putting Hands TogetherChapter: Prostration on the nose; Hadīth no. 1096.Sunan Ibn MājahBook of Performance of Prayer and its SunnahChapter: Prostration; Hadīth no. 884.

Chapter: Being straight in prostration, placing the palms on the ground, lifting the elbows away from the sides, and keeping the abdomen away from the thighs in prostration.

Anas (may Allah be pleased with him) reported that the Prophet (may Allah's peace and blessings be upon him) said: "Be straight in prostration, and let none of you spread his forearms on the ground like a dog."

Sahīh Al-BukhāriBook of AdhānChapter: He should not spread his forearms on the ground in prostration; Hadīth no. 822.Sahīh MuslimBook of PrayerChapter: Being straight in prostration, placing the palms on the ground, lifting the elbows away from the sides, and keeping the abdomen away from the thighs in prostration; Hadīth no. 493.Sunan Abu DāwudBook of PrayerChapter: Description of prostration; Hadīth no. 897.Jāmi' At-TirmidhiBook of Prayer as reported from the Prophet (PBUH)Chapter: What is reported on being straight in prostration; Hadīth no. 276.Sunan An-Nasā'iBook of Putting Hands TogetherChapter: Being straight in prostration; Hadīth no. 1110.Sunan Ibn MājahBook of Performance of Prayer and its SunnahChapter: Being straight in prostration; Hadīth no. 892.

Chapter: The Sutrah (shield) of a praying person

Abu Juhayfah (may Allah be pleased with him) reported: "I saw the Messenger of Allah (may Allah's peace and blessings be upon him) in a red leather tent and I saw Bilāl taking the remaining water from the ablution of the Messenger of Allah (may Allah's peace and blessings be upon him). I saw the people rushing to this water and whoever got some of it would rub it on his body and those who could not get any took the moisture from the others' hands. Then, I saw Bilāl carry a stick and plant it in the ground. The Prophet (may Allah's peace and blessings be upon him) came out tucking his red cloak and he led the people in prayer towards this stick, offering two Rak'ahs. I saw people and animals passing (in front of him) beyond the stick."

Sahīh Al-BukhāriBook of PrayerChapter: Praying while wearing red garment; Hadīth no. 376.Sahīh MuslimBook of PrayerChapter: The Sutrah (shield) of a praying person; Hadīth no. 503.Sunan Abu DāwudBook of PrayerChapter: The Muezzin turning right and left while reciting the Adhān; Hadīth no. 520.Jāmi' At-TirmidhiBook of Prayer as reported from the Prophet (PBUH)Chapter: What is reported on inserting finger in ear while reciting Adhān; Hadīth no. 197.Sunan An-Nasā'iBook of PurificationChapter: Making use of the water left over from ablution; Hadīth no. 137.Sunan Ibn MājahBook of Adhān and its SunnahChapter: The Sunnah related to the Adhān; Hadīth no. 711.

Abdullāh ibn 'Abbās (may Allah be pleased with him) reported: "Once I came riding a she-ass – when I had almost reached the age of puberty – as the Messenger of Allah (may Allah's peace and blessings be upon him) was leading people in prayer at Mina with no wall in front of him. I passed in front of part of the row. Then, I dismounted, let the she-ass loose to graze, and joined the row. No one criticized me for that."

Sahīh Al-BukhāriBook of PrayerChapter: The Imām's Sutrah (shield) is a Sutrah for those behind him; Hadīth no. 493.Sahīh MuslimBook of PrayerChapter: The Sutrah (shield) of a praying person; Hadīth no. 504.Sunan Abu DāwudBook of PrayerChapter: Those who hold that a donkey's passing does not interrupt prayer; Hadīth no. 715.Jāmi' At-TirmidhiBook of Prayer as reported from the Prophet (PBUH)Chapter: The Hadīth: Prayer is not interrupted by anything; Hadīth no. 337.Sunan An-Nasā'iBook of Qiblah (prayer direction)Chapter: Mention of what interrupts prayer and what does not interrupt it if there is no Sutrah in front of the praying person; Hadīth no. 752.Sunan Ibn MājahBook of Performance of Prayer and its SunnahChapter: What interrupts prayer; Hadīth no. 947.

Chapter: Preventing one who passes in front of a praying person

Busr ibn Sa'īd reported that Zayd ibn Khālid sent him to Abu Juhaym to ask him about what he had heard from the Prophet (may Allah's peace and blessings be upon him) on passing in front of a praying person. Abu Juhaym said: "The Prophet (may Allah's peace and blessings be upon him) said: 'If a person who passes in front of a praying one knew the extent of this sin, it would be better for him to wait for forty than to pass in front of him.'" Abu An-Nadr said: "I do not know whether he said forty days, months, or years."

Sahīh Al-BukhāriBook of PrayerChapter: The sin of passing in front of a praying person; Hadīth no. 510.Sahīh MuslimBook of PrayerChapter: Preventing one who passes in front of a praying person; Hadīth no. 507.Sunan Abu DāwudBook of PrayerChapter: What is forbidden in passing in front of a praying person; Hadīth no. 701.Jāmi' At-TirmidhiBook of Prayer as reported from the Prophet (PBUH)Chapter: What is reported on the dislike of passing in front of a praying person; Hadīth no.

336.Sunan An-Nasā'iBook of Qiblah (prayer direction)Chapter: Stressing the sin of passing between a praying person and his Sutrah; Hadīth no. 756.Sunan Ibn MājahBook of Performance of Prayer and its SunnahChapter: Passing in front of a praying person; Hadīth no. 945.

Chapter: Praying in one garment and how to wear it

'Umar ibn Abi Salamah (may Allah be pleased with him) reported: "I saw the Messenger of Allah (may Allah's peace and blessings be upon him) praying in Umm Salamah's house wrapped in a single garment, placing its two ends over his shoulders.

Sahīh Al-BukhāriBook of PrayerChapter: Praying wrapped up in one garment; Hadīth no. 356.Sahīh MuslimBook of PrayerChapter: Praying in one garment and how to wear it; Hadīth no. 517.Sunan Abu DāwudBook of PrayerChapter: Number of garments to be worn in prayer; Hadīth no. 628.Jāmi' At-TirmidhiBook of Prayer as reported from the Prophet (PBUH)Chapter: What is reported on praying in one garment; Hadīth no. 339.Sunan An-Nasā'iBook of QiblahChapter: Praying in one garment; Hadīth no. 764.Sunan Ibn MājahBook of Performance of Prayer and its SunnahChapter: Praying in one garment; Hadīth no. 1049.Book of Mosques and Places of PrayerChapter: The desirability of placing hands on the kneesin Rukū' and the abrogation of placing hands between the thighs

Mus'ab ibn Sa'd reported: "I once prayed by my father's side and I put my hands together and placed them between my thighs (in Ruku'). My father forbade me from doing so, saying: 'We used to do this then we were forbidden from doing it and commanded to place our hands on the knees.'"

Sahīh Al-BukhāriBook of AdhānChapter: Placing hands on the knees in Rukū'; Hadīth no. 790.Sahīh MuslimBook of Mosques and Places of PrayerChapter: The desirability of placing hands on the knees in Rukū' and the abrogation of putting hands together between thighs; Hadīth no. 535.Sunan Abu DāwudBook of PrayerChapters on Rukū' and prostrationChapter: Placing hands on the knees; Hadīth no. 867.Jāmi' At-TirmidhiBook of Prayer Times as reported from the Prophet (PBUH)Chapter: What is reported on placing the hands on the knees in Rukū'; Hadīth no. 259.Sunan An-Nasā'iBook of Putting Hands TogetherChapter: Putting hands together (between the thighs in Rukū'); Hadīth no.1032.Sunan Ibn MājahBook of Performance of Prayer and its SunnahChapter: Placing hands on the knees; Hadīth no. 873.

Chapter: The prohibition of talking during prayer and abrogation of the former permissibility.

Jābir ibn 'Abdullāh (may Allah be pleased with him) reported: "The Prophet (may Allah's peace and blessings be upon him) sent me on an errand. After completing it, I returned and greeted him, but he did not return the greeting. I felt anxious in a way that only Allah knows. I said to myself: 'Perhaps the Messenger of Allah (may Allah's peace and blessings be upon him) is upset with me because I did not come back quickly.' Then, I greeted him and he did not return the greeting. So, I felt even more anxious than the first time. Then, I greeted him and he returned the greeting and said: 'I could not return your greeting because I was praying.' He was on his camel facing a direction other than the Qiblah."

Sahīh Al-BukhāriBook of Action during PrayerChapter: Greeting is not returned during prayer; Hadīth no. 1217.Sahīh MuslimBook of Mosques and Places of PrayerChapter: Prohibition of talking during prayer and abrogation of the former permissibility; Hadīth no. 540.Sunan Abu DāwudBook of PrayerChapter: Returning greetings during prayer; Hadīth no. 926.Jāmi' At-TirmidhiBook of Prayer as reported from the Prophet (PBUH)Chapter: What is reported on praying on a mount whatever the direction it takes; Hadīth no. 351.Sunan An-Nasā'iBook of ForgetfulnessChapter: Returning greetings with a gesture during prayer; Hadīth no. 1189.Sunan Ibn MājahBook of Performance of Prayer and its SunnahChapter: How a praying person can return a greeting; Hadīth no. 1018.

Chapter: The dislike of wiping pebbles and leveling soil during prayer.

Abu Salamah reported: "Mu'ayqīb related to me that the Prophet (may Allah's peace and blessings be upon him) said regarding a man leveling the soil while prostrating himself: 'If you have to do so, then do it once.'"

Sahīh Al-BukhāriBook of Action during PrayerChapter: Wiping over pebbles during prayer; Hadīth no. 1207.Sahīh MuslimBook of Mosques and Places of PrayerChapter: The dislike of wiping over pebbles and leveling soil during prayer; Hadīth no. 546.Sunan Abu DāwudBook of PrayerChapter: Wiping pebbles during prayer; Hadīth no. 946.Jāmi' At-TirmidhiBook of Prayer as reported from the Prophet (PBUH)Chapter: What is reported on the dislike of wiping over pebbles during prayer; Hadīth no. 380.Sunan An-Nasā'iBook of ForgetfulnessChapter: The one-time concession for this; Hadīth no. 1192.Sunan Ibn MājahBook of Performance of Prayer and its SunnahChapter: Wiping over pebbles during prayer; Hadīth no. 1026.

Chapter: Forgetfulness during prayer and the prostration for it

Abu Hurayrah (may Allah be pleased with him) reported that the Prophet (may Allah's peace and blessings be upon him) said: "When anyone of you stands for prayer, the devil comes and confuses him till he forgets how many rak'ahs he has prayed. So, if this happens to anyone of you, he should perform two prostrations while sitting."

Sahīh Al-BukhāriBook of ForgetfulnessChapter: Forgetfulness in obligatory and supererogatory prayers; Hadīth no. 1232.Sahīh MuslimBook of Mosques and Places of PrayerChapter: Forgetfulness during prayer and the prostration for it; Hadīth no. 389.Sunan Abu DāwudBook of PrayerChapter: Those who say: He should complete prayer according to his stronger assumption; Hadīth no. 1030.Jāmi' At-TirmidhiBook of Prayer as reported from the Prophet (PBUH) - Chapters on forgetfulnessChapter: He who has doubt about increase or decrease in his prayer; Hadīth no. 397.Sunan An-Nasā'iBook of ForgetfulnessChapter: Estimating (what is most likely); Hadīth no. 1252.Sunan Ibn MājahBook of Performance of Prayer and its SunnahChapter: What is reported on the two prostrations of forgetfulness before Taslīm; Hadīth no. 1217.

'Abdullāh ibn Buhaynah (may Allah be pleased with him) reported: "The Messenger of Allah (may Allah's peace and blessings be upon him) once led us in prayer, and after he finished two Rak'ahs, he got up (for the third) without sitting (for Tashahhud), so the people got up with him. When he was about to finish his prayer and we waited for him to make Taslīm, he said Takbīr before Taslim and performed two prostrations while sitting and then finished the prayer with Taslīm."

Sahīh Al-BukhāriBook of ForgetfulnessChapter: What is reported on a praying person who forgetfully stands up and does not sit for Tashahhud after two Rak'ahs in an obligatory prayer; Hadīth no. 1224.Sahīh MuslimBook of Mosques and Places of PrayerChapter: Forgetfulness during prayer and the prostration for it; Hadīth no. 570.Sunan Abu DāwudBook of PrayerChapter: He who stands up after the second Rak'ah and does not sit for Tashahhud; Hadīth no. 1034.Jāmi' At-TirmidhiBook of Prayer as reported from the Prophet (PBUH)Chapter: What is reported on the two prostrations of forgetfulness before Taslīm; Hadīth no. 391.Sunan An-Nasā'iBook of ForgetfulnessChapter: What he should do if he forgetfully stands up after the second Rak'ah without sitting for Tashahhud; Hadīth no. 1222.Sunan Ibn MājahBook of Performance of Prayer and its SunnahChapter: What is reported on he who forgetfully stands up after the second Rak'ah; Hadīth no. 1207.

Ibrāhīm reported from 'Alqamah that he said: 'Abdullāh (may Allah be pleased with him) reported: The Prophet (may Allah's peace and blessings be upon him) offered prayer. Ibrāhīm (a sub-narrator) said: "I do not know whether he prayed more or less than usual." When he finished the prayer, he was asked: "O Messenger of Allah, has there been any change to prayer?" He said: "What is that?" The people said: "You have prayed such and such (number of Rak 'ahs)." Thereupon, he bent his legs, faced the Qiblah, offered two prostrations, and then made Taslīm. When he turned to face us, he said: "If there were any change to prayer, I would have surely informed you; but I am a human being like you and I forget just as you forget. So, if I forget, remind me; and if anyone of you is doubtful about his prayer, he should make an estimate and complete his prayer accordingly, then make Taslīm then offer two prostrations."

Sahīh Al-BukhāriBook of PrayerChapter: Facing the Qiblah wherever the praying person may be; Hadīth no. 401.Sahīh MuslimBook of Mosques and Places of PrayerChapter: Forgetfulness during prayer and the prostration for it; Hadīth no. 572.Sunan Abu DāwudBook of PrayerChapter: If he offers five Rak'ahs; Hadīth no. 1020.Jāmi' At-TirmidhiBook of Prayer as reported from the Prophet (PBUH)Chapter: What is reported on the two prostrations of forgetfulness after Taslīm and talk; Hadīth no. 392.Sunan An-Nasā'iBook of ForgetfulnessChapter: Estimating what is most likely; Hadīth no. 1242.Sunan Ibn MājahBook of Performance of Prayer and its SunnahChapter: Forgetfulness during prayer; Hadīth no. 1203.

Ibn Sīrīn reported that Abu Hurayrah (may Allah be pleased with him) reported: "The Messenger of Allah (may Allah's peace and blessings be upon him) led us in one of the two daytime prayers. (Ibn Sīrīn said: "Abu Hurayrah mentioned it by name but I forgot it.") He (the Prophet) prayed two Rak'ahs and then finished the prayer with Taslīm. Then, he went toward a beam of wood laying across the mosque and leaned upon it in such a way as if he was angry. He placed his right hand over the left and interlaced his fingers. The people who were in a haste left the mosque through its gates, saying: 'The prayer has been shortened.' Abu Bakr and 'Umar, who were present at that time, did not dare to talk to the Prophet. And among them was a long-handed man called Dhul-Yadayn who asked the Prophet: 'O Messenger of Allah, have you forgotten or has the prayer been shortened?' He replied: 'I have not forgotten, nor has it been shortened," then he said: 'Is what Dhul-Yadayn saying true?' They nswered in the affirmative. So he came forward and prayed what he missed, then finished the prayer with Taslīm. Then he made Takbīr and prostrated as he normally did or longer. Then he raised his head and made Takbīr. He made Takbīr again and prostrated as he normally did or longer. Then he raised his head and made Takbīr." When people asked Ibn Sīrīn if the Prophet offered Taslīm, he said: "I was informed that 'Imrān ibn Husayn reported: "he then offered Taslīm."

Sahīh Al-BukhāriBook of PrayerChapter: Intertwining fingers in the mosque and elsewhere; Hadīth no. 482.Sahīh MuslimBook of Mosques and Places of PrayerChapter: Forgetfulness during prayer and the prostration for it; Hadīth no. 573.Sunan Abu DāwudBook of PrayerChapter: Forgetfulness in the two prostrations; Hadīth no. 1008.Jāmi' At-TirmidhiBook of Prayer as reported from the Prophet (PBUH)Chapter: What is reported on a man making Taslīm after two Rak'ahs in 'Asr and Zhuhr prayers; Hadīth no. 399.Sunan An-Nasā'iBook of ForgetfulnessChapter: What he should do if he forgetfully makes Taslīm after the second Rak'ah and talks; Hadīth no. 1224.Sunan Ibn MājahBook of Performance of Prayer and its SunnahChapter: He who forgetfully makes Taslīm after two or three Rak'ahs; Hadīth no. 1214.Chapter: The prostration of recitation

Abu Rāfi' reported: I performed 'Ishā' prayer with Abu Hurayrah (may Allah be pleased with him), who recited Surat Al-Inshiqāq and made prostration. When I asked him about this, he replied: "I made prostration in it as I prayed behind Abu al-Qāsim (the Prophet, may Allah's peace and blessings be upon him), and I will keep prostrating in its recitation till I meet him."

Sahīh Al-BukhāriBook of AdhānChapter: Reciting Surat As-Sajdah in 'Ishā' prayer; Hadīth no. 768.Sahīh MuslimBook of Mosques and Places of PrayerChapter: The prostration of recitation; Hadīth no. 578.Sunan Abu DāwudBook of Prayer - Chapters on the Qur'an's recitation, its Tahzīb, and its TartīlChapter: Prostration in the recitation of Sūrat Al-Inshiqāq and Sūrat Al-'Alaq; Hadīth no. 1408.Jāmi' At-TirmidhiBook of Friday as reported from the Prophet (PBUH)Chapter: Prostration in the recitation of Sūrat Al-'Alaq and Sūrat Al-Inshiqāq; Hadīth no. 573.Sunan An-Nasā'iBook of Prayer CommencementChapter: Prostration in the obligatory prayers; Hadīth no. 968.Sunan Ibn MājahBook of Performance of Prayer and its SunnahChapter: The number of prostrations in the Qur'an; Hadīth no. 1059.Chapter: The desirability of coming to prayer in a solemnand calm manner and the prohibition of rushing to it.

Abu Hurayrah (may Allah be pleased with him) reported: "I heard the Prophet (may Allah's peace and blessings be upon him) say: 'When Iqāmah for prayer is pronounced, do not come to it running, but come walking calmly. Pray what you catch up with and complete what you miss.'"

Sahīh Al-BukhāriBook of FridayChapter: Walking to Friday prayer; Hadīth no. 908.Sahīh MuslimBook of Mosques and Places of PrayerChapter: The desirability of coming to prayer in a solemn and calm manner and the prohibition of rushing to it; Hadīth no. 602.Sunan Abu DāwudBook of PrayerChapter: Rushing to prayer; Hadīth no. 572.Jāmi' At-TirmidhiBook of Prayer as reported from the Prophet

(PBUH)Chapter: What is reported on walking to the mosque; Hadīth no. 327.Sunan An-Nasā'iBook of Leading People in PrayerChapter: Rushing to prayer; Hadīth no. 861.Sunan Ibn MājahBook of Mosques and Congregational PrayersChapter: Walking to prayer; Hadīth no. 775.

Chapter: He who catches up with one Rak'ah of a prayer has indeed caught up with that prayer.

Abu Hurayrah (may Allah be pleased with him) reported that the Prophet (may Allah's peace and blessings be upon him) said: "He who catches up with one Rak'ah of a prayer has indeed caught up with that prayer."

Sahīh Al-BukhāriBook of Prayer TimesChapter: He who catches up with one Rak'ah of prayer; Hadīth no. 580.Sahīh MuslimBook of Mosques and Places of PrayerChapter: He who catches up with one Rak'ah of a prayer has indeed caught up with that prayer; Hadīth no. 607.Sunan Abu DāwudBook of PrayerChapter: He who catches up with one Rak'ah of Friday prayer; Hadīth no. 1121.Jāmi' At-TirmidhiBook of Friday as reported from the Prophet (PBUH)Chapter: What is reported on he who catches up with one Rak'ah of Friday prayer; Hadīth no. 524.Sunan An-Nasā'iBook of Prayer TimesChapter: He who catches up with one Rak'ah of prayer; Hadīth no. 553.Sunan Ibn MājahBook of Performance of Prayer and its SunnahChapter: What is reported on he who catches up with one Rak'ah of Friday prayer; Hadīth no. 1122.

Abu Hurayrah (may Allah be pleased with him) reported that the Prophet (may Allah's peace and blessings be upon him) said: "He who catches up with one Rak'ah of Fajr prayer before sunrise has caught up with Fajr prayer, and he who catches up with one Rak'ah of 'Asr prayer before sunset has caught up with 'Asr prayer."

Sahīh Al-BukhāriBook of Prayer TimesChapter: He who catches up with one Rak'ah of Fajr prayer; Hadīth no. 579.Sahīh MuslimBook of Mosques and Places of PrayerChapter: He who catches up with one Rak'ah of a prayer has indeed caught up with that prayer; Hadīth no. 608.Sunan Abu DāwudBook of PrayerChapter: The time of 'Asr prayer; Hadīth no. 412.Jāmi' At-TirmidhiBook of Prayer as reported from the Prophet (PBUH)Chapter: What is reported on he who catches up with one Rak'ah of 'Asr prayer before sunset; Hadīth no. 186.Sunan An-Nasā'iBook of Prayer TimesChapter: He who catches up with two Rak'ahs of 'Asr prayer; Hadīth no. 515.Sunan Ibn MājahBook of Prayer - Chapters on prayer timesChapter: The time of prayer in case of excuse and necessity; Hadīth no. 699.

Chapter: The times of the five prayers.

'Ā'ishah (may Allah be pleased with her) reported that the Messenger of Allah (may Allah's peace and blessings be upon him) used to offer 'Asr prayer while sunlight was still inside her room and the shadow had not yet appeared in it.

Sahīh Al-BukhāriBook of Prayer TimesChapter: The times of prayer and its merit; Hadīth no. 522.Sahīh MuslimBook of Mosques and Places of PrayerChapter: The times of the five prayers; Hadīth no. 611.Sunan Abu DāwudBook of PrayerChapter: The time of 'Asr prayer; Hadīth no. 407.Jāmi' At-TirmidhiBook of Prayer as reported from the Prophet (PBUH)Chapter: What is reported on offering 'Asr prayer early; Hadīth no. 159.Sunan An-Nasā'iBook of Prayer TimesChapter: Offering 'Asr prayer early; Hadīth no. 505.Sunan Ibn MājahBook of Prayer - Chapters on prayer timesChapter: The time of 'Asr prayer; Hadīth no. 683.Chapter: The desirability of waiting for the air to cool down when it is very hot before offering Zhuhr prayerfor those going to the congregational prayer and suffering the heat on their way.

Abu Hurayrah (may Allah be pleased with him) reported that the Prophet (may Allah's peace and blessings be upon him) said: "When it is very hot, wait for it to cool down before you pray, for intense heat is from the flaring up of Hellfire."

Sahīh Al-BukhāriBook of Prayer TimesChapter: Waiting for the air to cool down when it is very hot before offering Zhuhr prayer; Hadīth no. 536.Sahīh MuslimBook of Mosques and Places of PrayerChapter: The desirability of waiting for the air to cool down when it is very hot before offering Zhuhr prayer for those going to the congregational prayer and suffering the heat on their way; Hadīth no. 615.Sunan Abu DāwudBook of PrayerChapter: The time of Zhuhr prayer; Hadīth no. 402.Jāmi' At-TirmidhiBook of Prayer as reported from the Prophet (PBUH)Chapter: What is reported on delaying Zhuhr prayer in intense heat; Hadīth no. 157.Sunan An-Nasā'iBook of Prayer TimesChapter: Waiting for the air to cool down when it is very hot before offering Zhuhr prayer; Hadīth no. 500.Sunan Ibn MājahBook of Prayer - Chapters on prayer timesChapter: Waiting for the air to cool down when it is very hot before offering Zhuhr prayer; Hadīth no. 677.

Chapter: The desirability of offering Zhuhr prayer at its earliest time if there is no intense heat.

Anas ibn Mālik (may Allah be pleased with him) reported: "We used to pray along with the Prophet (may Allah's peace and blessings be upon him) in intense heat. When anyone of us could not rest his face on the ground, he would spread his garment and prostrate himself on it."

Sahīh Al-BukhāriBook of Action during PrayerChapter: Spreading one's garment during prayer for prostration on it; Hadīth no. 1208.Sahīh MuslimBook of Mosques and Places of PrayerChapter: The desirability of offering Zhuhr prayer at its earliest time if there is no intense heat; Hadīth no. 620.Sunan Abu DāwudBook of PrayerChapter: A man prostrating himself on his garment; Hadīth no. 660.Jāmi' At-TirmidhiBook of Friday as reported from the Prophet (PBUH)Chapter: What is reported on the concession for prostration on clothing in heat and cold; Hadīth no. 584.Sunan An-Nasā'iBook of Putting Hands TogetherChapter: Prostration on clothing; Hadīth no. 1116.Sunan Ibn MājahBook of Performance of Prayer and its SunnahChapter: Prostration on clothing in heat and cold; Hadīth no. 1033.

Chapter: Stressing the sinfulness of missing 'Asr prayer.

Ibn 'Umar (may Allah be pleased with him) reported that the Prophet (may Allah's peace and blessings be upon him) said: "If a person misses 'Asr prayer, it is as if he lost his family and property."

Sahīh Al-BukhāriBook of Prayer TimesChapter: The sin of one who missed 'Asr prayer; Hadīth no. 552.Sahīh MuslimBook of Mosques and Places of PrayerChapter: Stressing the sinfulness of missing 'Asr prayer; Hadīth no. 626.Sunan Abu DāwudBook of PrayerChapter: The time of 'Asr prayer; Hadīth no. 414.Jāmi' At-TirmidhiBook of Prayer as reported from the Prophet (PBUH)Chapter: What is reported on forgetfully missing 'Asr prayer; Hadīth no. 175.Sunan An-Nasā'iBook of PrayerChapter: 'Asr prayer during travel; Hadīth no. 478.Sunan Ibn MājahBook of PrayerChapter: The strict observance of 'Asr prayer; Hadīth no. 685.

'Ali (may Allah be pleased with him) reported: "On the day of the Battle of the Confederates, the Messenger of Allah (may Allah's peace and blessings be upon him) said: 'May Allah fill their houses and graves with fire. They distracted us from the middle prayer until the sun has set.'"

Sahīh Al-BukhāriBook of Jihad and BiographiesChapter: Invoking Allah against the polytheists to be defeated and shaken; Hadīth no. 2931.Sahīh MuslimBook of Mosques and Places of PrayerChapter: Stressing the sinfulness of missing 'Asr prayer; Hadīth no. 627.Sunan Abu DāwudBook of PrayerChapter: The time of 'Asr prayer; Hadīth no. 409.Jāmi' At-TirmidhiBook of Interpretation of the Qur'an as reported from the Prophet (PBUH)Chapter: From Sūrat Al-Baqarah; Hadīth no. 2984.Sunan An-Nasā'iBook of PrayerChapter: The strict observance of 'Asr prayer; Hadīth no. 473.Sunan Ibn MājahBook of PrayerChapter: The strict observance of 'Asr prayer; Hadīth no. 684.Chapter: The desirability of offering Fajr prayer at its earliest time,which is called Taghlīs, and revealing the merit of recitation in it.

'Ā'ishah (may Allah be pleased with her) reported: "The Messenger of Allah (may Allah's peace and blessings be upon him) used to offer Fajr prayer and then the women would leave wrapped in their garments, unrecognizable in the darkness."

Sahīh Al-BukhāriBook of AdhānChapter: Women going out to the mosque in the night and the pre-dawn darkness; Hadīth no. 867.Sahīh MuslimBook of Mosques and Places of PrayerChapter: The desirability of offering Fajr prayer at its earliest time, which is called Taghlīs, and revealing the merit of recitation in it; Hadīth no. 645.Sunan Abu DāwudBook of PrayerChapter: The time of Fajr prayer; Hadīth no.

423.Jāmi' At-TirmidhiBook of Prayer as reported from the Prophet (PBUH)Chapter: What is reported on offering Fajr prayer in the pre-dawn darkness; Hadīth no. 153.Sunan An-Nasā'iBook of Prayer TimesChapter: Offering Fajr prayer in the pre-dawn darkness for non-travelers; Hadīth no. 545.Sunan Ibn MājahBook of Prayer - Chapters on prayer timesChapter: The time of Fajr prayer; Hadīth no. 669.

Sayyār ibn Salāmah reported: "My father and I visited Abu Barzah al-Aslami. My father asked him: 'How did the Messenger of Allah (may Allah's peace and blessings be upon him) use to perform the obligatory prayers?' Abu Barzah said: 'He used to pray Zhuhr, which you call 'the first one', as the sun declined at noon, and he would pray 'Asr at a time after which one of us could go to his house at the farthest place in Madīnah while the sun was still hot.' I forgot what he had said about Maghrib prayer. 'And he liked to delay 'Ishā' prayer, which you call 'Atamah, and disliked to sleep before it or talk after it. After Fajr prayer, he would leave when a man could recognize the person sitting beside him. He used to recite 60 to 100 verses.'"

Sahīh Al-BukhāriBook of Prayer TimesChapter: The time of 'Asr prayer; Hadīth no. 547.Sahīh MuslimBook of Mosques and Places of PrayerChapter: The desirability of offering Fajr prayer at its earliest time, which is called Taghlīs, and revealing the merit of recitation in it; Hadīth no. 647.Sunan Abu DāwudBook of PrayerChapter: The time and manner of the Prophet's prayer; Hadīth no. 398.Jāmi' At-TirmidhiBook of Prayer as reported from the Prophet (PBUH)Chapter: What is reported on the dislike of sleeping before 'Ishā' prayer and engaging in nightly chatting after it; Hadīth no. 168.Sunan An-Nasā'iBook of Prayer TimesChapter: The dislike of sleeping after Maghrib prayer; Hadīth no. 525.Sunan Ibn MājahBook of Prayer - Chapters on prayer timesChapter: The time of Zhuhr prayer; Hadīth no. 674.Chapter: The merit of congregational prayer and clarifyingthe sinfulness of failure to attend it

Abu Hurayrah (may Allah be pleased with him) reported that the Prophet (may Allah's peace and blessings be upon him) said: "A prayer offered in congregation is 25 times more meritorious than a prayer offered in his house or market. If one of you performs ablution properly and comes to the mosque for the sole purpose of praying, for each step he takes Allah will raise him by one degree and erase one sin from him, until he enters the mosque. And when he enters the mosque, he will be deemed in prayer as long as the prayer keeps him there, and the angels will invoke Allah's blessings and mercy upon him as long as he remains in the place where he prays, saying 'O Allah, forgive him; O Allah, show mercy to him', unless his ablution is broken."

Sahīh Al-BukhāriBook of PrayerChapter: Praying in the mosque of the market; Hadīth no. 477.Sahīh MuslimBook of Mosques and Places of PrayerChapter: The merit of congregational prayer and clarifying the sinfulness of failure to attend it; Hadīth no. 649.Sunan Abu DāwudBook of PrayerChapter: What is reported on the merit of walking to prayer; Hadīth no. 559.Jāmi' At-TirmidhiBook of Prayer as reported from the Prophet (PBUH)Chapter: What is reported on the merit of congregational prayer; Hadīth no. 216.Sunan An-Nasā'iBook of PrayerChapter: The merit of congregational prayer; Hadīth no. 486.Sunan Ibn MājahBook of Mosques and Congregational PrayersChapter: The merit of praying in congregation; Hadīth no. 786.

Abu Hurayrah (may Allah be pleased with him) reported that the Prophet (may Allah's peace and blessings be upon him) said: "By the One in Whose hand my soul is, I was about to order firewood to be collected and order that the Adhān be pronounced. Then, I would appoint a man to lead people in prayer then head to some men and burn their houses upon them. By the One in Whose hand my soul is, if anyone of them knew that he would get a meaty bone or some meat between two ribs, he would attend 'Ishā'."

Sahīh Al-BukhāriBook of AdhānChapter: The obligation of congregational prayer; Hadīth no. 644.Sahīh MuslimBook of Mosques and Places of PrayerChapter: The merit of congregational prayer and clarifying the sinfulness of failure to attend it; Hadīth no. 651.Sunan Abu DāwudBook of PrayerChapter: Stressing the sinfulness of abandoning the congregational prayer; Hadīth no. 548.Jāmi' At-TirmidhiBook of Prayer as reported from the Prophet (PBUH)Chapter: What is reported on he who hears Adhān yet does not respond to it; Hadīth no. 217.Sunan An-Nasā'iBook of Leading People in PrayerChapter: Stressing the sinfulness of failure to attend the congregational prayer; Hadīth no. 848.Sunan Ibn MājahBook of Mosques and Congregational PrayersChapter: Stressing the sinfulness of failure to attend the congregational prayer; Hadīth no. 791.

Chapter: Who is more worthy of being Imām

Mālik ibn al-Huwayrith (may Allah be pleased with him) reported: "I came to the Prophet (may Allah's peace and blessings be upon him) along with a group of men from my people. We stayed with him for twenty days, and he was merciful and compassionate. When he noticed our longing for our families, he said to us: 'Go back and stay amongst them and teach them the religion. Offer the prayer, and when its time comes, let one of you recite the Adhān and the eldest one of you should lead you in prayer.'"

Sahīh Al-BukhāriBook of AdhānChapter: Those who held that one Muezzin should make the Adhān during travel; Hadīth no. 628.Sahīh MuslimBook of Mosques and Places of PrayerChapter: Who is more worthy of being Imām; Hadīth no. 674.Sunan Abu DāwudBook of PrayerChapter: Who is more worthy of being Imām; Hadīth no. 589.Jāmi' At-TirmidhiBook of Prayer as reported from the Prophet (PBUH)Chapter: What is reported on the Adhān during travel; Hadīth no. 205.Sunan An-Nasā'iBook of AdhānChapter: For a non-traveler, the Adhān made by another person is sufficient; Hadīth no. 635.Sunan Ibn MājahBook of Performance of Prayer and its SunnahChapter: Who is more worthy of being Imām; Hadīth no. 979.

Chapter: Making up for the missed prayer and the desirability of doing this promptly

Anas (may Allah be pleased with him) reported that the Prophet (may Allah's peace and blessings be upon him) said: "Whoever forgets to offer a prayer should offer it when he remembers it. There is no other expiation for it except that - Allah says: {And establish prayer for My remembrance}."

Sahīh Al-BukhāriBook of Prayer TimesChapter: He who forgets a prayer should offer it when he remembers it and he should only offer this prayer; Hadīth no. 597.Sahīh MuslimBook of Mosques and Places of PrayerChapter: Making up for the missed prayer and the desirability of doing this promptly; Hadīth no. 684.Sunan Abu DāwudBook of PrayerChapter: He who misses a prayer due to sleeping or forgetfulness; Hadīth no. 442.Jāmi' At-TirmidhiBook of Prayer as reported from the Prophet (PBUH)Chapter: What is reported on a man forgetting prayer; Hadīth no. 178.Sunan An-Nasā'iBook of Prayer TimesChapter: He who forgets a prayer; Hadīth no. 613.Sunan Ibn MājahBook of PrayerChapter: He who misses a prayer due to sleeping or forgetfulness; Hadīth no. 696.

Book of Prayer by Travelers and Shortening it

Chapter: Prayer by Travelers and Shortening it

Ibn 'Umar (may Allah be pleased with him) reported: "I accompanied the Prophet (may Allah's peace and blessings be upon him) and I did not see him offer supererogatory prayers during travel; and Allah, the Almighty, says: {There has certainly been for you in the Messenger of Allah an excellent example}."

Sahīh Al-BukhāriBook of Shortening PrayerChapter: He who does not offer supererogatory prayers during travel before or after the obligatory prayers; Hadīth no. 1101.Sahīh MuslimBook of Prayer by Travelers and Shortening itChapter: Prayer by travelers and shortening it; Hadīth no. 689.Sunan Abu DāwudBook of PrayerChapter: Offering supererogatory prayers during travel; Hadīth no.1223.Jāmi' At-TirmidhiBook of Friday as reported from the Prophet (PBUH) - Chapters on travelChapter: Shortening prayer during travel; Hadīth no. 544.Sunan An-Nasā'iBook of Shortening Prayer During TravelChapter: Not offering supererogatory prayers during travel; Hadīth no.1458.Sunan Ibn MājahBook of Performance of Prayer and its SunnahChapter: Offering supererogatory prayers during travel; Hadīth no.1071.

Anas (may Allah be pleased with him) reported: "We traveled with the Prophet (may Allah's peace and blessings be upon him) from Madīnah to Makkah. He shortened the prayers to two Rak'ahs until we came back to Madīnah." I (sub-narrator) asked: "Did you stay in Makkah for a while?" He replied: "We stayed there for ten days."

Sahīh Al-BukhāriBook of Shortening PrayerChapter: What is reported on shortening prayer and the length of stay that allows shortening; Hadīth no. 1081.Sahīh MuslimBook of Prayer by Travelers and

Shortening itChapter: Prayer by travelers and shortening it; Hadīth no. 693.Sunan Abu DāwudBook of Prayer - Chapter on prayer during travelChapter: When a traveler should offer complete prayers; Hadīth no. 1233.Jāmi' At-TirmidhiBook of Friday as reported from the Prophet (PBUH) - Chapters on travelChapter: What is reported on the duration of shortening prayer; Hadīth no. 548.Sunan An-Nasā'iBook of Shortening Prayer During TravelChapter: The stay during which prayer is to be shortened; Hadīth no.1452.Sunan Ibn MājahBook of Performance of Prayer and its SunnahChapter: How long a traveler can shorten prayer if he stays in some town; Hadīth no. 1077.Chapter: The permissibility to offer supererogatory prayers on riding animalsduring travel, in any direction they are facing.

Ibn 'Umar (may Allah be pleased with him) reported: "The Prophet (may Allah's peace and blessings be upon him) used to pray during travel on his mount in whatever direction it took, nodding his head (for Rukū' and prostration). He would offer the night prayer, but not the obligatory prayers, and would pray Witr on his mount."

Sahīh Al-BukhāriBook of WitrChapter: Praying Witr during travel; Hadīth no.1000.Sahīh MuslimBook of Prayer by Travelers and Shortening itChapter: The permissibility to offer supererogatory prayers during travel on riding animals in any direction they face; Hadīth no. 700.Sunan Abu DāwudBook of PrayerChapter: Offering supererogatory prayers and Witr on riding animals; Hadīth no. 1224.Jāmi' At-TirmidhiBook of Interpretation of the Qur'an as reported from the Prophet (PBUH)Chapter: From Sūrat Al-Baqarah; Hadīth no. 2958.Sunan An-Nasā'iBook of PrayerChapter: The condition in which a person can face a direction other than the Qiblah; Hadīth no. 490.Sunan Ibn MājahBook of Establishing the Prayerand the Sunnah Acts Related to itChapter: What is reported on praying Witr on a riding animal; Hadīth no. 1200.

Chapter: The desirability of greeting the mosque by offering two Rak'ahs, the dislike of sitting before performing them, and the permissibility of this prayer at all times

Abu Qatādah as-Salami (may Allah be pleased with him) reported that the Prophet (may Allah's peace and blessings be upon him) said: "When anyone of you enters the mosque, let him offer two Rak'ahs before he sits down."

Sahīh Al-BukhāriBook of PrayerChapter: When anyone of you enters the mosque, let him offer two Rak'ahs before he sits down; Hadīth no. 444.Sahīh MuslimBook of Prayer by Travelers and Shortening itChapter: The desirability of greeting the mosque by offering two Rak'ahs, the dislike of sitting before performing them, and the permissibility of this prayer at all times; Hadīth no. 714.Sunan Abu DāwudBook of PrayerChapter: What is reported on offering prayer upon entering the mosque; Hadīth no. 467.Jāmi' At-TirmidhiBook of Prayer as reported fromthe Messenger of Allah (PBUH)Chapter: The Hadīth: When anyone of you enters the mosque, let him offer two Rak'ahs; Hadīth no. 316.Sunan An-Nasā'iBook of MosquesChapter: The order to pray before sitting in the mosque; Hadīth no. 730.Sunan Ibn MājahBook of Establishing the Prayerand the Sunnah Acts Related to itChapter: Whoever enters the mosque should not sit down before he prays; Hadīth no. 1013.Chapter: The merit and number of the regular Sunnah prayersbefore and after the obligatory prayers

Ibn 'Umar (may Allah be pleased with him) reported: "I prayed along with the Prophet (may Allah's peace and blessings be upon him) two Rak'ahs before Zhuhr prayer, two Rak'ahs after Zhuhr prayer, two Rak'ahs after Maghrib prayer, two Rak'ahs after 'Ishā' prayer, and two Rak'ahs after Friday prayer. As for those after Maghrib and 'Ishā' prayers, they were offered in his house."

Sahīh Al-BukhāriBook of Tahajjud (Midnight prayer)Chapter: Offering supererogatory prayers after the obligatory ones; Hadīth no. 1172.Sahīh MuslimBook of Prayer by Travelers and Shortening itChapter: The merit and number of the regular Sunnah prayers before and after the obligatory prayers; Hadīth no. 729.Sunan Abu DāwudBook of PrayerChapters on the supererogatory and Sunnah prayers; Hadīth no. 1252.Jāmi' At-TirmidhiBook of Prayer as reported from the Prophet (PBUH)Chapter: What is reported that he offered them at home; Hadīth no. 433.Sunan An-Nasā'iBook of Leading People in

PrayerChapter: The prayer after Zhuhr prayer; Hadīth no. 873.Sunan Ibn MājahBook of Performance of Prayer and its SunnahChapter: What is reported on the prayer after Friday prayer; Hadīth no. 1131.

Chapter: The permissibility of offering supererogatory prayers standing or sitting

and performing part of the Rak'ah standing and part of it sitting.

'Ā'ishah (may Allah be pleased with her) reported: "I did not see the Prophet (may Allah's peace and blessings be upon him) reciting in the night prayer while sitting until he became old, as he would recite while sitting and when thirty or forty verses remained from the Sūrah, he would get up and recite them then make Rukū'."

Sahīh Al-BukhāriBook of TahajjudChapter: The Prophet's night prayer during Ramadan and outside it; Hadīth no. 1148.Sahīh MuslimBook of Prayer by Travelers and Shortening itChapter: The permissibility of offering supererogatory prayers standing or sitting and performing part of the Rak'ah standing and part of it sitting; Hadīth no. 731.Sunan Abu DāwudBook of PrayerChapter: Prayer while sitting; Hadīth no. 953.Jāmi' At-TirmidhiBook of Prayer as reported from the Prophet (PBUH)Chapter: He who offers supererogatory prayer while sitting; Hadīth no. 374.Sunan An-Nasā'iBook of Supererogatory Prayer During the Night and DayChapter: What he should do if he starts prayer while standing and mention of the difference between the narrations reported from 'A'ishah in this regard; Hadīth no. 1649.Sunan Ibn MājahBook of Performance of Prayer and its SunnahChapter: Offering supererogatory prayer while sitting; Hadīth no. 1227.

Chapter: The night prayer and the number of the Prophet's Rak'ahs in the night,

that Witr is one Rak'ah, and that one Rak'ah is a valid prayer.

'Ā'ishah (may Allah be pleased with her) reported: "The Messenger of Allah (may Allah's peace and blessings be upon him) used to offer eleven Rak'ahs. That was his prayer (in the night). He would prostrate himself for as long as one of you would recite fifty verses before he would raise his head. He would also offer two Rak'ahs before Fajr prayer, after which he would lie on his right side till the Muezzin came to him for prayer."

Sahīh Al-BukhāriBook of WitrChapter: What is reported on Witr; Hadīth no. 994.Sahīh MuslimBook of Prayer by Travelers and Shortening itChapter: The night prayer and the number of the Prophet's Rak'ahs in the night, that Witr is one Rak'ah, and that one Rak'ah is a valid prayer; Hadīth no. 736.Sunan Abu DāwudBook of PrayerChapter: The night prayer; Hadīth no. 1336.Jāmi' At-TirmidhiBook of Prayer as reported from the Prophet (PBUH)Chapter: What is reported on the description of the Prophet's night prayer; Hadīth no. 440.Sunan An-Nasā'iBook of AdhānChapter: The Muezzins notifying the Imams of prayer; Hadīth no. 685.Sunan Ibn MājahBook of Performance of Prayer and its SunnahChapter: What is reported on the number of Rak'ahs of the night prayer; Hadīth no. 1358.

'A'ishah (may Allah be pleased with her) reported: "The Messenger of Allah (may Allah's peace and blessings be upon him) offered Witr in every part of the night, and the latest he offered Witr was in the time right before dawn."

Sahīh Al-BukhāriBook of WitrChapter: The times of Witr; Hadīth no. 996.Sahīh MuslimBook of Prayer by Travelers and Shortening itChapter: The night prayer and number of the Prophet's Rak'ahs in the night, that Witr is one Rak'ah, and that one Rak'ah is a valid prayer; Hadīth no. 745.Sunan Abu DāwudBook of PrayerChapter: The time of Witr; Hadīth no. 1435.Jāmi' At-TirmidhiBook of Prayer as reported from the Prophet (PBUH) - Chapters on WitrChapter: What is reported on offering Witr in the first and last parts of the night; Hadīth no. 457.Sunan An-Nasā'iBook of Supererogatory Prayer During the Night and DayChapter: The time of Witrr; Hadīth no. 1681.Sunan Ibn MājahBook of Performance of Prayer and its SunnahChapter: What is reported on offering Witr in the last part of the night; Hadīth no. 1185.

Chapter: The night prayer offered in sets of two Rak'ahs and Witr is one Rak'ah in the later part of the night.

Ibn 'Umar (may Allah be pleased with him) reported that a man asked the Messenger of Allah (may Allah's peace and blessings be upon him) about the night prayer, and he said: "The night prayer is to be offered in sets of two Rak'ahs, and if you fear that Fajr is approaching, let him offer one Rak'ah as Witr for what he has prayed."

Sahīh Al-BukhāriBook of WitrChapter: What is reported on Witr; Hadīth no. 990.Sahīh MuslimBook of Prayer by Travelers and Shortening itChapter: The night prayer offered in sets of two Rak'ahs and Witr is one Rak'ah in the last part of the night; Hadīth no. 749.Sunan Abu DāwudBook of PrayerChapter: The night prayer offered in sets of two Rak'ahs; Hadīth no. 1326.Jāmi' At-TirmidhiBook of Prayer as reported from the Prophet (PBUH)Chapter: What is reported on offering the night prayer in sets of two Rak'ahs; Hadīth no. 437.Sunan An-Nasā'iBook of Supererogatory Prayer During the Night and DayChapter: How to offer the night prayer; Hadīth no. 1667.Sunan Ibn MājahBook of Establishing the Prayerand the Sunnah Acts Related to itChapter: What is reported on offering the night prayer in sets of two Rak'ahs; Hadīth no. 1320.

Chapter: Encouragement of offering Ramadan night prayer known as Tarāwih.

Abu Hurayrah (may Allah be pleased with him) reported that the Prophet (may Allah's peace and blessings be upon him) said: "Whoever fasts Ramadan out of faith and in pursuit of divine reward, his past sins will be forgiven."

Sahīh Al-BukhāriBook of FaithChapter: Offering the supererogatory night prayer in Ramadan is part of faith; Hadīth no. 37.Sahīh MuslimBook of Prayer by Travelers and Shortening itChapter: Encouragement of offering Ramadan night prayer known as Tarāwih; Hadīth no. 759.Sunan Abu DāwudBook of Prayer - Chapters on the month of RamadanChapter: Offering the night prayer in Ramadan; Hadīth no. 1371.Jāmi' At-TirmidhiBook of Fasting as reported from the Prophet (PBUH)Chapter: What is reported on the merit of the month of Ramadan; Hadīth no. 683.Sunan An-Nasā'iBook of Supererogatory Prayer During the Night and DayChapter: The reward for he who offers Ramadan night prayer out of faith and in pursuit of divine reward; Hadīth no. 1602.Sunan Ibn MājahBook of Performance of Prayer and its SunnahChapter: What is reported on offering Ramadan night prayer; Hadīth no. 1326.

Chapter: Supplication in the night prayer

'Abdullāh ibn 'Abbās (may Allah be pleased with him) reported: "I stayed a night in the house of Maymūnah, (his maternal aunt) the Prophet's wife. I lay down across the cushion and the Messenger of Allah (may Allah's peace and blessings be upon him) and his wife lay down on it lengthwise. The Messenger of Allah (may Allah's peace and blessings be upon him) slept till midnight, or shortly before or after that. He woke up and sat up, wiping the effect of sleep off his face with his hands. Then, he recited ten last verses of Sūrat Āl-'Imrān, after which he moved toward a hanging water-skin and made ablution from it, properly. Then, he stood for prayer. So I got up and did as he did. Then, I moved and stood beside him. He put his right hand on my head and took hold of my right ear, twisting it. He offered two Rak'ahs, followed by two Rak'ahs, then two Rak'ahs, then two, then two, and then two. Then, he performed Witr, and after that he lay down until the Muezzin came to him. So, he got up, offered two brief Rak'ahs then went out and performed Fajr prayer."

Sahīh Al-BukhāriBook of AblutionChapter: Reciting the Qur'an after breaking the ablution and so on; Hadīth no. 183.Sahīh MuslimBook of Prayer by Travelers and Shortening itChapter: Supplication in the night prayer; Hadīth no. 763.Sunan Abu DāwudBook of PrayerChapter: The night prayer; Hadīth no. 1367.Jāmi' At-TirmidhiBook of Prayer as reported from the Prophet (PBUH)Chapter: What is reported on a man praying with another man; Hadīth no. 232.Sunan An-Nasā'iBook of Supererogatory Prayer During the Night and DayChapter: Mention of that with which a person commences the night prayer; Hadīth no. 1620.Sunan Ibn MājahBook of Performance of Prayer and its SunnahChapter: What is reported on the number of Rak'ahs of the night prayer; Hadīth no. 1363.

Ibn 'Abbās (may Allah be pleased with him) reported: "The Prophet (may Allah's peace and blessings be upon him) used to make this supplication at night: 'O Allah, our Lord, all praise is due to You. You are the Lord of the heavens and earth. All praise is due to You. You are the Sustainer of the heavens and earth and all what lies therein. All praise is due to You. You are the Light of the heavens and earth. Your speech is truth, Your promise is truth, meeting with You is true, Paradise is true, Hellfire is true, and the Hour is true. O Allah, to You I submit, in You I believe, upon You I rely, to You I turn in repentance, by Your help I contend with my foes, and to You I refer for judgment. So, forgive me my past and future sins and those sins which I did secretly and those which I did openly. You are my God. I have no other god but You.'"

Sahīh Al-BukhāriBook of MonotheismChapter: Allah says: {And it is He who created the heavens and earth in truth} - Hadīth no. 7385.Sahīh MuslimBook of Prayer by Travelers and Shortening itChapter: Supplication in the night prayer; Hadīth no. 769.Sunan Abu DāwudBook of PrayerChapter: The opening supplication in prayer; Hadīth no. 771.Jāmi' At-TirmidhiBook of Supplications as reported from the Prophet (PBUH)Chapter: What is reported on what a person should say when he gets up for prayer at night; Hadīth no. 3418.Sunan An-Nasā'iBook of Supererogatory Prayer During the Night and DayChapter: Mention of that with which a person opens the night prayer; Hadīth no. 1619.Sunan Ibn MājahBook of Establishing the Prayerand the Sunnah Acts Related to itChapter: What is reported on the supplication a person makes when he gets up for prayer at night; Hadīth no. 1355.Chapter: The desirability of offering the supererogatory prayerat home and the permissibility of offering it in the mosque

Ibn 'Umar (may Allah be pleased with him) reported that the Prophet (may Allah's peace and blessings be upon him) said: "Offer some of your prayers in your houses and do not take them as graves."

Sahīh Al-BukhāriBook of PrayerChapter: The dislike of praying in graveyards; Hadīth no. 432.Sahīh MuslimBook of Prayer by Travelers and Shortening itChapter: The desirability of offering the supererogatory prayer at home and the permissibility of offering it in the mosque; Hadīth no. 777.Sunan Abu DāwudBook of PrayerChapter: A man offering supererogatory prayers at home; Hadīth no. 1043.Jāmi' At-TirmidhiBook of Prayer as reported from the Prophet (PBUH)Chapter: What is reported on the merit of offering supererogatory prayers at home; Hadīth no. 451.Sunan An-Nasā'iBook of Supererogatory Prayer During the Night and DayChapter: Encouraging the performance of prayer at home and the merit of doing this; Hadīth no. 1598.Sunan Ibn MājahBook of Establishing the Prayerand the Sunnah Acts Related to itChapter: What is reported on offering supererogatory prayers at home; Hadīth no. 1377.Chapter: Commanding the one who feels drowsy during prayer or finds it hard to recite or understand the Qur'anor Dhikr (due to drowsiness) to lie or sit down until this condition goes away.

'A'isha (may Allah be pleased with her) reported that the Prophet (may Allah's peace and blessings be upon him) said: "If anyone of you feels drowsy during prayer, he should lie down until the drowsiness goes away from him, because if a person performs prayer while feeling drowsy, he might curse himself while asking for forgiveness."

Sahīh Al-BukhāriBook of AblutionChapter: Ablution is invalidated by sleep, and those who held that it is not invalidated by dozing off once or twice or after nodding in slumber; Hadīth no. 212.Sahīh MuslimBook of Prayer by Travelers and Shortening itChapter: Commanding one who feels drowsy during prayer or finds it hard to recite or understand the Qur'an or Dhikr (due to drowsiness) to lie or sit down until this condition goes away; Hadīth no. 786.Sunan Abu DāwudBook of PrayerChapter: Drowsiness during prayer; Hadīth no. 1310.Jāmi' At-TirmidhiBook of Prayer as reported from the Prophet (PBUH)Chapter: What is reported on praying while feeling drowsy; Hadīth no. 355.Sunan An-Nasā'iBook of PurificationChapter: Drowsiness; Hadīth no.162.Sunan Ibn MājahBook of Performance of Prayer and its SunnahChapter: What is reported on a praying person who feels drowsy; Hadīth no. 1370.

Chapter: The merit of the Qur'an memorizer

Abu Mūsa al-Ash'ari (may Allah be pleased with him) reported that the Prophet (may Allah's peace and blessings be upon him) said: "The example of a believer who recites the Qur'an is like that of a citron; it smells good and tastes good. And the example of a believer who does not recite the Qur'an is like that of a date; it has no smell and tastes good. And the example of a hypocrite who recites the Qur'an is like that of a sweet basil; it smells good and tastes bitter. And the example of a hypocrite who does not recite the Qur'an is like that of a colocynth; it has no smell and tastes bitter."

Sahīh Al-BukhāriBook of FoodsChapter: Mention of food; Hadīth no. 5427.Sahīh MuslimBook of Prayer by Travelers and Shortening itChapter: The merit of the Qur'an memorizer; Hadīth no. 797.Sunan Abu DāwudBook of Good MannersChapter: Whom a person should sit with; Hadīth no. 4830.Jāmi' At-TirmidhiBook of Good Manners as reported from the Prophet (PBUH)Chapter: What is reported on the example of a believer who recites the Qur'an and a believer who does not recite it; Hadīth no. 2865.Sunan An-Nasā'iBook of Faith and Its TeachingsChapter: The example of a believer and a hypocrite who recite the Qur'an; Hadīth no. 5038.Sunan Ibn MājahIntroduction of Ibn MājahChapter: The merit of the one who learns the Qur'an and teaches it; Hadīth no. 214.

Chapter: The times during which prayer is forbidden.

Ibn 'Abbās (may Allah be pleased with him) reported: "Virtuous men, and the most virtuous of them in my sight is 'Umar, affirmed in my presence that the Prophet (may Allah's peace and blessings be upon him) forbade prayer between Fajr and sunrise and between 'Asr and sunset."

Sahīh Al-BukhāriBook of Prayer TimesChapter: Prayer between Fajr and sunrise; Hadīth no. 581.Sahīh MuslimBook of Prayer by Travelers and Shortening itChapter: The times during which prayer is forbidden; Hadīth no. 826.Sunan Abu DāwudBook of PrayerChapter: Those who deem it permissible if the sun is high in the sky; Hadīth no. 1276.Jāmi' At-TirmidhiBook of Prayer as reported from the Prophet (PBUH)Chapter: The dislike of praying after 'Asr and after Fajr; Hadīth no. 183.Sunan An-Nasā'iBook of Prayer TimesChapter: The prohibition of praying after Fajr; Hadīth no. 562.Sunan Ibn MājahBook of Performance of Prayer and its SunnahChapter: The prohibition of praying after Fajr and after 'Asr; Hadīth no. 1250.

Chapter: There is a prayer between every two Adhāns.

'Abdullah ibn Mughaffal (may Allah be pleased with him) reported that the Prophet (may Allah's peace and blessings be upon him) said: "There is a prayer between every two Adhāns; there is a prayer between every two Adhāns." And in the third time, he added: "For those who wish."

Sahīh Al-BukhāriBook of AdhānChapter: There is a prayer between every two Adhāns for those who wish; Hadīth no. 627.Sahīh MuslimBook of Prayer by Travelers and Shortening itChapter: There is a prayer between every two Adhāns; Hadīth no. 838.Sunan Abu DāwudBook of PrayerChapter: Praying before Maghrib; Hadīth no. 1283.Jāmi' At-TirmidhiBook of Prayer as reported from the Prophet (PBUH)Chapter: What is reported on praying before Maghrib; Hadīth no. 185.Sunan An-Nasā'iBook of AdhānChapter: Prayer between Adhān and Iqāmah; Hadīth no. 681.Sunan Ibn MājahBook of Performance of Prayer and its SunnahChapter: What is reported on the two Rak'ahs before Maghrib; Hadīth no. 1162.

Chapter: The Fear Prayer

'Abdullah ibn 'Umar (may Allah be pleased with him) reported: The Messenger of Allah (may Allah's peace and blessings be upon him) led one of the two groups in prayer while the other group was facing the enemy. Then, they left and took the place of their comrades, who came and he led them in one Rak'ah and made Taslīm. Then, they stood and offered the missed Rak'ah, and the others stood and offered their missed Rak'ah.

Sahīh Al-BukhāriBook of BattlesChapter: The Battle of Dhāt ar-Riqā'; Hadīth no. 4133.Sahīh MuslimBook of Prayer by Travelers and Shortening itChapter: The fear prayer; Hadīth no. 839.Sunan Abu DāwudBook of PrayerChapter: Those who held that Imām should lead each group in one Rak'ah and make Taslīm and then each group should stand and offer the missed Rak'ah; Hadīth no. 1243.Jāmi' At-TirmidhiBook of Friday as reported from the Prophet (PBUH)Chapter: What is reported on the fear prayer; Hadīth no. 564.Sunan An-Nasā'iChapter: The Fear Prayer;Hadīth no. 1538.Sunan Ibn MājahBook of Establishing the Prayerand the Sunnah Acts Related to itChapter: What is reported on the fear prayer; Hadīth no. 1258.

Sahl ibn Abi Hathmah (may Allah be pleased with him) said: "The Imām stands in the direction of the Qiblah, leading one group in prayer and the other group is opposite the enemy, facing them. He offers one Rak'ah with the group behind him, after which they stand up and offer one Rak'ah alone and make two prostrations in their place. Then, they go to the place of the others, and he leads the others in one Rak'ah, the second for himself. Then, they offer one Rak'ah and make two prostrations." In another version: "The Prophet (may Allah's peace and blessings be upon him) prayed during the Battle of Banu Anmār."

Sahīh Al-BukhāriBook of BattlesChapter: The Battle of Dhāt ar-Riqā'; Hadīth no. 4131.Sahīh MuslimBook of Prayer by Travelers and Shortening itChapter: The fear prayer; Hadīth no. 841.Sunan Abu DāwudBook of PrayerChapter: Those who say: He offers one Rak'ah and keeps standing, and they perform another Rak'ah alone, make Taslīm, leave, and stand facing the enemy; but there is disagreement over Taslīm; Hadīth no. 1239.Jāmi' At-TirmidhiBook of Friday as reported from the Prophet (PBUH)Chapter: What is reported on the fear prayer; Hadīth no. 565.Sunan An-Nasā'iChapter: The Fear Prayer;Hadīth no. 1536.Sunan Ibn MājahBook of Establishing the Prayerand the Sunnah Acts Related to itChapter: What is reported on the fear prayer; Hadīth no. 1259.

Book of Friday

Chapter: Perfume and the tooth-stick on Fridays.

Abu Hurayrah (may Allah be pleased with him) reported that the Prophet (may Allah's peace and blessings be upon him) said: "Whoever performs Ghusl (ritual bath) on Friday then goes to the mosque early, it is as if he sacrificed a camel; if he goes in the second hour (i.e. later than that), it is as if he sacrificed a cow; if he goes in the third hour, it is as if he sacrificed a horned ram; if he goes in the fourth part of time, it is as if he sacrificed a hen; and if he goes in the fifth part of time, it is as if he sacrificed an egg; and when the Imām comes out, the angels attend to listen to Dhikr."

Sahīh Al-BukhāriBook of FridayChapter: The merit of Friday prayer; Hadīth no. 881.Sahīh MuslimBook of FridayChapter: Perfume and the tooth-stick on Friday; Hadīth no. 850.Sunan Abu DāwudBook of PurificationChapter: The ritual bath on Friday; Hadīth no. 351.Jāmi' At-TirmidhiBook of Friday as reported from the Prophet (PBUH)Chapter: What is reported on going to Friday prayer early; Hadīth no. 499.Sunan An-Nasā'iBook of FridayChapter: The time of Friday prayer; Hadīth no. 1388.Sunan Ibn MājahBook of Performance of Prayer and its SunnahChapter: What is reported on going to Friday prayer at the earliest time; Hadīth no. 1092.

Chapter: Listening attentively during Friday sermon.

Abu Hurayrah (may Allah be pleased with him) reported that the Prophet (may Allah's peace and blessings be upon him) said: "If you say to your companion: 'Listen carefully!' on Friday while the Imām is delivering the sermon, you have thus engaged in idle talk."

Sahīh Al-BukhāriBook of FridayChapter: Listening attentively on Friday while the Imām is giving the sermon; Hadīth no. 934.Sahīh MuslimBook of FridayChapter: Listening attentively during Friday sermon; Hadīth no. 851.Sunan Abu DāwudBook of PrayerChapter: Talking while the Imām is giving the sermon; Hadīth no. 1112.Jāmi' At-TirmidhiBook of Friday as reported from the Prophet (PBUH)Chapter: What is reported on the dislike of talking while the Imām is giving the sermon; Hadīth no. 512.Sunan An-Nasā'iBook of FridayChapter: Listening attentively to the sermon on Friday; Hadīth no. 1402.Sunan Ibn MājahBook of Establishing the Prayerand the Sunnah Acts Related to itChapter: What is reported on listening attentively to the sermon; Hadīth no. 1110.

Chapter: Mention of the two sermons before prayer and the sitting between them.

Ibn 'Umar (may Allah be pleased with him) reported: "The Prophet (may Allah's peace and blessings be upon him) used to give the sermon while standing and then sit down and then stand up again, as you do nowadays."

Sahīh Al-BukhāriBook of FridayChapter: Giving the sermon while standing; Hadīth no. 920.Sahīh MuslimBook of FridayChapter: Mention of the two sermons before prayer and the sitting between them; Hadīth no. 861.Sunan Abu DāwudBook of PrayerChapter: Sitting when he the Imām ascends the pulpit; Hadīth no. 1092.Jāmi' At-TirmidhiBook of Friday as reported from the Prophet (PBUH)Chapter: What is reported on sitting between the two sermons; Hadīth no. 506.Sunan An-Nasā'iBook of FridayChapter: Separating the two sermons by sitting; Hadīth no. 1416.Sunan Ibn MājahBook of Performance of Prayer and its SunnahChapter: What is reported on Friday sermon; Hadīth no. 1103.

Chapter: Giving a greeting while the Imām is delivering the sermon.

Jābir ibn 'Abdullāh (may Allah be pleased with him) reported that the Messenger of Allah (may Allah's peace and blessings be upon him) said while delivering a sermon: "If any of you comes while the Imām is giving the sermon or has come out, let him offer two Rak'ahs."

Sahīh Al-BukhāriBook of TahajjudChapter: What is reported on offering supererogatory prayers in sets of two Rak'ahs; Hadīth no. 1166.Sahīh MuslimBook of FridayChapter: Giving a greeting while the Imām is delivering the sermon; Hadīth no. 875.Sunan Abu DāwudBook of PrayerChapter: When a man comes in while the Imām is giving the sermon; Hadīth no. 1115.Jāmi' At-TirmidhiBook of Friday as reported from the Prophet (PBUH)Chapter: What is reported on the two Rak'ahs when a man comes in while the Imām is giving the sermon; Hadīth no. 510.Sunan An-Nasā'iBook of FridayChapter: Prayer on Friday for a man who comes while the Imām is giving the sermon; Hadīth no. 1400.Sunan Ibn MājahBook of Establishing the Prayerand the Sunnah Acts Related to itChapter: What is reported on a man who enters the mosque while the Imām is giving the sermon; Hadīth no. 1112.

Book on the Prayer of the Two Eids

Ibn 'Abbās (may Allah be pleased with him) reported: "The Prophet (may Allah's peace and blessings be upon him) offered two Rak'ahs on the day of Eid al-Fitr and prayed nothing before or after it. Then, he went to the women, along with Bilāl and ordered them to give charity, so they started giving right away; a woman would give her earrings and her necklace."

Sahīh Al-BukhāriBook of the Two EidsChapter: The sermon after Eid prayer; Hadīth no. 964.Sahīh MuslimBook on the Prayer of the Two EidsHadīth no. 884.Sunan Abu DāwudBook of PrayerChapter: Prayer after the Eid prayer; Hadīth no. 1159.Jāmi' At-TirmidhiBook of Friday as reported from the Prophet (PBUH) - Chapters on the two EidsChapter: No prayer before or after Eid prayer; Hadīth no. 537.Sunan An-Nasā'iBook of the Prayer of the Two EidsChapter: Prayer before and after the two Eid prayers; Hadīth no. 1587.Sunan Ibn MājahBook of Establishing the Prayerand the Sunnah Acts Related to itChapter: What is reported on the prayer of the two Eids; Hadīth no. 1273.

Chapter: Mention of the permissibility for women to go out in the two Eids

to the praying place and to attend the sermon, separately from men.

Umm 'Atiyyah (may Allah be pleased with her) reported: "We were ordered to bring out the menstruating women and the virgins staying in seclusion amongst us on the two Eids to attend the Muslim gathering and invocations; and that menstruating women should keep away from the praying place. A woman asked: 'O Messenger of Allah, what about if one of us does not have a Jilbāb (cloak)?' He said: 'Let her companion dress her in one of her cloaks.'"

Sahīh Al-BukhāriBook of PrayerChapter: The obligation to offer prayer while dressed; Hadīth no. 351.Sahīh MuslimBook on the Prayer of the Two EidsChapter: Mention of the permissibility for women to go out on the two Eids to the praying place and to attend the sermon, separately from men; Hadīth no. 890.Sunan Abu DāwudBook of PrayerChapter: Women going out to Eid prayer; Hadīth no. 1136.Jāmi' At-TirmidhiBook of Friday as reported from the Prophet (PBUH) - Chapters on the two EidsChapter: Women going out to the two Eid prayers; Hadīth no. 539.Sunan An-Nasā'iBook of Menstruation and Istihādah (bleeding)Chapter: Menstruating women attend the two Eid prayers and the Muslim invocations; Hadīth no. 390.Sunan Ibn MājahBook of Establishing the Prayerand the Sunnah Acts Related to itChapter: What is reported on women going out to the two Eid prayers; Hadīth no. 1307.

Book of the Prayer for Rain

'Abdullāh ibn Zayd (may Allah be pleased with him) reported: "I saw the Prophet (may Allah's peace and blessings be upon him) the day he went out to pray for rain. He turned his back to the people, faced the Qiblah, and invoked Allah. Then, he turned his cloak inside out and led us in a two-Rak'ah prayer in which he recited the Qur'an aloud."

Sahīh Al-BukhāriBook of the Prayer for RainChapter: How the Prophet (PBUH) turned his back to the people; Hadīth no. 1025.Sahīh MuslimBook of the Prayer for RainHadīth no. 894.Sunan Abu DāwudBook of PrayerChapters on the prayer for rain; Hadīth no. 1161.Jāmi' At-TirmidhiBook of Friday as reported from the Prophet (PBUH)Chapter: What is reported on the prayer for rain; Hadīth no. 556.Sunan An-Nasā'iBook of the Prayer for RainChapter: The Imām turning his back to the people when he supplicates during the prayer for rain; Hadīth no. 1509.Sunan Ibn MājahBook of Performance of Prayer and its SunnahChapter: What is reported on the prayer for rain; Hadīth no. 1267.

Book of Eclipses

Chapter: Eclipse prayer.

'Ā'ishah (may Allah be pleased with her) reported: "The sun was eclipsed in the lifetime of the Messenger of Allah (may Allah's peace and blessings be upon him), so he led the people in prayer. He stood for long, bowed for long, then stood for long, but it was shorter than the previous one, and then he bowed for long, but it was shorter than the previous one. Then, he prostrated himself for long. He did in the second Rak'ah as he did in the first one. He finished the prayer as the sun became clear. Starting with praising Allah, he addressed the people, saying: 'Indeed, the sun and the moon are two of the signs of Allah. They are not eclipsed due to the death or birth of anyone. So, if you see that, supplicate Allah, proclaim His greatness (say Allahu Akbar), pray, and give charity.' Then, he said: 'O followers of Muhammad, by Allah, no one is more jealous than Allah that any of His servants, male or female, should commit adultery. O followers of Muhammad, by Allah, if you knew what I know, you would laugh little and cry a lot.'"

Sahīh Al-BukhāriBook of EclipsesChapter: Giving charity at the time of eclipse; Hadīth no. 1044.Sahīh MuslimBook of EclipsesChapter: Eclipse prayer; Hadīth no. 901.Sunan Abu DāwudBook of PrayerChapter: Eclipse prayer; Hadīth no. 1177.Jāmi' At-TirmidhiBook of Friday as reported from the Prophet (PBUH)Chapter: The eclipse prayer; Hadīth no. 561.Sunan An-Nasā'iBook of EclipsesChapter: Another type of it reported from 'Ā'ishah (may Allah be pleased with her); Hadīth no. 1474.Sunan Ibn MājahBook of Performance of Prayer and its SunnahChapter: The eclipse prayer; Hadīth no. 1263.

Book of Funerals

Chapter: Patience over affliction at the first shock.

Anas ibn Mālik (may Allah be pleased with him) reported: "The Prophet (may Allah's peace and blessings be upon him) passed by a woman who was weeping at the side of a grave. He said to her: 'Fear Allah and be patient.' In reply, she said: 'Leave me alone, for you have not been afflicted with a calamity like mine,' not recognizing him. When she was informed that he was the Prophet (may Allah's peace and blessings be upon him), she went to his house, and there she did not find any doormen. She said to him: 'I did not recognize you.' He said: 'Indeed, patience is at the first shock.'"

Saḥīḥ Al-BukhāriBook of FuneralsChapter: Visiting the graves; Hadīth no. 1283.Saḥīḥ MuslimBook of FuneralsChapter: Patience over affliction at the first shock; Hadīth no. 926.Sunan Abu DāwudBook of FuneralsChapter: Patience at the first shock; Hadīth no. 3124.Sunan At-TirmidhiBook of Funerals as reported from the Prophet (PBUH)Chapter: The Hadīth: Patience is at the first shock; Hadīth no. 988.Sunan An-Nasā'iBook of FuneralsChapter: The order to seek divine reward and be patient when calamity strikes; Hadīth no. 1869.Sunan Ibn MājahBook of FuneralsChapter: What is reported on enduring affliction patiently; Hadīth no. 1596.

Chapter: The deceased suffers punishment due to his family weeping over him.

'Ā'ishah (may Allah be pleased with her), wife of the Prophet (may Allah's peace and blessings be upon him) reported: "The Messenger of Allah (may Allah's peace and blessings be upon him) passed by (the grave) of a Jewish woman whose family was weeping over her, so he said: 'They are weeping over her and she is being punished in her grave.'"

Saḥīḥ Al-BukhāriBook of FuneralsChapter: The Prophet's statement: "The deceased suffers punishment due to some weeping of his family over him" if lamentation was his habit; Hadīth no. 1289.Saḥīḥ MuslimBook of FuneralsChapter: The deceased suffers punishment due to his family weeping over him; Hadīth no. 931.Sunan Abu DāwudBook of FuneralsChapter: Wailing; Hadīth no. 3129.Jāmi' At-TirmidhiBook of Funerals as reported from the Prophet (PBUH)Chapter: What is reported on the concession for weeping over the dead; Hadīth no. 1004.Sunan An-Nasā'iBook of FuneralsChapter: Wailing over the dead; Hadīth no. 1856.Sunan Ibn MājahBook of FuneralsChapter: What is reported on the dead suffering punishment due to the wailing over him; Hadīth no. 1595.

Chapter: Washing the dead.

Umm 'Atiyyah (may Allah be pleased with her) reported: "One of the daughters of the Prophet (may Allah's peace and blessings be upon him) passed away. He came to us and said: 'Wash her with lotus leaves for an odd number of times; three, five, or more, as you see appropriate. In the last time, put camphor - or some camphor - on her, and when you finish, notify me.' When we finished, we informed him, and he gave us his waist-sheet (to shroud her). We braided her hair in three braids and let them fall at her back."

Saḥīḥ Al-BukhāriBook of FuneralsChapter: Hair of a dead woman is let to fall behind her; Hadīth no. 1263.Saḥīḥ MuslimBook of FuneralsChapter: Washing the dead; Hadīth no. 939.Sunan Abu DāwudBook of FuneralsChapter: How to wash the dead; Hadīth no. 3143.Jāmi' At-TirmidhiBook of Funerals as reported from the Prophet (PBUH)Chapter: What is reported on washing the dead; Hadīth no. 990.Sunan An-Nasā'iBook of FuneralsChapter: Using camphor in washing the dead; Hadīth no. 1890.Sunan Ibn MājahBook of FuneralsChapter: What is reported on washing the dead; Hadīth no. 1458.

Chapter: Shrouding the dead.

'Ā'ishah (may Allah be pleased with her) reported: "The Prophet (may Allah's peace and blessings be upon him) was shrouded in three sheets of white Yemeni cotton cloth, which included no shirt or turban."

Saḥīḥ Al-BukhāriBook of FuneralsChapter: White cloth for shrouding; Hadīth no. 1264.Saḥīḥ MuslimBook of FuneralsChapter: Shrouding the dead; Hadīth no. 941.Sunan Abu DāwudBook of FuneralsChapter: Shrouding; Hadīth no. 3151.Jāmi' At-TirmidhiBook of Funerals as reported from the Prophet (PBUH)Chapter: What is reported on shrouding the Prophet (PBUH); Hadīth no. 996.Sunan

An-Nasā'iBook of FuneralsChapter: Shrouding the Prophet (PBUH); Hadīth no. 1899.Sunan Ibn MājahBook of FuneralsChapter: What is reported on shrouding the Prophet (PBUH); Hadīth no. 1469.

Chapter: Hastening the funeral

Abu Hurayrah (may Allah be pleased with him) reported that the Prophet (may Allah's peace and blessings be upon him) said: "Hasten the funeral, for if the dead person is righteous, then you are hastening him to something good, and if he is otherwise, then it is an evil you are laying off your necks."

Sahīh Al-BukhāriBook of FuneralsChapter: Hastening the funeral; Hadīth no. 1315.Sahīh MuslimBook of FuneralsChapter: Hastening the funeral; Hadīth no. 944.Sunan Abu DāwudBook of FuneralsChapter: Hastening the funeral; Hadīth no. 3181.Jāmi' At-TirmidhiBook of Funerals as reported from the Prophet (PBUH)Chapter: What is reported on hastening the funeral; Hadīth no. 1015.Sunan An-Nasā'iBook of FuneralsChapter: Hastening the funeral; Hadīth no. 1910.Sunan Ibn MājahBook of FuneralsChapter: What is reported on following the funeral procession; Hadīth no. 1477.

Chapter: The merit of joining the funeral prayer and procession.

Abu Hurayrah (may Allah be pleased with him) reported that the Prophet (may Allah's peace and blessings be upon him) said: "Whoever follows a funeral procession till he offers the funeral prayer will have one Qirāt of reward, and whoever follows it till burial will have two Qirāts." It was asked: "What are the two Qirāts?" He said: "Like two huge mountains."

Sahīh Al-BukhāriBook of FuneralsChapter: One who remains with the funeral till burial; Hadīth no. 1325.Sahīh MuslimBook of FuneralsChapter: Merit of joining the funeral prayer and procession; Hadīth no. 945.Sunan Abu DāwudBook of FuneralsChapter: Merit of joining the funeral prayer and procession; Hadīth no. 3168.Jāmi' At-TirmidhiBook of Funerals as reported from the Prophet (PBUH)Chapter: What is reported on the merit of offering the funeral prayer; Hadīth no. 1040.Sunan An-Nasā'iBook of FuneralsChapter: The reward of offering the funeral prayer; Hadīth no. 1994.Sunan Ibn MājahBook of FuneralsChapter: What is reported on the reward of offering the funeral prayer and waiting till burial; Hadīth no. 1539.

Chapter: Making Takbīr over funeral (i.e. offering funeral prayer).

Abu Hurayrah (may Allah be pleased with him) reported that the Prophet (may Allah's peace and blessings be upon him) announced the death of the Negus on the day he died. He came out to the place of prayer, lined them up, and made Takbīr four times (i.e. offered the funeral prayer).

Sahīh Al-BukhāriBook of FuneralsChapter: Reporting the death of someone to his family; Hadīth no. 1245.Sahīh MuslimBook of FuneralsChapter: Making Takbīr over funeral (i.e. offering funeral prayer); Hadīth no. 951.Sunan Abu DāwudBook of FuneralsChapter: Offering funeral prayer for a Muslim who dies in a non-Muslim country; Hadīth no. 3204.Jāmi' At-TirmidhiBook of Funerals as reported from the Prophet (PBUH)Chapter: What is reported on making Takbīr over the funeral (i.e. offering the funeral prayer); Hadīth no. 1022.Sunan An-Nasā'iBook of FuneralsChapter: Forming rows for the funeral prayer; Hadīth no. 1971.Sunan Ibn MājahBook of FuneralsChapter: What is reported on offering the funeral prayer for the Negus; Hadīth no. 1534.

Chapter: Prayer at the grave.

Sulaymān ash-Shaybāni reported: "I heard Ash-Sha'bi say: 'I was informed by someone who passed along with the Prophet (may Allah's peace and blessings be upon him) by a secluded grave that he lined them up and led them in prayer there.' I said: 'Who reported that to you, O Abu 'Amr?' He replied: 'Ibn 'Abbās.'"

Sahīh Al-BukhāriBook of AdhānChapter: The ablution of boys and when they are required to take a ritual bath, purify themselves, and attend the congregational prayer, the two Eids, funerals, and their rows; Hadīth no. 857.Sahīh MuslimBook of FuneralsChapter: Prayer at the grave; Hadīth no. 954.Sunan Abu DāwudBook of FuneralsChapter: Making Takbīr over the funeral (i.e. offering funeral prayer); Hadīth no. 3196.Jāmi' At-TirmidhiBook of Funerals as reported from the Prophet (PBUH)Chapter: What is reported on praying at the grave; Hadīth no. 1037.Sunan An-Nasā'iBook of FuneralsChapter: Prayer at the grave; Hadīth no. 2024.Sunan Ibn MājahBook of FuneralsChapter: What is reported on praying at the grave; Hadīth no. 1530.

Chapter: Standing for a funeral procession.

'Āmir ibn Rabī'ah (may Allah be pleased with him) reported that the Prophet (may Allah's peace and blessings be upon him) said: "When you see a funeral procession, stand up till it passes you by." In another version: "till it passes you by or the coffin is put down."

Sahīh Al-BukhāriBook of FuneralsChapter: Standing up for a funeral procession; Hadīth no. 1307.Sahīh MuslimBook of FuneralsChapter: Standing up for a funeral procession; Hadīth no. 958.Sunan Abu DāwudBook of FuneralsChapter: Standing up for a funeral procession; Hadīth no. 3172.Jāmi' At-TirmidhiBook of Funerals as reported from the Prophet (PBUH)Chapter: What is reported on standing up for a funeral procession; Hadīth no. 1042.Sunan An-Nasā'iBook of FuneralsChapter: The order to stand up for a funeral procession; Hadīth no. 1916.Sunan Ibn MājahBook of FuneralsChapter: What is reported on standing up for a funeral procession; Hadīth no. 1542.

Chapter: Where the Imām stands in relation to the deceased during the funeral prayer.

Samurah ibn Jundub (may Allah be pleased with him) reported: "I offered the funeral prayer behind the Prophet (may Allah's peace and blessings be upon him) for a woman who died in her postpartum period. He stood before the middle of her body."

Sahīh Al-BukhāriBook of FuneralsChapter: Offering the funeral prayer for a woman who died in her postpartum period; Hadīth no. 1331.Sahīh MuslimBook of FuneralsChapter: Where the Imām stands in relation to the deceased during the funeral prayer; Hadīth no. 964.Sunan Abu DāwudBook of FuneralsChapter: Where the Imām stands from the deceased during the funeral prayer; Hadīth no. 3195.Jāmi' At-TirmidhiBook of Funerals as reported from the Prophet (PBUH)Chapter: What is reported on where the Imām stands from the dead man or woman during the funeral prayer; Hadīth no. 1035.Sunan An-Nasā'iBook of FuneralsChapter: The funerals of men and women together; Hadīth no. 1979.Sunan Ibn MājahBook of FuneralsChapter: What is reported on where the Imām stands during the funeral prayer; Hadīth no. 1493.

Book of Zakah

Abu Sa'īd (may Allah be pleased with him) reported: "The Prophet (may Allah's peace and blessings be upon him) said: 'Zakah is not due on what is less than five ounces, nor on what is less than five camels, nor on what is less than five Wasaqs.'"

Sahīh Al-BukhāriBook of ZakahChapter: Wealth whose Zakah is paid is not considered hoarded wealth; Hadīth no. 1405.Sahīh MuslimBook of ZakahHadīth no. 979.Sunan Abu DāwudBook of ZakahChapter: The Zakatable wealth; Hadīth no. 1558.Jāmi' At-TirmidhiBook of Zakah as reported from the Prophet (PBUH)Chapter: What is reported on the Zakah on plants, dates, and grains; Hadīth no. 626.Sunan An-Nasā'iBook of ZakahChapter: Zakah on camels; Hadīth no. 2445.Sunan Ibn MājahBook of ZakahChapter: The Zakatable wealth; Hadīth no. 1793.

Chapter: A Muslim is not required to pay Zakah on his slave or horse.

Abu Hurayrah (may Allah be pleased with him) reported: "The Prophet (may Allah's peace and blessings be upon him) said: 'A Muslim is not required to pay Zakah on his horse or slave.'"

Sahīh Al-BukhāriBook of ZakahChapter: A Muslim is not required to pay Zakah on his horse; Hadīth no. 1463.Sahīh MuslimBook of ZakahChapter: A Muslim is not required to pay Zakah on his slave or horse; Hadīth no. 982.Sunan Abu DāwudBook of ZakahChapter: Zakah on slaves; Hadīth no. 1595.Jāmi' At-TirmidhiBook of Zakah as reported from the Messenger of Allah (PBUH)Chapter: What is reported that there is no Zakah on horses or slaves; Hadīth no. 628.Sunan An-Nasā'iBook of ZakahChapter: Zakah on horses; Hadīth no. 2467.Sunan Ibn MājahBook of ZakahChapter: Zakah on horses and slaves; Hadīth no. 1812.

Chapter: Zakat al-Fitr on Muslims in the form of dates and barley.

Ibn 'Umar (may Allah be pleased with him) reported: "The Prophet (may Allah's peace and blessings be upon him) ordained Zakat al-Fitr as one Sā' (2.5 - 3 kg) of dates or barley, upon the slaves and the free, males and females, and young and old among the Muslims. He ordered that it be given out before people go out for Eid prayer."

Sahīh Al-BukhāriBook of ZakahChapter: Ordaining Zakat al-Fitr; Hadīth no. 1503.Sahīh MuslimBook of ZakahChapter: Zakat al-Fitr on Muslims in the form of dates and barley; Hadīth no. 984.Sunan Abu DāwudBook of ZakahChapter: How much is Zakat al-Fitr?; Hadīth no. 1611.Jāmi' At-TirmidhiBook of Zakah as reported from the Prophet (PBUH)Chapter: What is reported on Zakat al-Fitr; Hadīth no. 676.Sunan An-Nasā'iBook of ZakahChapter: Ordaining Zakah of Ramadān (Zakat al-Fitr) upon children; Hadīth no. 2502.Sunan Ibn MājahBook of ZakahChapter: Zakat al-Fitr; Hadīth no. 1826.

Abu Sa'īd al-Khudri (may Allah be pleased with him) reported: "We used to give it during the Prophet's lifetime as one Sā' (2.5 - 3 kg) of food or one Sā' of dates or one Sā' of barley or one Sā' of raisins. But when Mu'āwiyah became Caliph and wheat was available in abundance, he said: 'I see that one Mudd of this equals two Mudds.'"

Sahīh Al-BukhāriBook of ZakahChapter: One Sā' of raisins; Hadīth no. 1508.Sahīh MuslimBook of ZakahChapter: Zakat al-Fitr on Muslims in the form of dates and barley; Hadīth no. 985.Sunan Abu DāwudBook of ZakahChapter: How much is Zakat al-Fitr?; Hadīth no. 1616.Jāmi' At-TirmidhiBook of Zakah as reported from the Prophet (PBUH)Chapter: What is reported on Zakat al-Fitr; Hadīth no. 673.Sunan An-Nasā'iBook of ZakahChapter: Raisins; Hadīth no. 2512.Sunan Ibn MājahBook of ZakahChapter: Zakat al-Fitr; Hadīth no. 1829.

Chapter: Reward of the honest storekeeper and the woman who gives charity from her husband's house, without being extravagant, and with his explicit or customary approval.

'Ā'ishah (may Allah be pleased with her) reported that the Messenger of Allah (may Allah's peace and blessings be upon him) said: "If a woman gives some of the food of her house in charity, without being extravagant, she will receive a reward for what she has spent, her husband will receive a reward due to his earning, and the storekeeper will be similarly rewarded. The reward of one will not decrease the reward of the others."

Sahīh Al-BukhāriBook of ZakahChapter: The one who orders his servant to give charity and does not hand it out himself; Hadīth no. 1425.Sahīh MuslimBook of ZakahChapter: Reward of the honest storekeeper and the woman who gives charity from her husband's house, without being extravagant, and with his explicit or customary approval; Hadīth no. 1024.Sunan Abu DāwudBook of ZakahChapter: A woman gives charity from her husband's house; Hadīth no. 1685.Jāmi' At-TirmidhiBook of Zakah as reported from the Messenger of Allah (PBUH)Chapter: A woman spending from her husband's house; Hadīth no. 671.Sunan An-Nasā'iBook of ZakahChapter: A woman giving charity from her husband's house; Hadīth no. 2539.Sunan Ibn MājahBook of TradeChapter: The right of a woman in her husband's wealth; Hadīth no. 2294.

Book of Fasting

Chapter: Do not fast the day or two days before Ramadan.

Abu Hurayrah (may Allah be pleased with him) reported that the Prophet (may Allah's peace and blessings be upon him) said: "Do not fast the day or two days before Ramadan, except if someone used to fast it; then he may fast that day."

Sahīh Al-BukhāriBook of FastingChapter: Do not fast the day or two days before Ramadan; Hadīth no. 1914.Sahīh MuslimBook of FastingChapter: Do not fast the day or two days before Ramadan; Hadīth no. 1082.Sunan Abu DāwudBook of FastingChapter: He who joins Sha'bān to Ramadan (in fasting); Hadīth no. 2335.Jāmi' At-TirmidhiBook of Fasting as reported from the Prophet (PBUH)Chapter: What is reported: Do not fast just before Ramadan; Hadīth no. 685.Sunan An-Nasā'iBook of FastingChapter: Mentioning the difference between the Hadīths narrated in this regard by Yahya ibn Abi Kathīr and Muhammad ibn 'Amr about Abu Salamah; Hadīth no. 2173.Sunan Ibn MājahBook of FastingChapter: What is reported on the prohibition to fast just before Ramadan, except if that coincides with someone's usual fasting; Hadīth no. 1650.

Chapter: Validity of fasting of someone in a state of ritual impurity as dawn rises.

'Ā'ishah and Umm Salamah (may Allah be pleased with both of them) reported thật the dawn would rise while the Prophet (may Allah's peace and blessings be upon him) was ritually impure and then he would take a bath and observe the fast. Marwān said to 'Abdur-Rahmān: "I swear by Allah that you should relate it to Abu Hurayrah by way of rebuke." Marwān was the governor of Madinah at the time. Abu Bakr said: "'Abdur-Rahmān disliked the idea. Then, it happened that we got together in Dhul-Hulayfah, where Abu Hurayrah owned a piece of land. 'Abdur-Rahmān said to Abu Hurayrah: 'I am telling you something which I would not tell you if it were not for Marawān's oath to do so.' Then, he related to him the statement of 'Ā'ishah and Umm Salamah. Thereupon, he said: 'Al-Fadl ibn 'Abbas related this to me, and they ('Ā'ishah and Umm Salamah) know better.'"

Sahīh Al-BukhāriBook of FastingChapter: Morning comes as a fasting person is ritually impure; Hadīth no. 1925, 1926.Sahīh MuslimBook of FastingChapter: Validity of fasting of someone in a state of ritual impurity as dawn rises; Hadīth no. 1109.Sunan Abu DāwudBook of FastingChapter: Morning comes as a person is ritually impure during Ramadan; Hadīth no. 2388.Jāmi' At-TirmidhiBook of Fasting as reported from the Prophet (PBUH)Chapter: What is reported on dawn rising on a ritually impure person who wants to fast; Hadīth no. 779.Sunan An-Nasā'iBook of PurificationChapter: Ceasing to perform ablution after eating anything changed by fire; Hadīth no. 183.Sunan Ibn MājahBook of FastingChapter: What is reported on a person who is ritually impure as morning comes and he wants to fast; Hadīth no. 1703, 1704.

Chapter: Giving the option to fast or not to fast during travel.

'Ā'ishah (may Allah be pleased with her), the Prophet's wife reported: "Hamzah ibn 'Amr al-Aslami asked the Prophet (may Allah's peace and blessings be upon him): 'May I fast while traveling?,' and he used to fast often. He replied: "Fast if you wish, and do not fast if you wish.'"

Sahīh Al-BukhāriBook of FastingChapter: Fasting and not fasting during travel; Hadīth no.1943.Sahīh MuslimBook of FastingChapter: Giving the option to fast or not to fast during travel; Hadīth no. 1121.Sunan Abu DāwudBook of FastingChapter: Fasting during travel; Hadīth no. 2402.Jāmi' At-TirmidhiBook of Fasting as reported from the Prophet (PBUH)Chapter: What is reported on the concession regarding fasting during travel; Hadīth no. 711.Sunan An-Nasā'iBook of FastingChapter: Mentioning the difference over Hishām ibn 'Urwah; Hadīth no. 2305.Sunan Ibn MājahBook of FastingChapter: What is reported on fasting during travel; Hadīth no. 1662.

Chapter: Making up for the missed days of Ramadan during Sha'bān.

'Ā'ishah (may Allah be pleased with her) said: "I would miss some days of fast in Ramadan and could not make up for them except during Sha'bān." Yahya said: "Because of her many duties towards the Prophet (may Allah's peace and blessings be upon him)."

Sahīh Al-BukhāriBook of FastingChapter: When to make up for the missed fast in Ramadan; Hadīth no. 1950.Sahīh MuslimBook of FastingChapter: Making up for missed fast of Ramadan during Sha'bān; Hadīth no. 1146.Sunan Abu DāwudBook of FastingChapter: Delaying the observance of the missed fast of Ramadan; Hadīth no. 2399.Jāmi' At-TirmidhiBook of Fasting as reported from the Prophet (pbuh)Chapter: What is reported on delaying the observance of the missed fast of Ramadan; Hadīth no. 783.Sunan An-Nasā'iBook of FastingChapter: Exempting menstruating women from fasting; Hadīth no. 2319.Sunan Ibn MājahBook of FastingChapter: What is reported on making up for the missed fast in Ramadan; Hadīth no. 1669.

Chapter: The merit of fasting.

Abu Hurayrah (may Allah be pleased with him) reported that the Prophet (may Allah's peace and blessings be upon him) said: "Allah said: 'All deeds of the son of Adam are for himself, except for fasting; it is for Me, and I give the reward for it. Fasting is a shield. When anyone of you is fasting, he should avoid obscene language and loud voice, and if anyone curses him or quarrels with him, he should say: "I am fasting." By the One in whose hand the soul of Muhammad is, the breath of a fasting person is more pleasant to Allah than the fragrance of musk. A fasting person has two occasions of joy: When he breaks his fast, he feels joy, and when he meets his Lord, he feels joy for his fast."

Sahīh Al-BukhāriBook of FastingChapter: Should a person say "I am fasting" if someone curses him?; Hadīth no. 1904.Sahīh MuslimBook of FastingChapter: Merit of fasting; Hadīth no. 1151.Sunan Abu DāwudBook of FastingChapter: Backbiting in the case of a fasting person; Hadīth no. 2363.Jāmi' At-TirmidhiBook of Fasting as reported from the Prophet (PBUH)Chapter: What is reported on the merit of fasting; Hadīth no. 764.Sunan An-Nasā'iBook of FastingChapter: Mentioning the difference on Abu Sālih in this Hadīth; Hadīth no. 2216.Sunan Ibn MājahBook of FastingChapter: What is reported on the merit of fasting; Hadīth no. 1638.

Chapter: Fasting of the Prophet (PBUH) outside Ramadan and the desirability not to keep a month free from fasting.

'Ā'ishah (may Allah be pleased with her) reported: "The Messenger of Allah (may Allah's peace and blessings be upon him) would observe fast till we would say: He will not stop fasting. And he would stop fasting till we would say: He will not observe fast. I did not see the Messenger of Allah (may Allah's peace and blessings be upon him) fast a complete month except for Ramadan, and I did not see him fast in a month more than he did in Sha'bān."

Sahīh Al-BukhāriBook of FastingChapter: Fasting in Sha'bān; Hadīth no. 1969.Sahīh MuslimBook of FastingChapter: The Prophet's fasting outside Ramadan and the desirability not to keep a month free from fasting; Hadīth no. 1156.Sunan Abu DāwudBook of FastingChapter: How was the Prophet's fasting?; Hadīth no. 2434.Jāmi' At-TirmidhiBook of Fasting as reported from the Prophet (pbuh)Chapter: What is reported on continuous fasting; Hadīth no. 768.Sunan An-Nasā'iBook of FastingChapter: Mention of the different versions of the Hadīth reported by 'Ā'ishah in this regard; Hadīth no. 2183.Sunan Ibn MājahBook of FastingChapter: What is reported on the Prophet's fasting; Hadīth no. 1710.

Chapter: The prohibition of observing continuous fast, if the fasting person suffers harm because of it,

or neglects some duty because of it, or does not break the fast during Eids and the Days of Tashrīq

and showing the desirability of fasting on alternate days.

'Abdullāh ibn 'Amr ibn al-'Ās (may Allah be pleased with him) reported: "The Messenger of Allah (may Allah's peace and blessings be upon him) said to me: 'I was informed that you observe fast during the day and pray at night. Is it true?' I said: 'Yes, O Messenger of Allah.' He said: 'Do not do that! Fast and stop fasting, and pray and sleep. Indeed, your body has a right upon you, your eyes have a right upon you, your wife has a right upon you, and your visitor has a right upon you. It is enough for you to fast three days every month. You get a ten-fold reward for any good deed, and thus this is tantamount to fasting the whole month.' But I favored what is harder and so things were made harder for me. I said: 'O Messenger of Allah, I have strength (to fast more).' He said: 'Then, observe the fast of Prophet David, (peace be upon him) and no more than that.' I said: 'How was the fast of Prophet David (peace be upon him)?' He said: 'Half of the month.' 'Abdullāh used to say after growing old: 'I wish I had taken the Prophet's dispensation.'"

Sahīh Al-BukhāriBook of FastingChapter: What is reported on the right of one's body in relation to fasting; Hadīth no. 1975.Sahīh MuslimBook of FastingChapter: The prohibition of observing continuous fast if the fasting person suffers harm or neglects some duty because of it or does not break the fast during Eids and the Days of Tashrīq; and showing the desirability of fasting on alternate days; Hadīth no. 1159.Sunan Abu DāwudBook of FastingChapter: Observing continuous fast on a voluntary basis; Hadīth no. 2427.Jāmi' At-TirmidhiBook of Fasting as reported from the Prophet (pbuh)Chapter: What is reported on continuous fasting; Hadīth no. 770.Sunan An-Nasā'iBook of FastingChapter: Fasting on alternate days and mention of different versions of the Hadīth reported by 'Abdullāh ibn 'Amr; Hadīth no. 2390.Sunan Ibn MājahBook of FastingChapter: What is reported on Prophet Dāwud's fasting; Hadīth no. 1712.

Book of I'tikāf (Retreat in Ramadhan)

Chapter: When should a person who wants to observe I'tikāf enter his place of I'tikāf.

'Ā'ishah (may Allah be pleased with her) reported: "The Prophet (may Allah's peace and blessings be upon him) used to observe I'tikāf in the last ten days of Ramadan, and I used to pitch a tent for him. He would offer the Fajr prayer then enter the tent. Hafsah asked permission from 'Ā'ishah to pitch a tent for her, which she gave and she pitched the tent. When Zaynab bint Jahsh saw it, she pitched another tent. In the morning, the Prophet (may Allah's peace and blessings be upon him) saw the tents and said: "What is this?" He was told about it and, thereupon, he said: "Do you think that they intended to do righteousness by this?" He, therefore, abandoned I'tikāf in that month and observed it for ten days in the month of Shawwāl.

Sahīh Al-BukhāriBook of I'tikāf (Retreat in Ramadhan)Chapter: The I'tikāf of women; Hadīth no. 2033.Sahīh MuslimBook of I'tikāfChapter: When should a person who wants to observe I'tikāf enter his place of I'tikāf; Hadīth no. 1173.Sunan Abu DāwudBook of FastingChapter: I'tikāf; Hadīth no. 2464.Jāmi' At-TirmidhiBook of Fasting as reported from the Prophet (pbuh)Chapter: What is reported on I'tikāf; Hadīth no. 791.Sunan An-Nasā'iBook of MosquesChapter: Pitching tents in the mosque; Hadīth no. 709.Sunan Ibn MājahBook of FastingChapter: When to start I'tikāf and making up for missed I'tikāf; Hadīth no. 1771.

Book of Hajj

Chapter: What is permissible and what is impermissible for a pilgrim for Hajj or 'Umrah and pointing out the prohibition of using perfume by him.

'Abdullāh ibn 'Umar (may Allah be pleased with him) reported that a man asked: "O Messenger of Allah, what kind of clothes should a pilgrim wear?" The Messenger of Allah (may Allah's peace and blessings be upon him) replied: "He should not wear shirts, turbans, trousers, hooded cloaks, or leather socks except if he cannot find sandals; he may wear leather socks after cutting them to make them lower than the ankles. And do not wear clothes to which saffron or Wars (kind of perfume) was applied."

Saḥīḥ Al-BukhāriBook of HajjChapter: What a Muhrim should not wear; Hadīth no. 1543.Saḥīḥ MuslimBook of HajjChapter: What is permissible and what is impermissible for a Muhrim for Hajj or 'Umrah and pointing out the prohibition of using perfume by him; Hadīth no. 1177.Sunan Abu DāwudBook of RitualsChapter: What a Muhrim may wear; Hadīth no. 1823.Jāmi' At-TirmidhiBook of Hajj as reported from the Prophet (pbuh)Chapter: What is reported on the clothes a Muhrim should not wear; Hadīth no. 833.Sunan An-Nasā'iBook of Rituals of HajjChapter: prohibition of wearing clothes to which saffron and Wars were applied while in the state of Ihrām; Hadīth no. 2667.Sunan Ibn MājahBook of RitualsChapter: What a Muhrim may wear; Hadīth no. 2929.

Ibn 'Abbās (may Allah be pleased with him) reported: "I heard the Prophet (may Allah's peace and blessings be upon him) deliver a sermon at 'Arafāt, in which he said: 'A Muhrim who cannot find sandals may wear leather socks and who cannot find an Izār (waist-wrapper) may wear pants.'"

Saḥīḥ Al-BukhāriBook of the Penalty of Hunting during IhrāmChapter: A Muhrim may wear leather socks if he cannot find sandals; Hadīth no. 1841.Saḥīḥ MuslimBook of HajjChapter: What is permissible and what is impermissible for a Muhrim for Hajj or 'Umrah and pointing out the prohibition of using perfume by him; Hadīth no. 1178.Sunan Abu DāwudBook of RitualsChapter: What a Muhrim may wear; Hadīth no. 1829.Jāmi' At-TirmidhiBook of Hajj as reported from the Prophet (pbuh)Chapter: What is reported on a Muhrim wearing leather socks and pants if he cannot find a waist-wrapper and sandals; Hadīth no. 834.Sunan An-Nasā'iBook of AdornmentChapter: Wearing pants; Hadīth no. 5325.Sunan Ibn MājahBook of RitualsChapter: A Muhrim may wear pants and leather socks if he cannot find a waist-wrapper or sandals; Hadīth no. 2931.

Chapter: The Mīqāt (place where Muhrim assumes Ihrām) for Hajj and 'Umrah.

'Abdullāh ibn 'Umar (may Allah be pleased with him) reported that a man stood up in the mosque and said: "O Messenger of Allah, from where do you command us to assume Ihrām?" He said: "The people of Madinah should assume Ihrām from Dhul-Hulayfah, the people of the Levant should assume Ihrām from Al-Juhfah, and the people of Najd should assume Ihrām from Qarn." Ibn 'Umar said: "And they claim that the Messenger of Allah (may Allah's peace and blessings be upon him) said: 'The people of Yemen should assume Ihrām from Yalamlam.'" Ibn 'Umar used to say: "I did not hear this from the Messenger of Allah (may Allah's peace and blessings be upon him)."

Saḥīḥ Al-BukhāriBook of KnowledgeChapter: Mention of knowledge and Fatwas in the mosque; Hadīth no. 133.Saḥīḥ MuslimBook of HajjChapter: The Mīqāt of Hajj and 'Umrah; Hadīth no. 1182.Sunan Abu DāwudBook of RitualsChapter: Regarding the Mīqāt; Hadīth no. 1737.Jāmi' At-TirmidhiBook of Hajj as reported from the Prophet (pbuh)Chapter: What is reported on the times of Ihrām for the people coming from afar; Hadīth no. 831.Sunan An-Nasā'iBook of Rituals of HajjChapter: The Mīqāt for the people of the Levant; Hadīth no. 2652.Sunan Ibn MājahBook of RitualsChapter: The Mīqāt for the people coming from afar; Hadīth no. 2914.

Chapter: Talbiyah and its description and time.

'Abdullāh ibn 'Umar (may Allah be pleased with him) reported that the Talbiyah of the Messenger of Allah (may Allah's peace and blessings be upon him) was: "Labbayk Allāhumma labbayk. Labbayk lā sharīka laka labbayk. Inn al-Hamda wan-ni'mata laka wal-mulk. Lā sharīka lak (At Your service, O Lord,

At Your service. At Your service, You have no partner, At Your service. All Praise and all Bounty are Yours alone, and all Sovereignty. You have no partner)."

Sahīh Al-BukhāriBook of HajjChapter: Talbiyah; Hadīth no. 1549.Sahīh MuslimBook of HajjChapter: Talbiyah and its description and time; Hadīth no. 1184.Sunan Abu DāwudBook of RitualsChapter: How to make Talbiyah; Hadīth no. 1812.Jāmi' At-TirmidhiBook of Hajj as reported from the Prophet (PBUH)Chapter: What is reported on Talbiyah; Hadīth no. 825.Sunan An-Nasā'iBook of Rituals of HajjChapter: How to make Talbiyah; Hadīth no. 2748.Sunan Ibn MājahBook of RitualsChapter: Talbiyah; Hadīth no. 2918.

Chapter: Assuming Ihrām from where the journey begins

'Abdullāh ibn 'Umar (may Allah be pleased with him) reported: "I saw the Messenger of Allah (may Allah's peace and blessings be upon him) get on his camel at Dhul-Hulayfah then make Talbiyah as it stood upright."

Sahīh Al-BukhāriBook of HajjChapter: The statement of Allah Almighty: {They will come to you on foot and on every lean camel; they will come from every distant pass; that they may witness benefits for themselves}; Hadīth no. 1514.Sahīh MuslimBook of HajjChapter: Assuming Ihrām from where the journey begins; Hadīth no. 1187.Sunan Abu DāwudBook of RitualsChapter: The time of Ihrām; Hadīth no. 1771.Jāmi' At-TirmidhiBook of Hajj as reported from the Prophet (PBUH)Chapter: What is reported on the place where the Prophet (PBUH) assumed Ihrām; Hadīth no. 818.Sunan An-Nasā'iBook of Rituals of HajjChapter: What to do in Talbiyah; Hadīth no. 2758.Sunan Ibn MājahBook of RitualsChapter: Ihrām; Hadīth no. 2916.

Chapter: A Muhrim wearing perfume when entering Ihrām.

'Ā'ishah (may Allah be pleased with her) reported: "I used to apply perfume to the Messenger of Allah (may Allah's peace and blessings be upon him) before he entered Ihrām and when he ended Ihrām, before circumambulating the Ka'bah."

Sahīh Al-BukhāriBook of HajjChapter: Applying perfume upon entering Ihrām and what a person should wear if he wants to enter Ihrām and comb and oil his hair; Hadīth no. 1539.Sahīh MuslimBook of HajjChapter: A Muhrim wearing perfume upon entering Ihrām; Hadīth no. 1189.Sunan Abu DāwudBook of RitualsChapter: A Muhrim wearing perfume upon entering Ihrām; Hadīth no. 1745.Jāmi' At-TirmidhiBook of Hajj as reported from the Prophet (PBUH)Chapter: What is reported on wearing perfume upon ending Ihrām and before circumambulation of the Ka'bah; Hadīth no. 917.Sunan An-Nasā'iBook of Rituals of HajjChapter: The permissibility of applying perfume when entering Ihrām; Hadīth no. 2684.Sunan Ibn MājahBook of RitualsChapter: A Muhrim wearing perfume when entering Ihrām; Hadīth no. 2926.

Chapter: Prohibition of hunting for a Muhrim.

'Abdullāh ibn Abi Qatādah reported: "My father set out in the year of Al-Hudaybiyah and his companions assumed Ihrām but he did not. He (Abu Qatādah) said: 'The Prophet (may Allah's peace and blessings be upon him) was informed that an enemy would attack him. So, he proceeded onwards. While I was among my companions, with some of them laughing among themselves, I looked up and saw an onager. I attacked it, stabbed it, and caught it. I asked my companions for help, but they refused. Then, we all ate its meat and were afraid that we might lag far behind and be separated from the Prophet (may Allah's peace and blessings be upon him). So, I went in search of him and made my horse run at a great speed then at a normal speed alternately till I met a man from the tribe of Banu Ghifār at midnight. I asked him: "Where did you leave the Prophet (may Allah's peace and blessings be upon him)?" He replied: "I left him at Ta'han, and he intended to take the midday nap at As-Suqya." I followed the trace and reached the Prophet (may Allah's peace and blessings be upon him). I said: "O Messenger of Allah, your people send their greetings to you and invoke Allah's blessings upon you. They are afraid they might be left behind. So, please wait for them." I added: "O Messenger of Allah, I hunted an onager and some of its meat is with me." The Prophet (may Allah's peace and blessings be upon him) told the people to eat it, and all of them were in the state of Ihrām.'"

Saḥīḥ Al-Bukhārī Book of the Penalty of Hunting (while in state of Iḥrām) Chapter: Penalty for hunting and the like during Iḥrām; Ḥadīth no. 1821. Saḥīḥ Muslim Book of Hajj Chapter: Prohibition of hunting for a Muhrim; Ḥadīth no. 1196. Sunan Abu Dāwud Book of Rituals Chapter: Prohibition of the meat of game for a Muhrim; Ḥadīth no. 1852. Jāmi' At-Tirmidhi Book of Hajj as reported from the Prophet (PBUH) Chapter: What is reported on eating hunted animals in Iḥrām; Ḥadīth no. 847. Sunan An-Nasā'i Book of Rituals of Hajj Chapter: If a Muhrim laughs and this alerts a non-Muhrim to a prey, which he kills, may the Muhrim eat from it or not? Hadith no. 2824. Sunan Ibn Mājah Book of Rituals Chapter: The concession in this regard if it was not hunted for him; Ḥadīth no. 3093.

Chapter: Permissibility of shaving a Muhrim's head if it has some ailment, the obligation of paying a ransom for shaving his head, and stating how much it is.

'Abdullāh ibn Ma'qil reported: "I sat with Ka'b ibn 'Ujrah in this mosque, i.e. the Kufa Mosque, and asked him about the meaning of the verse: {Pay a ransom of fasting}. He said: 'I was taken to the Prophet (may Allah's peace and blessings be upon him) while lice were falling on my face. He said: "I did not think that your trouble reached such an extent. Can you afford to slaughter a sheep?" I said: "no." He said: "Then fast three days or feed six poor people by giving half a Sā' of food for each and shave your head." So, this verse was revealed concerning me in particular and for all of you in general.'"

Saḥīḥ Al-Bukhārī Book of Interpretation of the Qur'an Sūrat al-Baqarah Chapter: The verse: {And whoever among you is ill or has an ailment of the head}; Ḥadīth no. 4517. Saḥīḥ Muslim Book of Hajj Chapter: Permissibility of shaving a Muhrim's head if it has some ailment, the obligation of paying a ransom for shaving his head, and stating how much it is; Ḥadīth no. 1201. Sunan Abu Dāwud Book of Rituals Chapter: Ransom; Ḥadīth no. 1856. Jāmi' At-Tirmidhi Book of Interpretation of the Qur'an as reported from the Prophet (PBUH) Chapter: From Sūrat al-Baqarah; Ḥadīth no. 2973. Sunan An-Nasā'i Book of Rituals of Hajj Chapter: A Muhrim who is hurt by lice in his head; Ḥadīth no. 2851. Sunan Ibn Mājah Book of Rituals Chapter: The ransom if one is prevented from completing the rituals; Ḥadīth no. 3079.

Chapter: Permissibility of cupping during Iḥrām.

Ibn 'Abbās (may Allah be pleased with him) reported: "The Messenger of Allah (may Allah's peace and blessings be upon him) was cupped while in the state of Iḥrām."

Saḥīḥ Al-Bukhārī Book of the Penalty of Hunting (while in state of Iḥrām) Chapter: Cupping during Iḥrām; Ḥadīth no. 1835. Saḥīḥ Muslim Book of Hajj Chapter: Permissibility of cupping during Iḥrām; Ḥadīth no. 1202. Sunan Abu Dāwud Book of Rituals Chapter: Cupping in the state of Iḥrām; Ḥadīth no. 1835. Jāmi' At-Tirmidhi Book of Hajj as reported from the Prophet (PBUH) Chapter: What is reported on cupping during Iḥrām; Ḥadīth no. 839. Sunan An-Nasā'i Book of the Rituals of Hajj Chapter: Cupping in the state of Iḥrām; Ḥadīth no. 2845. Sunan Ibn Mājah Book of Trade Chapter: The earning of a cupping practitioner; Ḥadīth no. 2162.

Chapter: What to do with a Muhrim who dies.

Ibn 'Abbās (may Allah be pleased with him) reported: "While a man was standing at 'Arafah, he fell off his mount and it snapped his neck. The Messenger of Allah (may Allah's peace and blessings be upon him) said: 'Wash him with water and lotus leaves and shroud him in two sheets; do not perfume him or cover his head, for he will be resurrected on the Day of Judgment making Talbiyah.'"

Saḥīḥ Al-Bukhārī Book of Funerals Chapter: Shrouding in two sheets; Ḥadīth no. 1265. Saḥīḥ Muslim Book of Hajj Chapter: What to do with a Muhrim who dies; Ḥadīth no. 1206. Sunan Abu Dāwud Book of Funerals Chapter: What to do with a Muhrim who dies; Ḥadīth no. 3238. Jāmi' At-Tirmidhi Book of Hajj as reported from the Prophet (PBUH) Chapter: What is reported on a Muhrim passing away; Ḥadīth no. 951. Sunan An-Nasā'i Book of Rituals of Hajj Chapter: Washing the dead Muhrim with lotus leaves; Ḥadīth no. 2853. Sunan Ibn Mājah Book of Rituals Chapter: A Muhrim passing away; Ḥadīth no. 3084.

Chapter: Standing at 'Arafah and the verse: {Then depart from the place from where the people depart}.

'Ā'ishah (may Allah be pleased with her) reported: "Quraysh and those who followed its religion would stand at Muzdalifah, and they were called Al-Hums; whereas the rest of the Arabs used to stand at 'Arafāt. When Islam came, Allah commanded His Prophet to come to 'Arafāt, stand there, and then depart from there. This is revealed in the verse: {Then depart from the place from where the people depart.}."

Sahīh Al-BukhāriBook of Interpretation of the Qur'anSūrat al-BaqarahChapter: {Then depart from where the people depart}; Hadīth no. 4520.Sahīh MuslimBook of HajjChapter: Standing at 'Arafah and the verse: {Then depart from where the people depart}; Hadīth no. 1219.Sunan Abu DāwudBook of RitualsChapter: Standing at 'Arafah; Hadīth no. 1910.Jāmi' At-TirmidhiBook of Hajj as reported from the Prophet (PBUH)Chapter: What is reported on standing at 'Arafah and the supplication there; Hadīth no. 884.Sunan An-Nasā'iBook of Rituals of HajjChapter: Raising hands during the supplication at 'Arafah; Hadīth no. 3012.Sunan Ibn MājahBook of RitualsChapter: Moving on from 'Arafah; Hadīth no. 3018.

Chapter: Desirability of Ramal during Tawāf, 'Umrah, and the first Tawāf in Hajj.

Ibn 'Abbās (may Allah be pleased with him) reported: "When the Messenger of Allah (may Allah's peace and blessings be upon him) and his Companions came (to Makkah), the polytheists said: 'A group of people will come to you whom the fever of Yathrib has weakened.' So, the Prophet (may Allah's peace and blessings be upon him) ordered them to do Ramal (walk hurriedly or run lightly) in the first three rounds of Tawāf and walk at a normal pace between the two corners. Nothing prevented him from ordering them to do Ramal in all rounds except his compassion for them."

Sahīh Al-BukhāriBook of HajjChapter: How did Ramal start? Hadīth no. 1602.Sahīh MuslimBook of HajjChapter: Desirability of Ramal during Tawāf, 'Umrah, and the first Tawāf in Hajj; Hadīth no. 1266.Sunan Abu DāwudBook of RitualsChapter: Regarding Ramal; Hadīth no. 1886.Jāmi' At-TirmidhiBook of Hajj as reported from the Prophet (PBUH)Chapter: What is reported on Sa'i between Safa and Marwah; Hadīth no. 863.Sunan An-Nasā'iBook of Rituals of HajjChapter: The reason behind the Prophet's Sa'i (walking diligently) around the Ka'bah; Hadīth no. 2945.Sunan Ibn MājahBook of RitualsChapter: Ramal around the Ka'bah; Hadīth no. 2953.

Chapter: Permissibility of circumambulating around the Ka'bah on a camel or the like and touching the Black Stone with a stick or the like for a rider.

Ibn 'Abbās (may Allah be pleased with him) reported: "The Prophet (may Allah's peace and blessings be upon him) circumambulated the Ka'bah in the Farewell Hajj on a camel, touching the Corner with a stick."

Sahīh Al-BukhāriBook of HajjChapter: Touching the Corner with a stick; Hadīth no. 1607.Sahīh MuslimBook of HajjChapter: Permissibility of circumambulating around the Ka'bah on a camel or the like and touching the Black Stone with a stick or the like for a rider; Hadīth no. 1272.Sunan Abu DāwudBook of RitualsChapter: The obligatory Tawāf; Hadīth no. 1877.Jāmi' At-TirmidhiBook of Hajj as reported from the Prophet (PBUH)Chapter: What is reported on performing Tawāf while riding; Hadīth no. 865.Sunan An-Nasā'iBook of MosquesChapter: Letting a camel into the mosque; Hadīth no. 713.Sunan Ibn MājahBook of RitualsChapter: The one who touches the Corner with a stick; Hadīth no. 2948.

Chapter: Clarifying that Sa'i between Safa and Marwah is a pillar necessary for the validity of Hajj.

'Urwah reported: "I asked 'Ā'ishah (may Allah be pleased with her): 'How do you interpret the verse: {Indeed, Safa and Marwah are among the symbols of Allah. So, whoever performs Hajj to the House or 'Umrah - there is no blame upon him for walking between them}? By Allah, there is no blame if one does not perform Tawāf between Safa and Marwah.' She replied: 'O my nephew, your interpretation is not correct. Had this interpretation of yours been correct, the verse should have been: there is no blame upon him for not walking between them. But, in fact, this verse was revealed concerning the Ansār who used to assume Ihrām for an idol called 'Manāt', which they used to worship at a place called Al-Mushallal, before embracing Islam; whoever assumed Ihrām for that idol would refrain from performing Tawāf between Safa and Marwah. When they embraced Islam, they asked the Messenger of Allah (may Allah's peace and blessings be upon him) regarding it, saying: "O Messenger of Allah, we used to refrain from Tawāf between Safa and Marwah." So, Allah revealed: {Indeed, Safa and Marwah are among the symbols of Alla}.' 'Ā'ishah added: 'Indeed, the Messenger of Allah (may Allah's peace and blessings be upon him) set the Sunnah of Tawāf between Safa and Marwah. So, nobody may omit the Tawāf between them.' Later on, I told Abu Bakr ibn 'Abdur-Rahmān about it and he said: 'I have not heard this information before, but I heard the learned men saying that all people, except those whom 'Ā'ishah mentioned, and who used to assume Ihrām for the sake of Manāt, used to perform Tawāf between Safa and Marwah. When Allah, the Almighty, mentioned the Tawāf of the Ka'bah and did not mention Safa and Marwah in the Qur'an, the people asked: "O Messenger of Allah, we used to perform Tawāf between Safa and Marwah and Allah has revealed verses concerning Tawāf of the Ka'bah and has not mentioned Safa and Marwah. Is there any harm if we perform Tawāf between Safa and Marwah?" So, Allah revealed: {Indeed, Safa and Marwah are among the symbols of Allah}. It seems that this verse was revealed concerning both groups; those who used to refrain from Tawāf between Safa and Marwah before Islam and those who used to perform Tawāf then but refrained from it after embracing Islam because Allah Almighty, enjoined Tawāf of the Ka'bah and did not mention Safa, until He mentioned that after mentioning Tawāf of the Ka'bah.'"

Sahīh Al-BukhāriBook of HajjChapter: Obligation of Sa'i between Safa and Marwah and making them among the rites of Allah; Hadīth no. 1643.Sahīh MuslimBook of HajjChapter: Clarifying that Sa'i between Safa and Marwah is a pillar necessary for the validity of Hajj; Hadīth no. 1277.Sunan Abu DāwudBook of RitualsChapter: The command to perform Sa'i between Safa and Marwah; Hadīth no. 1901.Jāmi' At-TirmidhiBook of Interpretation of the Qur'an as reported from the Messenger of Allah (PBUH)Chapter: From Sūrat al-Baqarah; Hadīth no. 2965.Sunan An-Nasā'iBook of Rituals of HajjChapter: Mention of Safa and Marwah; Hadīth no. 2968.Sunan Ibn MājahBook of RitualsChapter: Sa'i between Safa and Marwah; Hadīth no. 2986.

Chapter: It is recommended that a pilgrim keeps making Talbiyah

until he begins throwing Jamrat al-'Aqabah on the Day of Nahr.

Ibn 'Abbās, may Allah be pleased with him, reported that Al-Fadl rode behind the Prophet (may Allah's peace and blessings be upon him). Al-Fadl said that he (the Prophet) continued to recite Talbiyah until he threw the pebbles.

Sahīh Al-BukhāriBook of HajjChapter: Reciting Talbiyah and Takbīr on the morning of the Day of Nahr until one throws the pebbles, and co-riding; Hadīth no. 1685.Sahīh MuslimBook of HajjChapter: Recommendation that pilgrim recites Talbiyah continuously until he starts stoning Jamrat Al-'Aqabah on the Day of Nahr; Hadīth no. 1281.Sunan Abu DāwudBook of RitualsChapter: When the pilgrim should stop reciting Talbiyah; Hadīth no. 1815.Jāmi' At-TirmidhiBook of Hajj as reported from the Prophet (PBUH)Chapter: What is reported on when to stop reciting Talbiyah in Hajj; Hadīth no. 918.Sunan An-Nasā'iBook of Rituals of HajjChapter: Reciting Talbiyah during the journey; Hadīth no.

3055.Sunan Ibn MājahBook of RitualsChapter: When the pilgrim should stop reciting Talbiyah; Hadīth no. 3040.

Chapter: When the pilgrim should stop reciting Talbiyah; Hadīth no. 3040.

Chapter: Desirability of letting the weak among women and others to depart from Muzdalifah to Mina late at night ahead of the people to avoid the crowd, and the desirability for other than them to spend the night in Muzdalifah until they offer the Fajr prayer there.

Ibn 'Abbās (may Allah be pleased with him) said: "I was one of those whom the Prophet (may Allah's peace and blessings be upon him) allowed to depart Muzdalifah late at night ahead of the people along with the weak among their families."

Sahīh Al-BukhāriBook of HajjChapter: Sending the weak family members to Mina ahead of the people at night, so they stay at Muzdalifah and make supplications until the moon sets then they depart; Hadīth no. 1678.Sahīh MuslimBook of HajjChapter: Recommendation of letting the weak of women and others to depart from Muzdalifah to Mina late at night ahead of the people to avoid the crowd, and the recommendation that other than them spend the night in Muzdalifah until they offer the Fajr prayer there; Hadīth no. 1293.Sunan Abu DāwudBook of RitualsChapter: Leaving early from Jam'; Hadīth no. 1939.Jāmi' At-TirmidhiBook of Hajj as reported from the Prophet (PBUH)Chapter: What is reported on allowing the weak to depart from Jam' at night; Hadīth no. 892.Sunan An-Nasā'iBook of the Rituals of HajjChapter: Sending women and children ahead of others to their camping places in Muzdalifah; Hadīth no. 3032.Sunan Ibn MājahBook of RitualsChapter: Proceeding from Jam' to Mina for throwing the pebbles; Hadīth no. 3026.

Book of Hajj

Chapter: Sending the weak family members to Mina ahead of the people at night, so they stay at Muzdalifah and make supplications until the moon sets then they depart; Hadīth no. 1678.

Sahīh Muslim

Book of Hajj

Chapter: Recommendation of letting the weak of women and others to depart from Muzdalifah to Mina late at night ahead of the people to avoid the crowd, and the recommendation that other than them spend the night in Muzdalifah until they offer the Fajr prayer there; Hadīth no. 1293.

Sunan Abu Dāwud

Book of Rituals

Chapter: Leaving early from Jam'; Hadīth no. 1939.

Jāmi' At-Tirmidhi

Book of Hajj as reported from the Prophet (PBUH)

Chapter: What is reported on allowing the weak to depart from Jam' at night; Hadīth no. 892.

Sunan An-Nasā'i

Book of the Rituals of Hajj

Chapter: Sending women and children ahead of others to their camping places in Muzdalifah; Hadīth no. 3032.

Sunan Ibn Mājah

Book of Rituals

Chapter: Proceeding from Jam' to Mina for throwing the pebbles; Hadīth no. 3026.

Chapter: Stoning Jamrat Al-'Aqabah from the bottom of the valley with Makkah being to the left of the pilgrim and reciting Takbīr while throwing each pebble.

'Abdur-Rahmān ibn Yazīd reported that he performed Hajj with Ibn Mas'ūd (may Allah be pleased with him), and he saw him stoning Jamrat Al-'Aqabah with seven pebbles; he stood such that the Ka'bah was on his left and Mina was on his right then he said: "This is the standing place of the one to whom Surat Al-Baqarah was revealed."

Sahīh Al-BukhāriBook of HajjChapter: Stoning Jamrat Al-'Aqabah with the Ka'bah to one's left side; Hadīth no. 1749.Sahīh MuslimBook of HajjChapter: Stoning Jamrat Al-'Aqabah from the bottom of the valley with Makkah being to the left of the pilgrim and reciting Takbīr while throwing each pebble; Hadīth no.1296.Sunan Abu DāwudBook of RitualsChapter: Regarding stoning the Jamrāt; Hadīth no. 1974.Jāmi' At-TirmidhiBook of Hajj as reported from the Prophet (PBUH)Chapter: What is reported on the manner of throwing the pebbles; Hadīth no. 901.Sunan An-Nasā'iBook of Rituals of HajjChapter: Place from where Jamrat Al-'Aqabah is to be stoned; Hadīth no. 3071.Sunan Ibn MājahBook of RitualsChapter: Place from where Jamrat Al-'Aqabah is to be stoned; Hadīth no. 3030.

Book of Hajj

Chapter: Stoning Jamrat Al-'Aqabah with the Ka'bah to one's left side; Hadīth no. 1749.

Sahīh Muslim

Book of Hajj

Chapter: Stoning Jamrat Al-'Aqabah from the bottom of the valley with Makkah being to the left of the pilgrim and reciting Takbīr while throwing each pebble; Hadīth no.1296.

Sunan Abu Dāwud

Book of Rituals

Chapter: Regarding stoning the Jamrāt; Hadīth no. 1974.

Jāmi' At-Tirmidhi

Book of Hajj as reported from the Prophet (PBUH)

Chapter: What is reported on the manner of throwing the pebbles; Hadīth no. 901.

Sunan An-Nasā'i

Book of Rituals of Hajj

Chapter: Place from where Jamrat Al-'Aqabah is to be stoned; Hadīth no. 3071.

Sunan Ibn Mājah

Book of Rituals

Chapter: Place from where Jamrat Al-'Aqabah is to be stoned; Hadīth no. 3030.

Chapter: Desirability of sending sacrificial animals to the holy precincts in Makkah if one does not intend to go

himself, and the desirability of garlanding them and plaiting the garlands, and that the one who sends the sacrificial animals is not considered in a state of Ihrām thereby, and nothing becomes prohibited for him.

'Ā'ishah (may Allah be pleased with her) reported: "I plaited the garlands for the sacrificial animals of the Prophet (may Allah's peace and blessings be upon him) with my own hands, and then he garlanded them, marked them, and sent them to the Sacred House, and nothing was prohibited for him which was lawful for him before."

Sahīh Al-BukhāriBook of HajjChapter: Marking and garlanding the sacrificial animals at Dhul-Hulayfah then entering the state of Ihrām therefrom; Hadīth no. 1696.Sahīh MuslimBook of HajjChapter: Desirability of sending sacrificial animals to the holy precincts in Makkah if one does not intend to go himself, and the desirability of garlanding them and plaiting the garlands, and that the one who sends the sacrificial animals is not considered in a state of Ihrām thereby, and nothing becomes forbidden to him; Hadīth no. 1321.Sunan Abu DāwudBook of RitualsChapter: One who sends his sacrificial animal and remains in residence; Hadīth no. 1757.Jāmi' At-TirmidhiBook of Hajj as reported from the Prophet (PBUH)Chapter: What is reported on garlanding sheep; Hadīth no. 909.Sunan An-Nasā'iBook of the Rituals of HajjChapter: Garlanding camels; Hadīth no. 2783.Sunan Ibn MājahBook of RitualsChapter: Garlanding camels and cattle; Hadīth no. 3095.

Book of Hajj

Chapter: Marking and garlanding the sacrificial animals at Dhul-Hulayfah then entering the state of Ihrām therefrom; Hadīth no. 1696.

Sahīh Muslim

Book of Hajj

Chapter: Desirability of sending sacrificial animals to the holy precincts in Makkah if one does not intend to go himself, and the desirability of garlanding them and plaiting the garlands, and that the one who sends the sacrificial animals is not considered in a state of Ihrām thereby, and nothing becomes forbidden to him; Hadīth no. 1321.

Sunan Abu Dāwud

Book of Rituals

Chapter: One who sends his sacrificial animal and remains in residence; Hadīth no. 1757.

Jāmi' At-Tirmidhi

Book of Hajj as reported from the Prophet (PBUH)

Chapter: What is reported on garlanding sheep; Hadīth no. 909.

Sunan An-Nasā'i

Book of the Rituals of Hajj

Chapter: Garlanding camels; Hadīth no. 2783.

Sunan Ibn Mājah

Book of Rituals

Chapter: Garlanding camels and cattle; Hadīth no. 3095.

Chapter: Obligation of the Farewell Tawāf and exempting women in a state of menstruation from it.

'Ā'ishah (may Allah be pleased with her), wife of the Prophet (may Allah's peace and blessings be upon him), reported that she said to the Messenger of Allah (may Allah's peace and blessings be upon him) that Safiyyah bint Huyayy had had her menstruation. He (may Allah's peace and blessings be upon him) said: "Perhaps she would detain us! Did she not perform Tawāf with you?" They said: "She did." He said (to her): "Then, depart."

Sahīh Al-BukhāriBook of MenstruationChapter: A woman having her menstruation after performing Tawāf al-Ifādah; Hadīth no. 328.Sahīh MuslimBook of HajjChapter: Obligation of the Farewell Tawāf and exempting women in a state of menstruation from it; Hadīth no. 1211.Sunan Abu DāwudBook of RitualsChapter: A menstruating woman departing after performing Tawāf al-Ifādah (Hajj Tawāf); Hadīth no. 2003.Jāmi' At-TirmidhiBook of Hajj as reported from the Prophet (PBUH)Chapter: A woman having her menstruation after performing Tawāf al-Ifādah; Hadīth no. 943.Sunan An-Nasā'iBook of Menstruation and IstihādahChapter: A woman having her menstruation after performing Tawāf al-Ifādah; Hadīth no. 391.Sunan Ibn MājahBook of RitualsChapter: A menstruating woman departing before performing the Farewell Tawāf; Hadīth no. 3072.

Book of Menstruation

Chapter: A woman having her menstruation after performing Tawāf al-Ifādah; Hadīth no. 328.

Sahīh Muslim

Book of Hajj

Chapter: Obligation of the Farewell Tawāf and exempting women in a state of menstruation from it; Hadīth no. 1211.

Sunan Abu Dāwud

Book of Rituals

Chapter: A menstruating woman departing after performing Tawāf al-Ifādah (Hajj Tawāf); Hadīth no. 2003.

Jāmi' At-Tirmidhi

Book of Hajj as reported from the Prophet (PBUH)

Chapter: A woman having her menstruation after performing Tawāf al-Ifādah; Hadīth no. 943.

Sunan An-Nasā'i

Book of Menstruation and Istihādah

Chapter: A woman having her menstruation after performing Tawāf al-Ifādah; Hadīth no. 391.

Sunan Ibn Mājah

Book of Rituals

Chapter: A menstruating woman departing before performing the Farewell Tawāf; Hadīth no. 3072.

Chapter: Desirability of entering the Ka'bah for pilgrims and others,

praying therein, and offering supplications in all its sides.

Ibn 'Umar, may Allah be pleased with him, said: "The Prophet (may Allah's peace and blessings be upon him) arrived at Makkah in the year of the Conquest while Osāmah was riding behind him on his she-camel, Al-Qaswā'. Bilāl and 'Uthmān ibn Talhah were accompanying him. When he made his she-camel kneel down near the Ka'bah, he said to 'Uthman: 'Bring us the key of the Ka'bah.' He brought the key to him and opened the door for him. The Prophet, Osāmah, Bilāl and 'Uthmān entered the Ka'bah and closed the door behind them from inside. The Prophet (may Allah's peace and blessings be upon him) stayed therein for a long time then came out. The people rushed to get in, but I went in before them and found Bilāl standing behind the door, and I asked him: 'Where did the Messenger of Allah (may Allah's peace and blessings be upon him) pray?' He said: 'He prayed between those two front pillars,' and the Ka'bah was built on six pillars in two rows. 'He prayed between two pillars of the front row with the door of the Ka'bah at his back and facing the wall which faces the person when he enters the Ka'bah, leaving between himself and that wall (a distance of about three cubits).' But I forgot to ask him how many Rak'ahs the Prophet (may Allah's peace and blessings be upon him) prayed. There is a red piece of marble at the place where he offered the prayer."

Sahīh Al-BukhāriBook of Military ExpeditionsChapter: The Farewell Hajj; Hadīth no. 4400.Sahīh MuslimBook of HajjChapter: Desirability of entering the Ka'bah for pilgrims and others, praying therein, and offering supplications in all its sides; Hadīth no. 1329.Sunan Abu DāwudBook of RitualsChapter: Praying inside the Ka'bah; Hadīth no. 2023.Jāmi' At-TirmidhiBook of Hajj as reported from the Prophet (PBUH)Chapter: What is reported on praying inside the Ka'bah; Hadīth no. 874.Sunan An-Nasā'iBook of the QiblahChapter: The distance to be observed; Hadīth no. 749.Sunan Ibn MājahBook of RitualsChapter: Entering the Ka'bah; Hadīth no. 3063.

Book of Military Expeditions

Chapter: The Farewell Hajj; Hadīth no. 4400.

Sahīh Muslim

Book of Hajj

Chapter: Desirability of entering the Ka'bah for pilgrims and others, praying therein, and offering supplications in all its sides; Hadīth no. 1329.

Sunan Abu Dāwud

Book of Rituals

Chapter: Praying inside the Ka'bah; Hadīth no. 2023.

Jāmi' At-Tirmidhi

Book of Hajj as reported from the Prophet (PBUH)

Chapter: What is reported on praying inside the Ka'bah; Hadīth no. 874.

Sunan An-Nasā'i

Book of the Qiblah

Chapter: The distance to be observed; Hadīth no. 749.

Sunan Ibn Mājah

Book of Rituals

Chapter: Entering the Ka'bah; Hadīth no. 3063.

Chapter: Demolishing the Ka'bah and rebuilding it.

'Ā'ishah, may Allah be pleased with her, reported that the Prophet (may Allah's peace and blessings be upon him) said to her: "O 'Ā'ishah, were it not for the fact that your people are close to their time of Jāhiliyyah (pre-Islam), I would have ordered for the Ka'bah to be demolished, and would have included in it the portion which had been excluded, and would have made it at a level with the ground and would have made two doors for it, one towards the east and the other towards the west, and then by doing this it would have been built on the foundations laid by Abraham." That was what urged Ibn Az-Zubayr to demolish the Ka'bah. Yazīd said: "I saw Ibn Az-Zubayr when he demolished and rebuilt the Ka'bah and included in it a portion of Al-Hijr (the unroofed portion of Ka'bah which is at present in the form of a semi-circular wall to the northwest of the Ka'bah). I saw the original foundations of Abraham which were of stones resembling the humps of camels." Jarīr asked Yazīd: "Where was its place?" Yazīd said: "I will now show it to you." So Jarīr accompanied Yazīd and entered Al-Hijr, and Yazīd pointed to a place and said: "Here it is." Jarīr said: "It seemed to me to be about six cubits from Al-Hijr or so."

Sahīh Al-BukhāriBook of HajjChapter: The merit of Makkah and its buildings; Hadīth no.1586.Sahīh MuslimBook of HajjChapter: Demolishing the Ka'bah and rebuilding it; Hadīth no. 1333.Sunan Abu DāwudBook of RitualsChapter: Praying inside the Hijr; Hadīth no. 2028.Jāmi' At-TirmidhiBook of Hajj as reported from the Prophet (PBUH)Chapter: What is reported on praying inside the Hijr; Hadīth no. 876.Sunan An-Nasā'iBook of the Rituals of HajjChapter: Building the Ka'bah; Hadīth no. 2903.Sunan Ibn MājahBook of RitualsChapter: Tawāf at the Hijr; Hadīth no. 2955.

Book of Hajj

Chapter: The merit of Makkah and its buildings; Hadīth no.1586.

Sahīh Muslim

Book of Hajj

Chapter: Demolishing the Ka'bah and rebuilding it; Hadīth no. 1333.

Sunan Abu Dāwud

Book of Rituals

Chapter: Praying inside the Hijr; Hadīth no. 2028.

Jāmi' At-Tirmidhi

Book of Hajj as reported from the Prophet (PBUH)

Chapter: What is reported on praying inside the Hijr; Hadīth no. 876.

Sunan An-Nasā'i

Book of the Rituals of Hajj

Chapter: Building the Ka'bah; Hadīth no. 2903.

Sunan Ibn Mājah

Book of Rituals

Chapter: Tawāf at the Hijr; Hadīth no. 2955.

Chapter: Performing Hajj on behalf of someone who is incapable of doing it because of chronic illness, old age, or death.

'Abdullāh ibn 'Abbās (may Allah be pleased with him) reported: "Al-Fadl was riding behind the Messenger of Allah (may Allah's peace and blessings be upon him) and a woman from the tribe of Khath'am came and Al-Fadl kept looking at her and she at him. The Prophet (may Allah's peace and blessings be upon him) turned Al-Fadl's face to the other side. The woman said: 'O Messenger of Allah, the obligation of Hajj has been enjoined by Allah on His slaves while my father is old and weak, and he cannot sit firm on the mount. Can I perform Hajj on his behalf?' The Prophet (may Allah's peace and blessings be upon him) replied: 'Yes.' This was during the Farewell Hajj."

Sahīh Al-BukhāriBook of HajjChapter: The obligation of Hajj and its merit; Hadīth no. 1513Sahīh MuslimBook of HajjChapter: Performing Hajj on behalf of someone who is incapable of doing it because of chronic illness, old age, or death; Hadīth no. 1334.Sunan Abu DāwudBook of RitualsChapter: A man performing Hajj on behalf of another; Hadīth no. 1809.Jāmi' At-TirmidhiBook of Hajj as reported from the Prophet (PBUH)Chapter: What was reported on performing Hajj on behalf of an old or a deceased person; Hadīth no. 928.Sunan An-Nasā'iBook of Rituals of HajjChapter: A woman performing Hajj on behalf of a man; Hadīth no. 2641.Sunan Ibn MājahBook of RitualsChapter: Performing Hajj on behalf of a living person if he is unable to; Hadīth no. 2909.

Book of Hajj

Chapter: The obligation of Hajj and its merit; Hadīth no. 1513

Sahīh Muslim

Book of Hajj

Chapter: Performing Hajj on behalf of someone who is incapable of doing it because of chronic illness, old age, or death; Hadīth no. 1334.

Sunan Abu Dāwud

Book of Rituals

Chapter: A man performing Hajj on behalf of another; Hadīth no. 1809.

Jāmi' At-Tirmidhi

Book of Hajj as reported from the Prophet (PBUH)

Chapter: What was reported on performing Hajj on behalf of an old or a deceased person; Hadīth no. 928.

Sunan An-Nasā'i

Book of Rituals of Hajj

Chapter: A woman performing Hajj on behalf of a man; Hadīth no. 2641.

Sunan Ibn Mājah

Book of Rituals

Chapter: Performing Hajj on behalf of a living person if he is unable to; Hadīth no. 2909.

Chapter: Permissibility of staying in Makkah for those who emigrated from it

for no more than three days after Hajj and 'Umrah are over.

Al-'Alā' ibn al-Hadrami (may Allah be pleased with him) reported that the Messenger of Allah (may Allah's peace and blessings be upon him) said: "An immigrant may stay three days (in Makkah) after returning from Mina."

Sahīh Al-BukhāriBook of the Merits of the AnsārChapter: An immigrant staying in Makkah after finishing the rituals; Hadīth no. 3933.Sahīh MuslimBook of HajjChapter: Permissibility for an immigrant to stay in Makkah for three days and no more after finishing Hajj and 'Umrah; Hadīth no. 1352.Sunan Abu DāwudBook of RitualsChapter: Staying in Makkah; Hadīth no. 2022.Jāmi' At-TirmidhiBook of Hajj as reported from the Prophet (PBUH)Chapter: What is reported on an immigrant staying in Makkah for three days after returning from Mina; Hadīth no. 949.Sunan An-Nasā'iBook of Shortening Prayer While TravelingChapter: Duration of stay that makes shortening the prayer permissible; Hadīth no. 1454.Sunan Ibn MājahBook of Establishing the Prayerand the Sunnah Acts Related to itChapter: Length of time during which the traveler is allowed to shorten the prayer if he stays in a town; Hadīth no. 1073.

Book of the Merits of the Ansār

Chapter: An immigrant staying in Makkah after finishing the rituals; Hadīth no. 3933.

Sahīh Muslim

Book of Hajj

Chapter: Permissibility for an immigrant to stay in Makkah for three days and no more after finishing Hajj and 'Umrah; Hadīth no. 1352.

Sunan Abu Dāwud

Book of Rituals

Chapter: Staying in Makkah; Hadīth no. 2022.

Jāmi' At-Tirmidhi

Book of Hajj as reported from the Prophet (PBUH)

Chapter: What is reported on an immigrant staying in Makkah for three days after returning from Mina; Hadīth no. 949.

Sunan An-Nasā'i

Book of Shortening Prayer While Traveling

Chapter: Duration of stay that makes shortening the prayer permissible; Hadīth no. 1454.

Sunan Ibn Mājah

Book of Establishing the Prayer

and the Sunnah Acts Related to it

Chapter: Length of time during which the traveler is allowed to shorten the prayer if he stays in a town; Hadīth no. 1073.

Chapter: The sanctity of Makkah and the sanctity of its game, grasses, trees

and lost property, except for the one who announces it, is forever.

Abu Hurayrah (may Allah be pleased with him) reported: "In the year of the Conquest of Makkah, the tribe of Khuzā'ah killed a man from the tribe of Banu Layth in retaliation for a person who was killed from their tribe before Islam. So, the Messenger of Allah (may Allah 's peace and blessings be upon him) got up and said: 'Indeed, Allah Almighty, held back the elephant from Makkah, but He enabled His Messenger and the believers to conquer it. Behold! Fighting in it was not permitted for anyone before me, nor will it be permitted for anyone after me; it was permitted for me only for a short while during the day. Verily, it is from this moment a sanctuary; its trees should not be cut down, its grass should not be removed, its thorny shrubs should not be uprooted, and lost items found in it should not be taken except by one who intends to look for their owner. And if someone is killed therein, his heir has the option to either ask for retribution or accept blood money.' A man from Yemen named Abu Shāh stood up and said: 'Write that for me, O Messenger of Allah.' The Messenger of Allah (may Allah's peace and blessings be upon him) said: 'Write that for Abu Shāh.' Then a man from Quraysh stood up and said: 'O Messenger of Allah, except for Idhkhir (a pleasant-smelling grass), for we use it in our houses and graves.' The Messenger, may Allah's peace and blessings be upon him, said: 'Except for Idhkhir.'"

Sahīh Al-BukhāriBook of Blood MoneyChapter: Heir of the killed person has the right to choose one of two compensations; Hadīth no. 6880.Sahīh MuslimBook of HajjChapter: Permanent sanctity of Makkah and sanctity of its game, grasses, trees, and lost property, except for the one who announces it; Hadīth no. 1355.Sunan Abu DāwudBook of RitualsChapter: Sanctity of the precincts of Makkah; Hadīth no. 2017.Jāmi' At-TirmidhiBook of Blood Money as reported from the Prophet (PBUH)Chapter: What is reported on the heir of one who was killed deciding between retaliation or pardon; Hadīth no. 1405.Sunan An-Nasā'iBook of Qasāmah (Oath of liability of deliberate homicide)Chapter: Whether blood money should be taken from the one who kills deliberately if the heir of the murdered pardon him and does not seek retaliation; Hadīth no. 4786.Sunan Ibn MājahBook of Blood MoneyChapter: Heir of the murdered has the right to choose one of the three compensations; Hadīth no. 2624.

Book of Blood Money

Chapter: Heir of the killed person has the right to choose one of two compensations; Hadīth no. 6880.

Sahīh Muslim

Book of Hajj

Chapter: Permanent sanctity of Makkah and sanctity of its game, grasses, trees, and lost property, except for the one who announces it; Hadīth no. 1355.

Sunan Abu Dāwud

Book of Rituals

Chapter: Sanctity of the precincts of Makkah; Hadīth no. 2017.

Jāmi' At-Tirmidhi

Book of Blood Money as reported from the Prophet (PBUH)

Chapter: What is reported on the heir of one who was killed deciding between retaliation or pardon; Hadīth no. 1405.

Sunan An-Nasā'i

Book of Qasāmah (Oath of liability of deliberate homicide)

Chapter: Whether blood money should be taken from the one who kills deliberately if the heir of the murdered pardon him and does not seek retaliation; Hadīth no. 4786.

Sunan Ibn Mājah

Book of Blood Money

Chapter: Heir of the murdered has the right to choose one of the three compensations; Hadīth no. 2624.

Chapter: Permissibility of entering Makkah without Ihrām.

Anas ibn Mālik (may Allah be pleased with him) reported: "The Messenger of Allah (may Allah's peace and blessings be upon him) entered Makkah in the Year of the Conquest wearing a helmet on his head. When he took it off, a man came to him and said: 'Ibn Khatal is hanging on to the drapes of the Ka'bah,' so he said: 'Kill him.'"

Sahīh Al-BukhāriBook of Penalty of Hunting (while in state of Ihrām)Chapter: Entering the holy precincts and Makkah without Ihrām; Hadīth no. 1846.Sahīh MuslimBook of HajjChapter: Permissibility of entering Makkah without Ihrām; Hadīth no. 1357.Sunan Abu DāwudBook of JihādChapter: Killing a captive without inviting him to Islam; Hadīth no. 2685.Jāmi' At-TirmidhiBook of Jihād as reported from the Prophet (PBUH)Chapter: What is reported on the helmet; Hadīth no. 1693.Sunan An-Nasā'iBook of Rituals of HajjChapter: Entering Makkah without Ihrām; Hadīth no. 2867.Sunan Ibn MājahBook of JihādChapter: Weapons; Hadīth no. 2805.

Book of Penalty of Hunting (while in state of Ihrām)

Chapter: Entering the holy precincts and Makkah without Ihrām; Hadīth no. 1846.

Sahīh Muslim

Book of Hajj

Chapter: Permissibility of entering Makkah without Ihrām; Hadīth no. 1357.

Sunan Abu Dāwud

Book of Jihād

Chapter: Killing a captive without inviting him to Islam; Hadīth no. 2685.

Jāmi' At-Tirmidhī

Book of Jihād as reported from the Prophet (PBUH)

Chapter: What is reported on the helmet; Hadīth no. 1693.

Sunan An-Nasā'i

Book of Rituals of Hajj

Chapter: Entering Makkah without Ihrām; Hadīth no. 2867.

Sunan Ibn Mājah

Book of Jihād

Chapter: Weapons; Hadīth no. 2805.

Chapter: Merit of Madinah and the invocation of the Prophet (PBUH) that Allah bless it, stating its sanctity and the inviolability of its game and trees, and marking the borders of its sanctuary.

'Ali (may Allah be pleased with him) addressed the people while he was standing on a brick pulpit and carrying a sword from which was hanging a scroll. He said: "By Allah, we have no book to read except the Book of Allah and whatever is on this scroll," and he unrolled it, and behold, in it was written what sort of camels were to be given as blood money, and there was also written in it: "Madinah is a sanctuary from 'Ayr (a mountain) to such-and-such place, so whoever commits a sin therein or introduces a religious innovation, he will incur the curse of Allah, the angels, and all the people, and Allah will not accept his obligatory or optional good deeds." There was also written in it: "The asylum (pledge of protection) granted by any Muslim is one and the same, even a Muslim of the lowest status is to be secured and respected by all other Muslims, and whoever betrays a Muslim in this respect (by violating the pledge) will incur the curse of Allah, the angels, and all the people, and Allah will not accept his obligatory or optional good deeds." There was also written in it: "Any freed slave who takes as allies other than his real allies (his ex-owners who manumitted him) without their permission will incur the curse of Allah, the angels, and all the people, and Allah will not accept his obligatory or optional good deeds."

Sahīh Al-BukhāriBook of Holding Fast to the Qur'ān and SunnahChapter: Reprehensibility of going deep into knowledge and arguing about it, exaggerating in religion, and introducing Bid'ahs; Hadīth no. 7300.Sahīh MuslimBook of HajjChapter: Merit of Madinah and the invocation of the Prophet (PBUH) that Allah bless it, stating its sanctity and the inviolability of its game and trees, and marking the borders of its sanctuary; Hadīth no. 1370.Sunan Abu DāwudBook of RitualsChapter: Sanctity of Madinah; Hadīth no. 2034.Jāmi' At-TirmidhiBook of Walā' (loyalty) and Gifts as reported from the Prophet (PBUH)Chapter: What is reported on loyalty to other than one's real masters (his ex-owners who manumitted him) or attributing oneself to other than one's real father; Hadīth no. 2127.Sunan An-Nasā'iBook of Qasāmah (Oath of liability of deliberate homicide)Chapter: Executing retribution between free persons and slaves in murder cases; Hadīth no. 4734.Sunan Ibn MājahBook of Blood MoneyChapter: A believer is not to be killed in retaliation for a disbeliever; Hadīth no. 2658.

Book of Holding Fast to the Qur'ān and Sunnah

Chapter: Reprehensibility of going deep into knowledge and arguing about it, exaggerating in religion, and introducing Bid'ahs; Hadīth no. 7300.

Saḥīḥ Muslim

Book of Hajj

Chapter: Merit of Madinah and the invocation of the Prophet (PBUH) that Allah bless it, stating its sanctity and the inviolability of its game and trees, and marking the borders of its sanctuary; Ḥadīth no. 1370.

Sunan Abu Dāwud

Book of Rituals

Chapter: Sanctity of Madinah; Ḥadīth no. 2034.

Jāmi' At-Tirmidhi

Book of Walā' (loyalty) and Gifts as reported from the Prophet (PBUH)

Chapter: What is reported on loyalty to other than one's real masters (his ex-owners who manumitted him) or attributing oneself to other than one's real father; Ḥadīth no. 2127.

Sunan An-Nasā'i

Book of Qasāmah (Oath of liability of deliberate homicide)

Chapter: Executing retribution between free persons and slaves in murder cases; Ḥadīth no. 4734.

Sunan Ibn Mājah

Book of Blood Money

Chapter: A believer is not to be killed in retaliation for a disbeliever; Ḥadīth no. 2658.

Book of Marriage

Chapter: Desirability of marriage for whoever longs for it and can afford it, and the desirability of fasting for whoever cannot afford it.

'Alqamah reported: "While I was walking with 'Abdullah (may Allah be pleased with him), he said: 'We were in the company of the Prophet (may Allah's peace and blessings be upon him) when he said: "He who can afford to marry should marry because it helps refraining from unlawful gaze and more chaste for private parts; and he who cannot afford to marry should fast, as fasting will diminish his sexual desire."'"

Saḥīḥ Al-BukhāriBook of FastingChapter: Fasting for the one who fears committing sin if he stays unmarried; Ḥadīth no. 1905.Saḥīḥ MuslimBook of MarriageChapter: Desirability of marriage for whoever longs for it and can afford it, and the desirability of fasting for whoever cannot afford it; Ḥadīth no. 1400.Sunan Abu DāwudBook of MarriageChapter: Encouraging marriage; Ḥadīth no. 2046.Jāmi' At-TirmidhiBook of Marriage as Reported from the Prophet (PBUH)Chapter: What is reported on the merit of marriage and encouraging it; Ḥadīth no. 1081.Sunan An-Nasā'iBook of FastingChapter: Mentioning the difference in the reports from Muhammad ibn Abi Ya'qūb in the Ḥadīth of Abu Umāmah on the merit of the fasting person; Ḥadīth no. 2239.Sunan Ibn MājahBook of MarriageChapter: What is reported on the merit of marriage; Ḥadīth no. 1845.

Book of Fasting

Chapter: Fasting for the one who fears committing sin if he stays unmarried; Ḥadīth no. 1905.

Saḥīḥ Muslim

Book of Marriage

Chapter: Desirability of marriage for whoever longs for it and can afford it, and the desirability of fasting for whoever cannot afford it; Hadīth no. 1400.

Sunan Abu Dāwud

Book of Marriage

Chapter: Encouraging marriage; Hadīth no. 2046.

Jāmi' At-Tirmidhi

Book of Marriage as Reported from the Prophet (PBUH)

Chapter: What is reported on the merit of marriage and encouraging it; Hadīth no. 1081.

Sunan An-Nasā'i

Book of Fasting

Chapter: Mentioning the difference in the reports from Muhammad ibn Abi Ya'qūb in the Hadīth of Abu Umāmah on the merit of the fasting person; Hadīth no. 2239.

Sunan Ibn Mājah

Book of Marriage

Chapter: What is reported on the merit of marriage; Hadīth no. 1845.

Chapter: Prohibition of taking a woman and her paternal or maternal aunt as co-wives.

Abu Hurayrah (may Allah be pleased with him) reported that the Prophet (may Allah's peace and blessings be upon him) said: "One may not take as co-wives a woman and her paternal aunt or a woman and her maternal aunt."

Sahīh Al-BukhāriBook of MarriageChapter: A woman may not be co-wife to her paternal aunt; Hadīth no. 5109.Sahīh MuslimBook of MarriageChapter: Prohibition of taking as co-wives a woman and her paternal aunt or maternal aunt; Hadīth no. 1408.Sunan Abu DāwudBook of MarriageChapter: Women whom it is disliked to combine as co-wives; Hadīth no. 2066.Jāmi' At-TirmidhiBook of Marriage as Reported from the Prophet (PBUH)Chapter: What is reported on prohibition of taking a woman and her paternal aunt or maternal aunt as co-wives; Hadīth no.1125.Sunan An-Nasā'iBook of MarriageChapter: Prohibition of Taking a woman and her paternal aunt as co-wives; Hadīth no. 3288.Sunan Ibn MājahBook of MarriageChapter: What is reported on prohibition of taking a woman and her paternal aunt or maternal aunt as co-wives; Hadīth no.1929.

Book of Marriage

Chapter: A woman may not be co-wife to her paternal aunt; Hadīth no. 5109.

Sahīh Muslim

Book of Marriage

Chapter: Prohibition of taking as co-wives a woman and her paternal aunt or maternal aunt; Hadīth no. 1408.

Sunan Abu Dāwud

Book of Marriage

Chapter: Women whom it is disliked to combine as co-wives; Hadīth no. 2066.

Jāmi' At-Tirmidhi

Book of Marriage as Reported from the Prophet (PBUH)

Chapter: What is reported on prohibition of taking a woman and her paternal aunt or maternal aunt as co-wives; Hadīth no.1125.

Sunan An-Nasā'i

Book of Marriage

Chapter: Prohibition of Taking a woman and her paternal aunt as co-wives; Hadīth no. 3288.

Sunan Ibn Mājah

Book of Marriage

Chapter: What is reported on prohibition of taking a woman and her paternal aunt or maternal aunt as co-wives; Hadīth no.1929.

Chapter: Prohibition of getting married and dislike of proposing marriage for Muhrim (one in state of Ihrām).

Ibn 'Abbās (may Allah be pleased with him) reported: "The Prophet (may Allah's peace and blessings be upon him) married Maymūnah when he was in the state of Ihrām."

Sahīh Al-BukhāriBook of Penalty of Hunting (while in state of Ihrām)Chapter: Giving in marriage to a Muhrim; Hadīth no. 1837.Sahīh MuslimBook of MarriageChapter: Prohibition of getting married and dislike of proposing marriage for Muhrim (one in state of Ihrām); Hadīth no. 1410.Sunan Abu DāwudBook of RitualsChapter: A Muhrim getting married; Hadīth no. 1844.Jāmi' At-TirmidhiBook of Hajj as reported from the Prophet (PBUH)Chapter: What is reported on the dispensation in this regard; Hadīth no. 844.Sunan An-Nasā'iBook of Rituals of HajjChapter: Concession for a Muhrim to marry; Hadīth no. 2837.Sunan Ibn MājahBook of MarriageChapter: A Muhrim getting married; Hadīth no. 1965.

Book of Penalty of Hunting (while in state of Ihrām)

Chapter: Giving in marriage to a Muhrim; Hadīth no. 1837.

Sahīh Muslim

Book of Marriage

Chapter: Prohibition of getting married and dislike of proposing marriage for Muhrim (one in state of Ihrām); Hadīth no. 1410.

Sunan Abu Dāwud

Book of Rituals

Chapter: A Muhrim getting married; Hadīth no. 1844.

Jāmi' At-Tirmidhi

Book of Hajj as reported from the Prophet (PBUH)

Chapter: What is reported on the dispensation in this regard; Hadīth no. 844.

Sunan An-Nasā'i

Book of Rituals of Hajj

Chapter: Concession for a Muhrim to marry; Hadīth no. 2837.

Sunan Ibn Mājah

Book of Marriage

Chapter: A Muhrim getting married; Hadīth no. 1965.

Chapter: Prohibition of proposing to a woman whom a fellow Muslim has proposed to until the latter gives permission or withdraws his proposal.

Ibn 'Umar (may Allah be pleased with him) reported: "The Prophet (may Allah's peace and blessings be upon him) forbade that someone offers a higher price for something that has already been sold to his brother, or proposes marriage to a woman when someone else has already proposed to her, unless the previous suitor gives up the proposal or gives him permission."

Sahīh Al-BukhāriBook of MarriageChapter: None should propose to a woman whom a fellow Muslim has already proposed to until the first suitor either marries her or leaves her; Hadīth no. 5142.Sahīh MuslimBook of MarriageChapter: Prohibition of proposing to a woman whom a fellow Muslim has already proposed to until the first suitor gives permission or leaves her; Hadīth no. 1412.Sunan Abu DāwudBook of MarriageChapter: Dislike of proposing to a woman whom a fellow Muslim has already proposed to; Hadīth no. 2081.Jāmi' At-TirmidhiBook of Sales as reported from the Prophet (PBUH)Chapter: What is reported on forbiddance of selling over the sale of a fellow Muslim; Hadīth no. 1292.Sunan An-Nasā'iBook of MarriageChapter: A man proposing to a woman when her first suitor leaves her or gives him permission to propose to her; Hadīth no. 3243.Sunan Ibn MājahBook of MarriageChapter: A man does not propose to a woman already proposed to by a fellow Muslim; Hadīth no. 1868.

Book of Marriage

Chapter: None should propose to a woman whom a fellow Muslim has already proposed to until the first suitor either marries her or leaves her; Hadīth no. 5142.

Sahīh Muslim

Book of Marriage

Chapter: Prohibition of proposing to a woman whom a fellow Muslim has already proposed to until the first suitor gives permission or leaves her; Hadīth no. 1412.

Sunan Abu Dāwud

Book of Marriage

Chapter: Dislike of proposing to a woman whom a fellow Muslim has already proposed to; Hadīth no. 2081.

Jāmi' At-Tirmidhi

Book of Sales as reported from the Prophet (PBUH)

Chapter: What is reported on forbiddance of selling over the sale of a fellow Muslim; Hadīth no. 1292.

Sunan An-Nasā'i

Book of Marriage

Chapter: A man proposing to a woman when her first suitor leaves her or gives him permission to propose to her; Hadīth no. 3243.

Sunan Ibn Mājah

Book of Marriage

Chapter: A man does not propose to a woman already proposed to by a fellow Muslim; Hadīth no. 1868.

Chapter: Prohibition of Shighār marriage and its invalidity.

Ibn 'Umar (may Allah be pleased with him) reported that the Messenger of Allah (may Allah's peace and blessings be upon him) forbade Shighār marriage, which is when a man marries his daughter off to another man who, in turn, marries his daughter off to him, without a dower paid by either of them.

Sahīh Al-BukhāriBook of MarriageChapter: Shighār marriage; Hadīth no. 5112.Sahīh MuslimBook of MarriageChapter: Prohibition of Shighār marriage and its invalidity; Hadīth no. 1415.Sunan Abu DāwudBook of MarriageChapter: About Shighār marriage; Hadīth no. 2074.Jāmi' At-TirmidhiBook of Marriage as Reported from the Prophet (PBUH)Chapter: What is reported on the prohibition of Shighār marriage; Hadīth no. 1124.Sunan An-Nasā'iBook of MarriageChapter: Explanation of Shighār marriage; Hadīth no. 3337.Sunan Ibn MājahBook of MarriageChapter: Forbidding Shighār marriage; Hadīth no. 1883.

Book of Marriage

Chapter: Shighār marriage; Hadīth no. 5112.

Sahīh Muslim

Book of Marriage

Chapter: Prohibition of Shighār marriage and its invalidity; Hadīth no. 1415.

Sunan Abu Dāwud

Book of Marriage

Chapter: About Shighār marriage; Hadīth no. 2074.

Jāmi' At-Tirmidhi

Book of Marriage as Reported from the Prophet (PBUH)

Chapter: What is reported on the prohibition of Shighār marriage; Hadīth no. 1124.

Sunan An-Nasā'i

Book of Marriage

Chapter: Explanation of Shighār marriage; Hadīth no. 3337.

Sunan Ibn Mājah

Book of Marriage

Chapter: Forbidding Shighār marriage; Hadīth no. 1883.

Chapter: Fulfilling the conditions in marriage.

'Uqbah ibn 'Āamir (may Allah be pleased with him) reported that the Prophet (may Allah's peace and blessings be upon him) said: "The conditions that are the worthiest of being fulfilled are those which make sexual intercourse lawful for you."

Sahīh Al-BukhāriBook of ConditionsChapter: Conditions regarding the dower when concluding marriage contract; Hadīth no. 2721.Sahīh MuslimBook of MarriageChapter: Fulfilling conditions set in marriage contract; Hadīth no. 1418.Sunan Abu DāwudBook of MarriageChapter: A man who agrees to the condition of living in her place of residence; Hadīth no. 2139.Jāmi' At-TirmidhiBook of Marriage as Reported from the Prophet (PBUH)Chapter: Conditions regarding the dowry when concluding marriage contract; Hadīth no. 1127.Sunan An-Nasā'iBook of MarriageChapter: Conditions set in marriage contract; Hadīth no. 3282.Sunan Ibn MājahBook of MarriageChapter: Conditions set in marriage contract; Hadīth no. 1954.

Book of Conditions

Chapter: Conditions regarding the dower when concluding marriage contract; Hadīth no. 2721.

Sahīh Muslim

Book of Marriage

Chapter: Fulfilling conditions set in marriage contract; Hadīth no. 1418.

Sunan Abu Dāwud

Book of Marriage

Chapter: A man who agrees to the condition of living in her place of residence; Hadīth no. 2139.

Jāmi' At-Tirmidhi

Book of Marriage as Reported from the Prophet (PBUH)

Chapter: Conditions regarding the dowry when concluding marriage contract; Hadīth no. 1127.

Sunan An-Nasā'i

Book of Marriage

Chapter: Conditions set in marriage contract; Hadīth no. 3282.

Sunan Ibn Mājah

Book of Marriage

Chapter: Conditions set in marriage contract; Hadīth no. 1954.

Chapter: Seeking the permission of a previously-married woman for marriage by her verbal consent and that of a virgin by her remaining silent.

Abu Hurayrah (may Allah be pleased with him) reported that the Prophet (may Allah's peace and blessings be upon him) said: "A previously-married woman should not be married until her verbal consent is sought, and a virgin should not be married until her permission is sought." They said: "O Messenger of Allah, what is her permission?" He said: "When she remains silent."

Sahīh Al-BukhāriBook of MarriageChapter: A father or other than him cannot give a virgin or a previously-married woman in marriage without her consent; Hadīth no.5136.Sahīh MuslimBook of MarriageChapter: Seeking permission of a previously-married woman for marriage by getting her verbal consent, and that of a virgin by her silence; Hadīth no. 1419.Sunan Abu DāwudBook of MarriageChapter: Seeking the woman's permission to give her in marriage; Hadīth no. 2092.Jāmi' At-TirmidhiBook of Marriage as Reported from the Prophet (PBUH)Chapter: What is reported on seeking the permission of a virgin or a previously-married woman (for marriage); Hadīth no. 1107.Sunan An-Nasā'iBook of MarriageChapter: Seeking permission of a previously-married woman for her own marriage; Hadīth no. 3265.Sunan Ibn MājahBook of MarriageChapter: Seeking permission of a virgin and previously-married woman for marriage; Hadīth no. 1871.

Book of Marriage

Chapter: A father or other than him cannot give a virgin or a previously-married woman in marriage without her consent; Hadīth no.5136.

Sahīh Muslim

Book of Marriage

Chapter: Seeking permission of a previously-married woman for marriage by getting her verbal consent, and that of a virgin by her silence; Hadīth no. 1419.

Sunan Abu Dāwud

Book of Marriage

Chapter: Seeking the woman's permission to give her in marriage; Hadīth no. 2092.

Jāmi' At-Tirmidhi

Book of Marriage as Reported from the Prophet (PBUH)

Chapter: What is reported on seeking the permission of a virgin or a previously-married woman (for marriage); Hadīth no. 1107.

Sunan An-Nasā'i

Book of Marriage

Chapter: Seeking permission of a previously-married woman for her own marriage; Hadīth no. 3265.

Sunan Ibn Mājah

Book of Marriage

Chapter: Seeking permission of a virgin and previously-married woman for marriage; Hadīth no. 1871.

Chapter: Dowry and the permissibility of it being in the form of teaching the Qur'an or a ring

made of iron or other things whether much or little, and the desirability

of it being five hundred dirhams if not causing harm to the suitor.

Sahl ibn Sa'd As-Sā'idi, may Allah be pleased with him, reported: "A woman came to Allah's Messenger (PBUH) and said: 'O Messenger of Allah, I have come to you to give myself to you in marriage.' Allah's Messenger (PBUH) looked at her and cast a glance at her from head to foot. Allah's Messenger (PBUH) then lowered his head. When the woman saw that he had made no decision in regard to her, she sat down. There stood up a person from amongst his companions and said: 'O Messenger of Allah, marry her off to me if you have no need of her.' The Prophet (PBUH) said: 'Is there anything with you (which you can give as a dower)?' He said: 'No, Messenger of Allah, by Allah I have nothing.' Thereupon Allah's Messenger (PBUH) said: 'Go to your people (family) and see if you can find something.' He returned and said: 'I have found nothing.' The Messenger of Allah (PBUH) said: 'Look for even an iron ring.' He went and returned and said: No, by Allah, not even an iron ring, but only this lower garment of mine (Sahl said that he had no upper garment), half of which (I am prepared to part with) for her. Thereupon Allah's Messenger (PBUH) said: How can your lower garment serve your purpose, for if you wear it, she would not be able to make any use of it, and if she wears it there would not be anything upon you?' The man sat down and as the sitting prolonged he stood up (in disappointment) and as he was going back, Allah's Messenger (PBUH) ordered him to be called back, and as he came, he said to him: 'Do you know anything of the Qur'an?' He said: 'I know such-and-such surahs (and he counted them)', whereupon he (PBUH) said: 'Can you memorize them by heart ?' He said: 'Yes,' whereupon he (Allah's Messenger) said: 'Go, I have given her to you in marriage for the Qur'an which you know.'"

Sahīh Al-BukhāriBook of MarriageChapter: Giving in marriage to a poor man; Hadīth no. 5087.Sahīh MuslimBook of MarriageChapter: Dower and the permissibility of it being in the form of teaching the Qur'an or an iron ring or otherwise, whether much or little, and the desirability of it being five hundred dirhams if not causing harm to the suitor; Hadīth no. 1425.Sunan Abu DāwudBook of MarriageChapter: Dower in form of work suitor has to do; Hadīth no. 2111.Jāmi' At-TirmidhiBook of Marriage as Reported from the Prophet (PBUH)Chapter: Marriage; Hadīth no. 1114.Sunan An-Nasā'iBook of

MarriageChapter: The words by which marriage is concluded; Hadīth no. 1889Sunan Ibn MājahBook of MarriageChapter: Dower of women; Hadīth no. 1889.

Book of Marriage

Chapter: Giving in marriage to a poor man; Hadīth no. 5087.

Sahīh Muslim

Book of Marriage

Chapter: Dower and the permissibility of it being in the form of teaching the Qur'an or an iron ring or otherwise, whether much or little, and the desirability of it being five hundred dirhams if not causing harm to the suitor; Hadīth no. 1425.

Sunan Abu Dāwud

Book of Marriage

Chapter: Dower in form of work suitor has to do; Hadīth no. 2111.

Jāmi' At-Tirmidhi

Book of Marriage as Reported from the Prophet (PBUH)

Chapter: Marriage; Hadīth no. 1114.

Sunan An-Nasā'i

Book of Marriage

Chapter: The words by which marriage is concluded; Hadīth no. 1889

Sunan Ibn Mājah

Book of Marriage

Chapter: Dower of women; Hadīth no. 1889.

Anas (may Allah be pleased with him) reported: "When 'Abdur-Rahmān ibn 'Awf came to Madinah, the Prophet (may Allah's peace and blessings be upon him) established a bond of brotherhood between him and Sa'd ibn Ar-Rabī' al-Ansāri. Sa'd was a rich man, so he said to 'Abdur-Rahmān: 'I will give you half of my wealth and will help you marry.' 'Abdur-Rahmān said (to him): 'May Allah bless for you your family and wealth. Show me the way to the market.' So 'Abdur-Rahmān did not return (from the market) till he had gained some dried buttermilk (yogurt) and ghee (through trading). He brought that to his household. We stayed for sometime (or as long as Allah willed), and then 'Abdur-Rahmān came, scented with yellowish perfume. The Prophet (may Allah's peace and blessings be upon him) said (to him): 'What is this?' He replied: 'O Messenger of Allah, I married an Ansāri woman.' He asked: 'What did you give her (as dower)?' He replied: 'A gold stone, or gold equal to the weight of a date stone.' The Prophet (may Allah's peace and blessings be upon him) said: 'Give a wedding banquet even if with one sheep.'"

Sahīh Al-BukhāriBook of SalesChapter: What is reported on the statement of Allah Almighty: {And when the prayer has been concluded, disperse within the land and seek from the bounty of Allah, and remember Allah often that you may succeed. But when they see some merchandise or some amusement, they rush to it and leave you standing. Say, "What is with Allah is better than amusement and than merchandise, and Allah is the best of providers.} and His statement: {...do not consume one another's wealth unjustly but only [in lawful] business by mutual consent...}; Hadīth no. 2049.Sahih MuslīmBook of MarriageChapter: Dower and the permissibility of it being in the form of teaching the Qur'an or an iron ring or otherwise, whether much or little, and the desirability of it being five hundred dirhams if not causing harm to the suitor; Hadīth no. 1427.Sunan Abu DāwudBook of MarriageChapter: Paying a small dower; Hadīth no. 2109.Jāmi' At-TirmidhiBook of Marriage as Reported from the Prophet (PBUH)Chapter: What is reported on the marriage banquet; Hadīth no. 1094.Sunan An-Nasā'iBook of

MarriageChapter: Giving a gift to the one who got married; Hadīth no. 3388.Sunan Ibn MājahBook of MarriageChapter: Marriage banquet; Hadīth no.1907.

Book of Sales

Chapter: What is reported on the statement of Allah Almighty: {And when the prayer has been concluded, disperse within the land and seek from the bounty of Allah, and remember Allah often that you may succeed. But when they see some merchandise or some amusement, they rush to it and leave you standing. Say, "What is with Allah is better than amusement and than merchandise, and Allah is the best of providers.} and His statement: {...do not consume one another's wealth unjustly but only [in lawful] business by mutual consent...}; Hadīth no. 2049.

Sahih Muslīm

Book of Marriage

Chapter: Dower and the permissibility of it being in the form of teaching the Qur'an or an iron ring or otherwise, whether much or little, and the desirability of it being five hundred dirhams if not causing harm to the suitor; Hadīth no. 1427.

Sunan Abu Dāwud

Book of Marriage

Chapter: Paying a small dower; Hadīth no. 2109.

Jāmi' At-Tirmidhi

Book of Marriage as Reported from the Prophet (PBUH)

Chapter: What is reported on the marriage banquet; Hadīth no. 1094.

Sunan An-Nasā'i

Book of Marriage

Chapter: Giving a gift to the one who got married; Hadīth no. 3388.

Sunan Ibn Mājah

Book of Marriage

Chapter: Marriage banquet; Hadīth no.1907.

Chapter: Merit of freeing one's slave-girl then marrying her.

Anas ibn Mālik (may Allah be pleased with him) reported: "The Messenger of Allah (PBUH) conquered Khaybar, so we offered the morning prayer there in the darkness of early dawn. Then the Prophet of Allah (PBUH) rode (his mount). Abu Talhah rode his, and I rode behind Abu Talhah on the same mount. The Prophet of Allah (PBUH) rode through the alleys of Khaybar and (I rode so close to him that) my knee touched the thigh of the Prophet of Allah (PBUH). His Izār (waist wrapper) rolled back from his thigh, and I could see its whiteness. When he entered the town, he said: 'Allahu Akbar (God is Great). Khaybar is doomed to destruction. When we descend in the midst of a people, it is a bad day for them who have been warned (and have not taken heed).' He said these words thrice. The people of the town had just come out (from their houses) to go about their jobs. They said (in surprise): 'Muhammad has come.' 'Abdul-'Azīz (sub-narrator) said: 'some of our companions said: Muhammad and the army (have come).' He said: 'We seized it (the territory of Khaybar) by force, and the captives of war were rounded up. Dihyah al-Kalbi came and said: 'O Prophet of Allah, give me a girl from the captives.' He said: 'Go and take a girl.' Dihyah chose Safiyyah bint Huyayy. A man came to the Prophet (PBUH) and said: 'O Prophet of Allah, you have given to Dihyah Safiyyah bint Huyayy, the honorable lady of Qurayzhah and An-Nadīr. She is worthy of you alone.' He said: 'Call him along with her.' So he came along with her. When the Prophet (PBUH) saw her he said: 'Take a girl from the captives other than her.' He (the narrator) said: 'The Prophet (PBUH) then freed her and married her. Thābit said to him (the narrator):

'O Abu Hamzah, how much dower did he give her?' He said: 'Her self. He freed her and married her.' On the way, Umm Sulaym prepared her for him and sent her to him in the night. So the Prophet (PBUH) was a bridegroom in the morning and he said: 'He who has anything (to eat) should bring it.' A leather sheet was spread. One man came with cheese, another with dates, and another with refined butter, and they prepared Hays (a type of dish), and that was the wedding feast of the Messenger of Allah (PBUH)."

Sahīh Al-BukhāriBook of PrayerChapter: What is reported about the thigh; Hadīth no. 371.Sahīh MuslimBook of MarriageChapter: Merit of manumitting one's female slave then marrying her; Hadīth no. 1365.Sunan Abu DāwudBook of MarriageChapter: A man manumits his female slave then marries her; Hadīth no. 2054.Jāmi' At-TirmidhiBook of Marriage as Reported from the Prophet (PBUH)Chapter: A man manumits his female slave then marries her; Hadīth no. 1115.Sunan An-Nasā'iBook of MarriageChapter: Marriage with manumission as dower; Hadīth no. 3342.Sunan Ibn MājahBook of MarriageChapter: A man manumits his female slave then marries her; Hadīth no. 1957.

Book of Prayer

Chapter: What is reported about the thigh; Hadīth no. 371.

Sahīh Muslim

Book of Marriage

Chapter: Merit of manumitting one's female slave then marrying her; Hadīth no. 1365.

Sunan Abu Dāwud

Book of Marriage

Chapter: A man manumits his female slave then marries her; Hadīth no. 2054.

Jāmi' At-Tirmidhi

Book of Marriage as Reported from the Prophet (PBUH)

Chapter: A man manumits his female slave then marries her; Hadīth no. 1115.

Sunan An-Nasā'i

Book of Marriage

Chapter: Marriage with manumission as dower; Hadīth no. 3342.

Sunan Ibn Mājah

Book of Marriage

Chapter: A man manumits his female slave then marries her; Hadīth no. 1957.

Chapter: A woman divorced thrice is not lawful for her ex-husband in marriage until she marries

another man who has sexual intercourse with her, then he leaves her (by divorce or death) and her waiting period is over.

'Ā'ishah (may Allah be pleased with her) said: "The wife of Rifā'ah al-Qurazhi came to the Messenger of Allah (may Allah's peace and blessings be upon him) while I was sitting, and Abu Bakr was also there. She said: 'O Messenger of Allah, I was the wife of Rifā'ah and he divorced me irrevocably. Then I married 'Abdur-Rahmān ibn az-Zubayr who, by Allah, O Messenger of Allah, has only something like a fringe of a garment, showing the fringe of her dress (meaning that his male organ was very small). Khālid ibn Sa'īd, who was standing at the door as he was not permitted, heard her statement and said:

'O Abu Bakr, why do you not stop this woman from saying what she is saying openly before the Messenger of Allah?' No, by Allah, the Messenger of Allah (may Allah's peace and blessings be upon him) did no more than smile. Then he said to the woman: 'Perhaps you wish to return to Rifā'ah? That is impossible until he ('Abdur-Rahmān) consummates his marriage with you.' That became the followed practice from then onwards."

Sahīh Al-BukhāriBook of ClothingChapter: The fringed waist-wrapper; Hadīth no. 5792.Sahīh MuslimBook of MarriageChapter: A woman thrice-divorced is not lawful for her ex-husband in marriage until she marries another husband who has intercourse with her then leaves her (by divorces or death) and she completes her waiting period; Hadīth no. 1433.Sunan Abu DāwudBook of DivorceChapter: An irrivocably-divorced woman cannot be taken back in marriage by her ex-husband until she marries another man; Hadīth no. 2309.Jāmi' At-TirmidhiBook of Marriage as Reported from the Prophet (PBUH)Chapter: What is reported on one who divorces his wife thrice then another man marries her and divorces her before consummating marriage with her; Hadīth no. 1118.Sunan An-Nasā'iBook of DivorceChapter: Irrivocable divorce; Hadīth no. 3409.Sunan Ibn MājahBook of MarriageChapter: A man divorces his wife thrice then marries and new husband divorces her before consummating the marriage, may she return to her first husband?; Hadīth no.1932.

Book of Clothing

Chapter: The fringed waist-wrapper; Hadīth no. 5792.

Sahīh Muslim

Book of Marriage

Chapter: A woman thrice-divorced is not lawful for her ex-husband in marriage until she marries another husband who has intercourse with her then leaves her (by divorces or death) and she completes her waiting period; Hadīth no. 1433.

Sunan Abu Dāwud

Book of Divorce

Chapter: An irrivocably-divorced woman cannot be taken back in marriage by her ex-husband until she marries another man; Hadīth no. 2309.

Jāmi' At-Tirmidhi

Book of Marriage as Reported from the Prophet (PBUH)

Chapter: What is reported on one who divorces his wife thrice then another man marries her and divorces her before consummating marriage with her; Hadīth no. 1118.

Sunan An-Nasā'i

Book of Divorce

Chapter: Irrivocable divorce; Hadīth no. 3409.

Sunan Ibn Mājah

Book of Marriage

Chapter: A man divorces his wife thrice then marries and new husband divorces her before consummating the marriage, may she return to her first husband?; Hadīth no.1932.

Chapter: Ruling on coitus interruptus.

Abu Sa'īd (may Allah be pleased with him) said: "We set out with the Messenger of Allah (may Allah's peace and blessings be upon him) in the battle of Banu al-Mustaliq. We received captives from the Arab captives. We desired women and celibacy became hard on us. We wanted to practice coitus interruptus so we asked the Messenger of Allah (may Allah's peace and blessings be upon him) whether it was permissible. He said: 'It is better for you not to do so, for if any soul is predestined to exist up to the Day of Resurrection, it will exist.'"

Sahīh Al-BukhāriBook of Manumission of SlavesChapter: Whoever possesses Arab slaves then gives them as gifts, sells them, has sexual intercourse with them, ransoms them, or takes the offspring as captives; Hadīth no. 2542.Sahīh MuslimBook of MarriageChapter: Ruling on coitus interruptus; Hadīth no. 1438.Sunan Abu DāwudBook of MarriageChapter: What is reported on coitus interruptus; Hadīth no. 2172.Jāmi' At-TirmidhiBook of Marriage as Reported from the Prophet (PBUH)Chapter: What is reported on the dislike of coitus interruptus; Hadīth no. 1138.Sunan An-Nasā'iBook of MarriageChapter: Coitus interruptus; Hadīth no. 3327.Sunan Ibn MājahBook of MarriageChapter: Coitus interruptus; Hadīth no. 1926.

Book of Manumission of Slaves

Chapter: Whoever possesses Arab slaves then gives them as gifts, sells them, has sexual intercourse with them, ransoms them, or takes the offspring as captives; Hadīth no. 2542.

Sahīh Muslim

Book of Marriage

Chapter: Ruling on coitus interruptus; Hadīth no. 1438.

Sunan Abu Dāwud

Book of Marriage

Chapter: What is reported on coitus interruptus; Hadīth no. 2172.

Jāmi' At-Tirmidhi

Book of Marriage as Reported from the Prophet (PBUH)

Chapter: What is reported on the dislike of coitus interruptus; Hadīth no. 1138.

Sunan An-Nasā'i

Book of Marriage

Chapter: Coitus interruptus; Hadīth no. 3327.

Sunan Ibn Mājah

Book of Marriage

Chapter: Coitus interruptus; Hadīth no. 1926.

Book of Breastfeeding

Chapter: Unlawfulness of marriage due to kinship by birth is same in case of milk kinship.

'Amrah bint 'Abdur-Rahmān reported that 'Ā'ishah (may Allah be pleased with her), wife of the Prophet (PBUH), told her that the Prophet (PBUH) was at her home when she heard a man asking permission to be admitted into Hafsah's home. She said: "I said: 'O Messenger of Allah, a man is asking permission to enter your home!' The Messenger of Allah (PBUH) said: 'I believe he is so-and-so,' referring to Hafsah's paternal milk uncle (brother of her wet nurse's husband). 'Ā'ishah said: "If so-and-so (referring to her own milk uncle) was alive, would he enter upon me?" The Messenger of Allah (PBUH) said: "Yes, for milk kinship makes unlawful for marriage those who are unlawful for marriage by birth kinship."

Sahīh Al-BukhāriBook of WitnessesChapter: Giving witness concerning lineages, established milk kinship, and persons who died a long time ago; Hadīth no. 2646.Sahīh MuslimBook of Breastfeeding (Milk Kinship)Chapter: Unlawfulness of marriage due to kinship by birth is same in case of milk kinship;

Hadīth no. 1444.Sunan Abu DāwudBook of MarriageChapter: Unlawfulness of marriage due to kinship by birth is same in case of milk kinship; Hadīth no. 2055.Jāmi' At-TirmidhiBook of Breastfeeding (Milk Kinship) as reported from the Messenger of Allah (PBUH)Chapter: Unlawfulness of marriage due to kinship by birth is same in case of milk kinship; Hadīth no. 1147.Sunan An-Nasā'iBook of MarriageChapter: Laban al-Fahl (lit. Sire's milk); Hadīth no. 3313.Sunan Ibn MājahBook of MarriageChapter: Unlawfulness of marriage due to kinship by birth is same in case of milk kinship; Hadīth no. 1937.

Book of Witnesses

Chapter: Giving witness concerning lineages, established milk kinship, and persons who died a long time ago; Hadīth no. 2646.

Sahīh Muslim

Book of Breastfeeding (Milk Kinship)

Chapter: Unlawfulness of marriage due to kinship by birth is same in case of milk kinship; Hadīth no. 1444.

Sunan Abu Dāwud

Book of Marriage

Chapter: Unlawfulness of marriage due to kinship by birth is same in case of milk kinship; Hadīth no. 2055.

Jāmi' At-Tirmidhi

Book of Breastfeeding (Milk Kinship) as reported from the Messenger of Allah (PBUH)

Chapter: Unlawfulness of marriage due to kinship by birth is same in case of milk kinship; Hadīth no. 1147.

Sunan An-Nasā'i

Book of Marriage

Chapter: Laban al-Fahl (lit. Sire's milk); Hadīth no. 3313.

Sunan Ibn Mājah

Book of Marriage

Chapter: Unlawfulness of marriage due to kinship by birth is same in case of milk kinship; Hadīth no. 1937.

Chapter: Unlawfulness to marry milk siblings is related to Mā' al-Fahl (wet nurse husband's semen).

'Ā'ishah (may Allah be pleased with her) reported: "Aflah, the brother of Abul-Qu'ays (her wet nurse's husband) came and asked my permission (to enter the house) after Hijāb was ordained. I said I would not let him in until I get permission from the Prophet (PBUH), for it was not his brother, Abul-Qu'ays, who suckled me; rather, it was Abul-Qu'ays's wife who suckled me. The Prophet (PBUH) entered the house so I said to him: 'O Messenger of Allah, Aflah, the brother of Abul-Qu'ays, asked to come in and I refused to let him in until I get your permission.' The Prophet (PBUH) said: 'What prevented you from letting your paternal uncle in?' I said: 'O Messenger of Allah, it was not the man who suckled me; rather, it was Abul-Qu'ays's wife who suckled me.' He said: 'Let him in, for he is your paternal uncle, may your right hand be soiled with dust (an expression that indicates blame/reprimand)!'"

Sahīh Al-BukhāriBook of the (Prophetic) Commentary on the QuranSūrat Al-AhzābChapter: Allah's statement: {Whether you reveal something or conceal it, Allah is indeed All-Knowing of everything}; Hadīth no. 4796.Sahīh MuslimBook of Breastfeeding (Milk Kinship)Chapter: Unlawfulness to marry milk siblings is related to Mā' al-Fahl (wet nurse husband's semen); Hadīth no.1445.Sunan Abu DāwudBook of MarriageChapter: About Laban al-Fahl (lit. sire's milk); Hadīth no. 2057.Jāmi' At-TirmidhiBook of Breastfeeding (Milk Kinship) as reported from the Messenger of Allah (PBUH)Chapter: What is reported on Laban al-Fahl; Hadīth no. 1148.Sunan An-Nasā'iBook of MarriageChapter: Laban al-Fahl; Hadīth no. 3318.Sunan Ibn MājahBook of MarriageChapter: Laban al-Fahl; Hadīth no. 1948.

Book of the (Prophetic) Commentary on the Quran

Sūrat Al-Ahzāb

Chapter: Allah's statement: {Whether you reveal something or conceal it, Allah is indeed All-Knowing of everything}; Hadīth no. 4796.

Sahīh Muslim

Book of Breastfeeding (Milk Kinship)

Chapter: Unlawfulness to marry milk siblings is related to Mā' al-Fahl (wet nurse husband's semen); Hadīth no.1445.

Sunan Abu Dāwud

Book of Marriage

Chapter: About Laban al-Fahl (lit. sire's milk); Hadīth no. 2057.

Jāmi' At-Tirmidhi

Book of Breastfeeding (Milk Kinship) as reported from the Messenger of Allah (PBUH)

Chapter: What is reported on Laban al-Fahl; Hadīth no. 1148.

Sunan An-Nasā'i

Book of Marriage

Chapter: Laban al-Fahl; Hadīth no. 3318.

Sunan Ibn Mājah

Book of Marriage

Chapter: Laban al-Fahl; Hadīth no. 1948.

Chapter: Detecting lineage of an infant from physical features

'Ā'ishah (may Allah be pleased with her) reported: "The Messenger of Allah (may Allah's peace and blessings be upon him) entered upon me one day and he was looking pleased and said: 'O 'Ā'ishah! Don't you know that Mujazziz al-Mudliji entered upon me and saw Usāmah ibn Zayd and Zayd (his father) with a velvet cloth over them that covered their heads and left their feet visible, so he said: 'These feet are related to one another.'"

Sahīh Al-BukhāriBook of the Law of InheritanceChapter: The Qā'if (one skilled at detecting lineage through physical features); Hadīth no. 6771.Sahīh MuslimBook of BreastfeedingChapter: Detecting lineage of an infant from physical features; Hadīth no. 1459.Sunan Abu DāwudBook of DivorceChapter: Detecting lineage from physical features; Hadīth no. 2267.Jāmi' At-TirmidhiBook of Guardianship and Gifts as reported from the Prophet (PBUH)Chapter: What is reported on detecting lineage from physical features; Hadīth no. 2129.Sunan An-Nasā'iBook of DivorceChapter: Detecting lineage from physical features; Hadīth no. 3494.Sunan Ibn MājahBook of RulingsChapter: Detecting lineage from physical features; Hadīth no. 2349.

Book of the Law of Inheritance

Chapter: The Qā'if (one skilled at detecting lineage through physical features); Hadīth no. 6771.

Sahīh Muslim

Book of Breastfeeding

Chapter: Detecting lineage of an infant from physical features; Hadīth no. 1459.

Sunan Abu Dāwud

Book of Divorce

Chapter: Detecting lineage from physical features; Hadīth no. 2267.

Jāmi' At-Tirmidhi

Book of Guardianship and Gifts as reported from the Prophet (PBUH)

Chapter: What is reported on detecting lineage from physical features; Hadīth no. 2129.

Sunan An-Nasā'i

Book of Divorce

Chapter: Detecting lineage from physical features; Hadīth no. 3494.

Sunan Ibn Mājah

Book of Rulings

Chapter: Detecting lineage from physical features; Hadīth no. 2349.

Chapter: Desirability of marrying a virgin.

Jābir (may Allah be pleased with him) reported: "We were with the Prophet (PBUH) detecting lineage of infant from physical features on a military expedition. When we returned, I urged my camel to move quickly as it was slow. A rider caught up with me from behind and he goaded my camel with a stick he had with him. My camel moved forward like the best that you have ever seen. I turned and found that it was the Prophet (PBUH). I said: 'O Messenger of Allah, I am newly wedded.' He said: 'You married?' I said: 'Yes.' He asked: 'A virgin or previously married one?' I said: 'A previously married.' He said: 'Why not a virgin so that you could play with her and she could play with you?' Then when we arrived at Madinah and were about to enter, he said: 'Wait until you enter at night, meaning in the evening, so that the woman with dishevelled hair may comb it and the woman whose husband was away may shave her pubic hair.'"

Sahīh Al-BukhāriBook of MarriageChapter: The woman whose husband was away shaves her pubic hair and the woman with dishevelled hair combs it; Hadīth no. 5247. Sahīh MuslimBook of BreastfeedingChapter: Desirability of marrying a virgin; Hadīth no. 715.Sunan Abu DāwudBook of MarriageChapter: Marrying off virgins; Hadīth no. 2048.Jāmi' At-TirmidhiBook of Marriage as Reported from the Prophet (PBUH)Chapter: What is reported on marrying off virgins; Hadīth no. 1100.Sunan An-Nasā'iBook of MarriageChapter: Marrying virgins; Hadīth no. 3219.Sunan Ibn MājahBook of MarriageChapter: Marrying off virgins; Hadīth no. 1860.

Book of Marriage

Chapter: The woman whose husband was away shaves her pubic hair and the woman with dishevelled hair combs it; Hadīth no. 5247.

Sahīh Muslim

Book of Breastfeeding

Chapter: Desirability of marrying a virgin; Hadīth no. 715.

Sunan Abu Dāwud

Book of Marriage

Chapter: Marrying off virgins; Hadīth no. 2048.

Jāmi' At-Tirmidhi

Book of Marriage as Reported from the Prophet (PBUH)

Chapter: What is reported on marrying off virgins; Hadīth no. 1100.

Sunan An-Nasā'i

Book of Marriage

Chapter: Marrying virgins; Hadīth no. 3219.

Sunan Ibn Mājah

Book of Marriage

Chapter: Marrying off virgins; Hadīth no. 1860.

Book of Divorce

Chapter: Prohibition of divorcing a woman during her menses against her will and that

the divorce in this case is effective, and the husband is commanded to take her back.

'Abdullāh ibn 'Umar, may Allah be pleased with both of them, reported that he had divorced his wife while she was menstruating, and this happened during the lifetime of the Messenger of Allah (PBUH). 'Umar ibn Al-Khattāb asked the Messenger of Allah (PBUH) about that, so the Messenger of Allah (PBUH) said: "Order him to take her back and keep her till she is clean (by taking ritual bath at the end of menses), and then wait till she gets her next menses and then becomes clean again. Thereupon, if he wishes to keep her, he may do so, and if he wishes to divorce her, he may divorce her before having sexual intercourse with her. That is the prescribed waiting period that Allah has fixed for the women who are to be divorced."

Sahīh Al-BukhāriBook of DivorceChapter: The statement of Allah Almighty: {O Prophet, when you [Muslims] divorce women, divorce them at their prescribed waiting period and keep count of the waiting period...} Hadīth no. 5251.Sahīh MuslimBook of DivorceChapter: Prohibition of divorcing a woman during her menses against her will and that the divorce in this case is effective, and the husband is commanded to take her back; Hadīth no. 1471.Sunan Abu DāwudBook of DivorceChapter: The Sunnah-compliant divorce; Hadīth no. 2182.Jāmi' At-TirmidhiBook of Divorce and Oath of Condemnation as reported from the Prophet (PBUH)Chapter: What is reported on the Sunnah-compliant divorce; Hadīth no. 1176.Sunan An-Nasā'iBook of DivorceChapter: Time of divorce at the prescribed waiting period that Allah Almighty ordered that women may be divorced at; Hadīth no. 3390.Sunan Ibn MājahBook of DivorceChapter: The Sunnah-compliant divorce; Hadīth no. 2022.

Book of Divorce

Chapter: The statement of Allah Almighty: {O Prophet, when you [Muslims] divorce women, divorce them at their prescribed waiting period and keep count of the waiting period...} Hadīth no. 5251.

Sahīh Muslim

Book of Divorce

Chapter: Prohibition of divorcing a woman during her menses against her will and that the divorce in this case is effective, and the husband is commanded to take her back; Hadīth no. 1471.

Sunan Abu Dāwud

Book of Divorce

Chapter: The Sunnah-compliant divorce; Hadīth no. 2182.

Jāmi' At-Tirmidhi

Book of Divorce and Oath of Condemnation as reported from the Prophet (PBUH)

Chapter: What is reported on the Sunnah-compliant divorce; Hadīth no. 1176.

Sunan An-Nasā'i

Book of Divorce

Chapter: Time of divorce at the prescribed waiting period that Allah Almighty ordered that women may be divorced at; Hadīth no. 3390.

Sunan Ibn Mājah

Book of Divorce

Chapter: The Sunnah-compliant divorce; Hadīth no. 2022.

Chapter: Obligation of paying expiation on one who said his wife is unlawful for him without intending divorce thereby.

'Ā'ishah (may Allah be pleased with her) reported: "The Messenger of Allah (PBUH) liked honey and sweets. After offering the 'Asr prayer, he used to enter upon his wives and approach them. Once, he entered upon Hafsah bint 'Umar and stayed with her longer than his usual stay. I felt jealous so I asked about that and I was told that a woman from her kin had sent her a skinbag of honey as a gift, and she gave a drink from it to the Messenger of Allah (PBUH). I said: 'By Allah, we will play a trick on him.' I mentioned that to Sawdah and said: 'He will approach you. When he does, say to him: "Have you eaten Maghāfīr (bad-smelling gum)?" He would say: "no." Then say to him: "What is this smell I notice on you?" He would say: "Hafsah has given me a drink of honey." Then you should say to him: "The honey-bees must have sucked from the 'Urfut tree," and I would also say the same to him, and you, Safiyyah, say the same.' Sawdah said: "By Allah, when he was at the door, I wanted to say right away what you ('Ā'ishah) ordered me to do out of fear of you." So when he came near to Sawdah, she said: 'O Messenger of Allah, have you eaten Maghāfīr?' He said: 'no.' She said: 'Then what is this smell that I notice on you?' He said: 'Hafsah gave me a drink of honey.' She said: 'The honey-bees must have sucked from the 'Urfut tree.' When he came to me, I said the same thing. He then visited Safiyyah and she said the same thing. When he visited Hafsah, she said: 'O Messenger of Allah, should I get you a drink of it.' He said: 'I do not need it.' Sawdah said: 'By Allah, we have deprived him (of the honey).' I said to her: 'Be quiet.'"Sahīh Al-BukhāriBook of DivorceChapter: The statement of Allah Almighty: {O Prophet, why do you prohibit [yourself from] what Allah has made lawful for you...}; Hadīth no. 5268.Sahīh MuslimBook of DivorceChapter: Obligation of paying expiation by someone who said his wife is unlawful to him without intending divorce thereby; Hadīth no. 1474.Sunan Abu DāwudBook of DrinksChapter: Drinking honey; Hadīth no.3715.Jāmi' At-TirmidhiBook of Foods as reported from the Prophet (PBUH)Chapter: What is reported on love of the Prophet (PBUH) for sweets and honey; Hadīth no. 1831.Sunan An-Nasā'iBook of DivorceChapter: Interpreting this verse in another way; Hadīth no. 3421.Sunan Ibn MājahBook of FoodsChapter: Sweet foods; Hadīth no. 3323.

Sahīh Al-Bukhāri

Book of Divorce

Chapter: The statement of Allah Almighty: {O Prophet, why do you prohibit [yourself from] what Allah has made lawful for you...}; Hadīth no. 5268.

Sahīh Muslim

Book of Divorce

Chapter: Obligation of paying expiation by someone who said his wife is unlawful to him without intending divorce thereby; Hadīth no. 1474.

Sunan Abu Dāwud

Book of Drinks

Chapter: Drinking honey; Hadīth no.3715.

Jāmi' At-Tirmidhi

Book of Foods as reported from the Prophet (PBUH)

Chapter: What is reported on love of the Prophet (PBUH) for sweets and honey; Hadīth no. 1831.

Sunan An-Nasā'i

Book of Divorce

Chapter: Interpreting this verse in another way; Hadīth no. 3421.

Sunan Ibn Mājah

Book of Foods

Chapter: Sweet foods; Hadīth no. 3323.

Chapter: Clarifying that giving the choice to one's wife is not considered divorce unless he intends it.

'Ā'ishah, may Allah be pleased with her, reported: "The Prophet (may Allah's peace and blessings be upon him) gave us the choice (either to stay with him as wives or leave him) so we chose Allah and His Messenger, without this being counted as a divorce."

Sahīh Al-BukhāriBook of DivorceChapter: Giving the choice to one's wives; Hadīth no. 5262.Sahīh MuslimBook of DivorceChapter: Clarifying that giving the choice to one's wife is not considered a divorce unless he intends it; Hadīth no. 1477.Sunan Abu DāwudBook of DivorceChapter: Giving wife the choice; Hadīth no. 2203.Jāmi' At-TirmidhiBook of Divorce and Oath of Condemnation as reported from the Prophet (PBUH)Chapter: What is reported on (giving wife the) choice; Hadīth no. 1179.Sunan An-Nasā'iBook of DivorceChapter: A woman who is given the choice and chooses to stay with her husband; Hadīth no. 3441.Sunan Ibn MājahBook of DivorceChapter: A man giving his wife the choice; Hadīth no. 2052.

Book of Divorce

Chapter: Giving the choice to one's wives; Hadīth no. 5262.

Sahīh Muslim

Book of Divorce

Chapter: Clarifying that giving the choice to one's wife is not considered a divorce unless he intends it; Hadīth no. 1477.

Sunan Abu Dāwud

Book of Divorce

Chapter: Giving wife the choice; Hadīth no. 2203.

Jāmi' At-Tirmidhi

Book of Divorce and Oath of Condemnation as reported from the Prophet (PBUH)

Chapter: What is reported on (giving wife the) choice; Hadīth no. 1179.

Sunan An-Nasā'i

Book of Divorce

Chapter: A woman who is given the choice and chooses to stay with her husband; Hadīth no. 3441.

Sunan Ibn Mājah

Book of Divorce

Chapter: A man giving his wife the choice; Hadīth no. 2052.

Chapter: Obligation of mourning during the post-death waiting period and its prohibition beyond that except for the period of three days.

Humayd ibn Nāfi' reported that Zaynab bint Abi Salamah narrated to him the following three Hadīths: She said: "I went to Umm Habībah, the wife of Allah's Messenger (PBUH) when her father Abu Sufyān died. Umm Habībah sent for perfume that had a yellowness in it, saffron or otherwise, and she applied it to a girl and then rubbed some of it on her cheeks then said: 'By Allah, I have no need for perfume but I heard Allah's Messenger (PBUH) saying: "It is impermissible for a woman who believes in Allah and the Last Day to mourn for the dead beyond three days, except in case (of the death) of the husband; (she mourns) for four months and ten days." Zaynab said: "I then visited Zaynab bint Jahsh when her brother died and she sent for perfume and applied it then said: 'By Allah, I have no need for perfume but I heard Allah's Messenger (PBUH) say on the pulpit: "It is impermissible for a woman who believes in Allah and the Last Day to mourn the dead beyond three days except in case (of the death) of the husband; (she mourns) for four months and ten days." Zaynab said: "And I heard (my mother) Umm Salamah saying: 'A woman came to Allah's Messenger (PBUH) and said: "O Messenger of Allah, I have a daughter whose husband has died and she is suffering from sore eyes; should she apply (antimony) kohl to it?" The Messenger of Allah (PBUH) said: "No," repeating it twice or thrice, saying only "No" each time. Then he said: "It is only four mouths and ten days, whereas in the pre-Islamic period none of you threw away the dung until one year had passed." Humayd said: "I said to Zaynab: 'What is this throwing of dung until a year had passed?'" Zaynab said: "When a woman's husband died, she would go into a hut and put on her worst clothes, and would not apply perfume until a year has passed. Then an animal, like a donkey or a goat or a bird, would be brought to her and she would rub her skin with it. The animal with which she rubbed her body would scarcely survive. She then would come out and would be given a piece of dung and she would throw it away. Then, she could go back to using whatever she wishes of perfume or otherwise."

Sahīh Al-BukhāriBook of DivorceChapter: A widow mourns for her husband for four months and ten days; Hadīth no. 5334, 5335, 5336, 5337.Sahīh MuslimBook of DivorceChapter: Obligation of mourning during the post-death waiting period and its prohibition for other than that except for the period of three days; Hadīth no.1486,1487,1488,1489.Sunan Abu DāwudBook of DivorceChapter: Mourning of a widow; Hadīth no. 2299.Jāmi' At-TirmidhiBook of Divorce and Oath of Condemnation as reported from the Prophet (PBUH)Chapter: What is reported on the post-death waiting period of a widow; Hadīth no. 1195, 1196, 1197.Sunan An-Nasā'iBook of DivorceChapter: Giving up adornment for a mourning Muslim widow, not a Jew or a Christian one; Hadīth no. 3533.Sunan Ibn MājahBook of DivorceChapter: Dislike of adornment for a widow; Hadīth no. 2084.

Book of Divorce

Chapter: A widow mourns for her husband for four months and ten days; Hadīth no. 5334, 5335, 5336, 5337.

Sahīh Muslim

Book of Divorce

Chapter: Obligation of mourning during the post-death waiting period and its prohibition for other than that except for the period of three days; Hadīth no.1486,1487,1488,1489.

Sunan Abu Dāwud

Book of Divorce

Chapter: Mourning of a widow; Hadīth no. 2299.

Jāmi' At-Tirmidhi

Book of Divorce and Oath of Condemnation as reported from the Prophet (PBUH)

Chapter: What is reported on the post-death waiting period of a widow; Hadīth no. 1195, 1196, 1197.

Sunan An-Nasā'i

Book of Divorce

Chapter: Giving up adornment for a mourning Muslim widow, not a Jew or a Christian one; Hadīth no. 3533.

Sunan Ibn Mājah

Book of Divorce

Chapter: Dislike of adornment for a widow; Hadīth no. 2084.

Book of Li'ān (Oaths of Condemnation)

Ibn 'Umar (may Allah be pleased with him) reported: "The Prophet (may Allah's peace and blessings be upon him) said to the couple who were involved in a case of Li'ān (oaths of mutual condemnation): 'Your reckoning is with Allah. One of you two is a liar, and you (the husband) have no right over her (she is no longer your wife).' The man said: 'What about my money (i.e. the dower I paid)?' The Prophet (may Allah's peace and blessings be upon him) said: 'You have no right to any money. If you have told the truth about her, then it (the dower) was in return for the consummation of your marriage with her; and if you have lied about her, then you have even less right (to any money).'"

Sahīh Al-BukhāriBook of DivorceChapter: The Muslim ruler saying to the two parties involved in a case of Li'ān: "Surely one of you two is a liar; so will one of you repent (to Allah)?"; Hadīth no. 5312.Sahīh MuslimBook of Li'ān (Oaths of Condemnation)Hadīth no. 1493.Sunan Abu DāwudBook of DivorceChapter: Li'ān (Oaths of Condemnation); Hadīth no. 2257.Jāmi' At-TirmidhiBook of Divorce and Oath of Condemnation as reported from the Prophet (PBUH)Chapter: What is reported on Li'ān; Hadīth no. 1203.Sunan An-Nasā'iBook of DivorceChapter: Can the two who have engaged in a case of Li'ān stay together (as husband and wife)?; Hadīth no. 3476.Sunan Ibn MājahBook of DivorceChapter: Li'ān (Oaths of Condemnation); Hadīth no.2069.

Book of Divorce

Chapter: The Muslim ruler saying to the two parties involved in a case of Li'ān: "Surely one of you two is a liar; so will one of you repent (to Allah)?"; Hadīth no. 5312.

Sahīh Muslim

Book of Li'ān (Oaths of Condemnation)

Hadīth no. 1493.

Sunan Abu Dāwud

Book of Divorce

Chapter: Li'ān (Oaths of Condemnation); Hadīth no. 2257.

Jāmi' At-Tirmidhi

Book of Divorce and Oath of Condemnation as reported from the Prophet (PBUH)

Chapter: What is reported on Li'ān; Hadīth no. 1203.

Sunan An-Nasā'i

Book of Divorce

Chapter: Can the two who have engaged in a case of Li'ān stay together (as husband and wife)?; Hadīth no. 3476.

Sunan Ibn Mājah

Book of Divorce

Chapter: Li'ān (Oaths of Condemnation); Hadīth no.2069.

Abu Hurayrah (may Allah be pleased with him) reported that a man came to the Messenger of Allah (may Allah's peace and blessings be upon him) and said: "My wife has given birth to a black boy." He (the Prophet) asked him: "Do you have camels?" He replied: "Yes." The Prophet asked: "What color are they?" He replied: "Red." The Prophet asked: "Is any of them gray?" He replied: "Yes." The Prophet asked: "From where did that grayness come?" He said: "It might have inherited it from one of its ancestors." The Prophet said: "Perhaps this son of yours (also) inherited it (this color) from one of his ancestors."

Sahīh Al-BukhāriBook of DivorceChapter: If a husband suspects his paternity to a child; Hadīth no. 5305.Sahīh MuslimBook of Li'ān (Oaths of Condemnation)Hadīth no. 1500.Sunan Abu DāwudBook of DivorceChapter: If a husband suspects his paternity to a child; Hadīth no. 2260.Jāmi' At-TirmidhiBook of Walā' (Allegiance) and GiftsChapter: What is reported on a man denying his paternity to his child; Hadīth no. 2128.Sunan An-Nasā'iBook of DivorceChapter: If a man hints an accusation about his wife and wants to disown the child; Hadīth no. 3478.Sunan Ibn MājahBook of MarriageChapter: A man suspecting the paternity of his child; Hadīth no. 2002.

Book of Divorce

Chapter: If a husband suspects his paternity to a child; Hadīth no. 5305.

Sahīh Muslim

Book of Li'ān (Oaths of Condemnation)

Hadīth no. 1500.

Sunan Abu Dāwud

Book of Divorce

Chapter: If a husband suspects his paternity to a child; Hadīth no. 2260.

Jāmi' At-Tirmidhi

Book of Walā' (Allegiance) and Gifts

Chapter: What is reported on a man denying his paternity to his child; Hadīth no. 2128.

Sunan An-Nasā'i

Book of Divorce

Chapter: If a man hints an accusation about his wife and wants to disown the child; Hadīth no. 3478.

Sunan Ibn Mājah

Book of Marriage

Chapter: A man suspecting the paternity of his child; Hadīth no. 2002.

Book of Manumission of Slaves

'Abdullah ibn 'Umar (may Allah be pleased with him) reported that the Messenger of Allah (may Allah's peace and blessings be upon him) said: "Whoever frees his share of a common slave and he has sufficient money to free him completely, should let its price be estimated by a just man and give his partners the price of their shares and manumit the slave; otherwise (i.e. if he has not sufficient money) he manumits the slave partially."

Sahīh Al-BukhāriBook of Manumission of SlavesChapter: If one manumits a male slave co-owned by two or a female slave co-owned by several partners; Hadīth no. 2522.Sahīh MuslimBook of Manumission of SlavesHadīth no. 1501.Sunan Abu DāwudBook of Manumission of SlavesChapter: Those who reported that he (the slave) is not asked to work in return for manumitting himself; Hadīth no. 3940.Jāmi' At-TirmidhiBook of Rulings as reported from the Prophet (PBUH)Chapter: What is reported on a slave co-owned by two partners one of them manumits his share; Hadīth no. 1346.Sunan An-Nasā'iBook of SalesChapter: Partnership without money; Hadīth no. 4698.Sunan Ibn MājahBook of Manumission of SlavesChapter: One who manumits his share in a slave; Hadīth no. 2528.

Book of Manumission of Slaves

Chapter: If one manumits a male slave co-owned by two or a female slave co-owned by several partners; Hadīth no. 2522.

Sahīh Muslim

Book of Manumission of Slaves

Hadīth no. 1501.

Sunan Abu Dāwud

Book of Manumission of Slaves

Chapter: Those who reported that he (the slave) is not asked to work in return for manumitting himself; Hadīth no. 3940.

Jāmi' At-Tirmidhi

Book of Rulings as reported from the Prophet (PBUH)

Chapter: What is reported on a slave co-owned by two partners one of them manumits his share; Hadīth no. 1346.

Sunan An-Nasā'i

Book of Sales

Chapter: Partnership without money; Hadīth no. 4698.

Sunan Ibn Mājah

Book of Manumission of Slaves

Chapter: One who manumits his share in a slave; Hadīth no. 2528.

Chapter: Walā' (Allegiance) is for the one who manumits.

'Ā'ishah (may Allah be pleased with her) reported: "Barīrah came to me and said: 'I have agreed with my masters to pay them nine 'ūqiyyahs (of silver), one 'ūqiyyah per year; please help me.' I said: 'I am ready to pay the whole amount now provided that your masters agree that your Walā' will be for me.' So, Barīrah went to her masters and told them about that offer but they refused to accept it. She returned, and at that time, the Prophet (PBUH) was sitting with me. Barīrah said: 'I told them of the offer but they did not accept it, and insisted that the Walā' be for them.' The Prophet (PBUH) heard that. 'Ā'ishah told the whole story to the Prophet (PBUH). He said to her: "Take her and stipulate that her Walā' would be yours as the Walā' is for the one who manumits." 'Ā'ishah did so. Then the Messenger of Allah (PBUH) stood up in front of the people, and after glorifying and praising Allah, he said: 'What is the matter with some men who impose conditions which are not in Allah's Book? Any condition that is not in Allah's Book is invalid, even if they were one hundred conditions. Allah's judgment is more right and His conditions are firmer. Verily, Walā' is for the one who manumits.'"

Saḥīḥ Al-BukhāriBook of SalesChapter: If someone stipulates conditions in a sale that are unlawful; Hadīth no. 2168.Saḥīḥ MuslimBook of Manumission of SlavesChapter: Walā' is only for the one who manumits; Hadīth no. 1504.Sunan Abu DāwudBook of Manumission of SlavesChapter: Selling a Mukātab (a slave who made a contract to buy his freedom) if his contract of manumission is annulled; Hadīth no. 3929.Jāmi' At-TirmidhiBook of Wills and Testaments as reported from the Prophet (PBUH)Chapter: What is reported on a man who gives something as charity or manumits a slave at the time of his death; Hadīth no. 2124.Sunan An-Nasā'iBook of SalesChapter: Selling a Mukātab slave; Hadīth no. 4655.Sunan Ibn MājahBook of Manumission of SlavesChapter: The Mukātab; Hadīth no. 2521.

Book of Sales

Chapter: If someone stipulates conditions in a sale that are unlawful; Hadīth no. 2168.

Saḥīḥ Muslim

Book of Manumission of Slaves

Chapter: Walā' is only for the one who manumits; Hadīth no. 1504.

Sunan Abu Dāwud

Book of Manumission of Slaves

Chapter: Selling a Mukātab (a slave who made a contract to buy his freedom) if his contract of manumission is annulled; Hadīth no. 3929.

Jāmi' At-Tirmidhi

Book of Wills and Testaments as reported from the Prophet (PBUH)

Chapter: What is reported on a man who gives something as charity or manumits a slave at the time of his death; Hadīth no. 2124.

Sunan An-Nasā'i

Book of Sales

Chapter: Selling a Mukātab slave; Hadīth no. 4655.

Sunan Ibn Mājah

Book of Manumission of Slaves

Chapter: The Mukātab; Hadīth no. 2521.

Chapter: Forbiddance of selling Walā' or giving it as a gift.

Ibn 'Umar (may Allah be pleased with him) reported: "The Prophet, (may Allah's peace and blessings be upon him) forbade selling Walā' or giving it as a gift."

Saḥīḥ Al-BukhāriBook of the Law of InheritanceChapter: Sinfulness of the freed slave who disavows those who manumitted him; Hadīth no. 6756.Saḥīḥ MuslimBook of Manumission of SlavesChapter: Forbiddance of selling Walā' or giving it as a gift; Hadīth no. 1506.Sunan Abu DāwudBook of the Law of InheritanceChapter: Selling Walā' (Allegiance); Hadīth no. 2919.Jāmi' At-TirmidhiBook of Sales as reported from the Prophet (PBUH)Chapter: What is reported on the dislike of selling Walā' or giving it as a gift; Hadīth no. 1236.Sunan An-Nasā'iBook of SalesChapter: Selling Walā'; Hadīth no. 4657.Sunan Ibn MājahBook of the Law of InheritanceChapter: Forbiddance of selling Walā' or giving it as a gift; Hadīth no. 2747.

Book of the Law of Inheritance

Chapter: Sinfulness of the freed slave who disavows those who manumitted him; Hadīth no. 6756.

Sahīh Muslim

Book of Manumission of Slaves

Chapter: Forbiddance of selling Walā' or giving it as a gift; Hadīth no. 1506.

Sunan Abu Dāwud

Book of the Law of Inheritance

Chapter: Selling Walā' (Allegiance); Hadīth no. 2919.

Jāmi' At-Tirmidhi

Book of Sales as reported from the Prophet (PBUH)

Chapter: What is reported on the dislike of selling Walā' or giving it as a gift; Hadīth no. 1236.

Sunan An-Nasā'i

Book of Sales

Chapter: Selling Walā'; Hadīth no. 4657.

Sunan Ibn Mājah

Book of the Law of Inheritance

Chapter: Forbiddance of selling Walā' or giving it as a gift; Hadīth no. 2747.

Book of Sales

Chapter: Prohibition of selling Habal al-Habalah (the offspring of the offspring of a pregnant animal).

'Abdullāh ibn 'Umar (may Allah be pleased with him) reported that the Messenger of Allah (may Allah's peace and blessings be upon him) forbade the sale transaction called Habal al-Habalah. It was a sale that the people used to practice in the pre-Islamic era where a man would buy the unborn offspring of the unborn offspring of a pregnant she-camel.

Sahīh Al-BukhāriBook of SalesChapter: Gharar sale and Habal al-Habalah sale; Hadīth no. 2143.Sahīh MuslimBook of SalesChapter: Prohibition of Habal al-Habalah sale; Hadīth no. 1514.Sunan Abu DāwudBook of SalesChapter: Gharar sale; Hadīth no. 3380.Jāmi' At-TirmidhiBook of Sales as reported from the Prophet (PBUH)Chapter: What is reported on the forbiddance of the Habal al-Habalah sale; Hadīth no. 1229.Sunan An-Nasā'iBook of SalesChapter: The relevant explanation; Hadīth no. 4625.Sunan Ibn MājahBook of TradeChapter: Forbiddance of buying what is in the wombs of cattle, what is in their udders, and what a diver is going to bring; Hadīth no. 2197.

Book of Sales

Chapter: Gharar sale and Habal al-Habalah sale; Hadīth no. 2143.

Sahīh Muslim

Book of Sales

Chapter: Prohibition of Habal al-Habalah sale; Hadīth no. 1514.

Sunan Abu Dāwud

Book of Sales

Chapter: Gharar sale; Hadīth no. 3380.

Jāmi' At-Tirmidhi

Book of Sales as reported from the Prophet (PBUH)

Chapter: What is reported on the forbiddance of the Habal al-Habalah sale; Hadīth no. 1229.

Sunan An-Nasā'i

Book of Sales

Chapter: The relevant explanation; Hadīth no. 4625.

Sunan Ibn Mājah

Book of Trade

Chapter: Forbiddance of buying what is in the wombs of cattle, what is in their udders, and what a diver is going to bring; Hadīth no. 2197.

Chapter: Prohibition of making an offer in a sale of a fellow Muslim that is in progress, and of haggling

to compete with a fellow Muslim's haggling, and the prohibition of Najsh and leaving the animals unmilked (for sometime for the purpose of accumulation of milk to deceive the buyer).

Abu Hurayrah (may Allah be pleased with him) reported that the Prophet (may Allah's peace and blessings be upon him) said: "Do not go out to meet the riders (in a trade caravan to buy from it on the way before it reaches town), do not urge buyers to cancel a sale transaction to make a new one with you, do not bid against each other (to fool another bidder), a townsman must not sell on behalf of a Bedouin, and do not tie up the udders of sheep (so that they appear to have a lot of milk). If someone buys them while in this condition and has already milked them, then he has two options: If he is pleased with them, he may keep them, and if he is displeased with them, he may return them along with a Sā' of dates."

Sahīh Al-BukhāriBook of SalesChapter: Forbiddance that a seller keeps the camels, cows, sheep, or any animals, unmilked for a long time; Hadīth no. 2150.Sahīh MuslimBook of SalesChapter: Prohibition of making an offer in a sale of a fellow Muslim that is in progress, and of haggling to compete with a fellow Muslim's haggling, and the prohibition of Najsh and leaving the animals unmilked (for sometime for the purpose of accumulation of milk to deceive the buyer); Hadīth no. 1515.Sunan Abu DāwudBook of Sales - Chapters on IjārahChapter: The one who buys an animal that was unmilked for a long time, then he dislikes it; Hadīth no. 3443.Jāmi' At-TirmidhiBook of Sales as reported from the Prophet (PBUH)Chapter: What is reported on the animal that was left unmilked for a long time; Hadīth no. 1251.Sunan An-Nasā'iBook of SalesChapter: Forbiddance of (selling) a Musarrāh, which means to bind the udders of camels or sheep and avoid milking them for two or three days until the milk accumulates in them to deceive the buyer into increasing the price when he sees that it has a great amount of milk; Hadīth no. 4487.Sunan Ibn MājahBook of TradeChapter: Selling a Musarrāh; Hadīth no. 2239.

Book of Sales

Chapter: Forbiddance that a seller keeps the camels, cows, sheep, or any animals, unmilked for a long time; Hadīth no. 2150.

Sahīh Muslim

Book of Sales

Chapter: Prohibition of making an offer in a sale of a fellow Muslim that is in progress, and of haggling to compete with a fellow Muslim's haggling, and the prohibition of Najsh and leaving the animals unmilked (for sometime for the purpose of accumulation of milk to deceive the buyer); Hadīth no. 1515.

Sunan Abu Dāwud

Book of Sales - Chapters on Ijārah

Chapter: The one who buys an animal that was unmilked for a long time, then he dislikes it; Hadīth no. 3443.

Jāmi' At-Tirmidhi

Book of Sales as reported from the Prophet (PBUH)

Chapter: What is reported on the animal that was left unmilked for a long time; Hadīth no. 1251.

Sunan An-Nasā'i

Book of Sales

Chapter: Forbiddance of (selling) a Musarrāh, which means to bind the udders of camels or sheep and avoid milking them for two or three days until the milk accumulates in them to deceive the buyer into increasing the price when he sees that it has a great amount of milk; Hadīth no. 4487.

Sunan Ibn Mājah

Book of Trade

Chapter: Selling a Musarrāh; Hadīth no. 2239.

Chapter: Invalidity of selling an item before it being in the seller's possession.

Tāwūs reported: "I heard Ibn 'Abbās (may Allah be pleased with him) say: 'What the Prophet (may Allah's peace and blessings be upon him) forbade is the selling of foodstuff before receiving it. I believe that this applies to the selling of everything else.'"Sahīh Al-BukhāriBook of SalesChapter: Selling foodstuff before receiving it and selling what one does not have; Hadīth no. 2135.Sahīh MuslimBook of SalesChapter: Invalidity of selling something before having it in one's possession; Hadīth no. 1525.Sunan Abu DāwudBook of Sales - Chapters on IjārahChapter: Selling foodstuff before having it in one's possession; Hadīth no. 3496.Jāmi' At-TirmidhiBook of Sales as reported from the Prophet (PBUH)Chapter: What is reported on the dislike of selling foodstuff until having it in one's possession; Hadīth no. 1291.Sunan An-Nasā'iBook of SalesChapter: Selling foodstuff before having it in one's possession; Hadīth no. 4600.Sunan Ibn MājahBook of TradeChapter: Forbiddance of selling foodstuff before having it in one's possession; Hadīth no. 2227.

Sahīh Al-Bukhāri

Book of Sales

Chapter: Selling foodstuff before receiving it and selling what one does not have; Hadīth no. 2135.

Sahīh Muslim

Book of Sales

Chapter: Invalidity of selling something before having it in one's possession; Hadīth no. 1525.

Sunan Abu Dāwud

Book of Sales - Chapters on Ijārah

Chapter: Selling foodstuff before having it in one's possession; Hadīth no. 3496.

Jāmi' At-Tirmidhī

Book of Sales as reported from the Prophet (PBUH)

Chapter: What is reported on the dislike of selling foodstuff until having it in one's possession; Hadīth no. 1291.

Sunan An-Nasā'i

Book of Sales

Chapter: Selling foodstuff before having it in one's possession; Hadīth no. 4600.

Sunan Ibn Mājah

Book of Trade

Chapter: Forbiddance of selling foodstuff before having it in one's possession; Hadīth no. 2227.

Chapter: Affirming that both parties of a sale transaction have the option (to rescind it) before they part company.

Ibn 'Umar (may Allah be pleased with him) reported that the Messenger of Allah (may Allah's peace and blessings be upon him) said: "If two men engage in a sale transaction, then each of them has the option (to rescind it) as long as they have not parted, or one of them may give the other the option (for a longer period). If they both agreed on that, then the sale is confirmed. If they part after their agreement and neither of them rescinded the sale, then the sale is confirmed."

Sahīh Al-BukhāriBook of SalesChapter: If one of the two parties gives the other the option to rescind the sale after the transaction is concluded, then the sale is confirmed; Hadīth no. 2112.Sahīh MuslimBook of SalesChapter: Affirming that both parties of a transaction have the option (of rescinding it) before they part company; Hadīth no. 1531.Sunan Abu DāwudBook of Sales - Chapters on Ijārah (Lease)Chapter: About the option granted to the two parties of a sale transaction; Hadīth no. 3454.Jāmi' At-TirmidhiBook of Sales as reported from the Prophet (PBUH)Chapter: What is reported on: The buyer and seller retain the option (to rescind the sale) as long as they have not parted company; Hadīth no. 1245.Sunan An-Nasā'iBook of SalesChapter: Mentioning the difference in Nāfi''s wording of the Hadīth; Hadīth no. 4472.Sunan Ibn MājahBook of TradeChapter: The buyer and seller retain the option (to rescind the sale) as long as they have not parted company; Hadīth no. 2181.

Book of Sales

Chapter: If one of the two parties gives the other the option to rescind the sale after the transaction is concluded, then the sale is confirmed; Hadīth no. 2112.

Sahīh Muslim

Book of Sales

Chapter: Affirming that both parties of a transaction have the option (of rescinding it) before they part company; Hadīth no. 1531.

Sunan Abu Dāwud

Book of Sales - Chapters on Ijārah (Lease)

Chapter: About the option granted to the two parties of a sale transaction; Hadīth no. 3454.

Jāmi' At-Tirmidhi

Book of Sales as reported from the Prophet (PBUH)

Chapter: What is reported on: The buyer and seller retain the option (to rescind the sale) as long as they have not parted company; Hadīth no. 1245.

Sunan An-Nasā'i

Book of Sales

Chapter: Mentioning the difference in Nāfi''s wording of the Hadīth; Hadīth no. 4472.

Sunan Ibn Mājah

Book of Trade

Chapter: The buyer and seller retain the option (to rescind the sale) as long as they have not parted company; Hadīth no. 2181.

Chapter: Forbiddance of selling fruits before they are evidently

in a good state without the condition of them being cut.

'Abdullah ibn 'Umar (may Allah be pleased with him) reported: "The Messenger of Allah (may Allah's peace and blessings be upon him) forbade the selling of fruits until they are evidently in a good state. He forbade both the buyer and the seller (from engaging in such a transaction)."

Sahīh Al-BukhāriBook of SalesChapter: Selling fruits before they are evidently in a good state; Hadīth no. 2194.Sahīh MuslimBook of SalesChapter: Forbiddance of selling fruits before they are evidently in a good state without the condition of them being cut; Hadīth no.1534.Sunan Abu DāwudBook of SalesChapter: Selling fruits before they are evidently in a good state; Hadīth no. 3367.Jāmi' At-TirmidhiBook of Sales as reported from the Prophet (PBUH)Chapter: What is reported on the dislike of selling fruits until they are evidently in a good state; Hadīth no. 1226.Sunan An-Nasā'iBook of SalesChapter: Selling fruits before they are evidently in a good state; Hadīth no. 4519.Sunan Ibn MājahBook of TradeChapter: Forbiddance of selling fruits before they are evidently in a good state; Hadīth no. 2214.

Book of Sales

Chapter: Selling fruits before they are evidently in a good state; Hadīth no. 2194.

Sahīh Muslim

Book of Sales

Chapter: Forbiddance of selling fruits before they are evidently in a good state without the condition of them being cut; Hadīth no.1534.

Sunan Abu Dāwud

Book of Sales

Chapter: Selling fruits before they are evidently in a good state; Hadīth no. 3367.

Jāmi' At-Tirmidhi

Book of Sales as reported from the Prophet (PBUH)

Chapter: What is reported on the dislike of selling fruits until they are evidently in a good state; Hadīth no. 1226.

Sunan An-Nasā'i

Book of Sales

Chapter: Selling fruits before they are evidently in a good state; Hadīth no. 4519.

Sunan Ibn Mājah

Book of Trade

Chapter: Forbiddance of selling fruits before they are evidently in a good state; Hadīth no. 2214.

Chapter: Prohibition of selling fresh dates in exchange for dry dates except in the case of 'Arāya.

Zayd ibn Thābit (may Allah be pleased with him) reported that the Messenger of Allah (may Allah's peace and blessings be upon him) gave concession to the owner of 'Arāya to sell the fruits on the trees by means of estimating them.

Sahīh Al-BukhāriBook of SalesChapter: Muzābanah transaction which is to sell dry dates for fresh dates on the trees, raisins for fresh grapes and to sell the 'Arāya; Hadīth no. 2188.Sahīh MuslimBook of SalesChapter: Prohibition of selling fresh dates in exchange for dry dates except in the case of 'Arāya.Sunan Abu DāwudBook of SalesChapter: Regarding selling (fruits of) 'Arāya; Hadīth no. 3362.Jāmi' At-TirmidhiBook of Sales as reported from the Prophet (PBUH)Chapter: What is reported on the 'Arāya and the concession given in this regard; Hadīth no. 1302.Sunan An-Nasā'iBook of SalesChapter: Selling (fruits of) 'Arāya for dried dates by estimation; Hadīth no. 4538.Sunan Ibn MājahBook of TradeChapter: Selling (fruits of) 'Arāya for dried dates by estimation; Hadīth no. 2268.

Book of Sales

Chapter: Muzābanah transaction which is to sell dry dates for fresh dates on the trees, raisins for fresh grapes and to sell the 'Arāya; Hadīth no. 2188.

Sahīh Muslim

Book of Sales

Chapter: Prohibition of selling fresh dates in exchange for dry dates except in the case of 'Arāya.

Sunan Abu Dāwud

Book of Sales

Chapter: Regarding selling (fruits of) 'Arāya; Hadīth no. 3362.

Jāmi' At-Tirmidhi

Book of Sales as reported from the Prophet (PBUH)

Chapter: What is reported on the 'Arāya and the concession given in this regard; Hadīth no. 1302.

Sunan An-Nasā'i

Book of Sales

Chapter: Selling (fruits of) 'Arāya for dried dates by estimation; Hadīth no. 4538.

Sunan Ibn Mājah

Book of Trade

Chapter: Selling (fruits of) 'Arāya for dried dates by estimation; Hadīth no. 2268.

'Abdullah ibn 'Umar (may Allah be pleased with him) reported: "The Messenger of Allah (may Allah's peace and blessings be upon him) forbade the Muzābanah sale transaction which is to sell fresh dates for dry dates by measure, and raisins for fresh grapes by measure."

Sahīh Al-BukhāriBook of SalesChapter: Selling raisins for raisins and foodstuff for foodstuff; Hadīth no. 2171.Sahīh MuslimBook of SalesChapter: Prohibition of selling fresh dates in exchange for dry dates except in the case of 'Arāya; Ḥadīth no.1542.Sunan Abu DāwudBook of SalesChapter: Regarding Muzābanah; Ḥadīth no. 3361.Jāmi' At-TirmidhiBook of Sales as reported from the Prophet (PBUH)Chapter: What was reported on 'Arāya and the concession given in this regard; Ḥadīth no. 1300.Sunan An-Nasā'iBook of SalesChapter: Selling fresh dates for dry dates; Ḥadīth no. 4533.Sunan Ibn MājahBook of TradeChapter: Muzābanah and Muḥāqalah; Ḥadīth no. 2265.

Book of Sales

Chapter: Selling raisins for raisins and foodstuff for foodstuff; Ḥadīth no. 2171.

Saḥīḥ Muslim

Book of Sales

Chapter: Prohibition of selling fresh dates in exchange for dry dates except in the case of 'Arāya; Ḥadīth no.1542.

Sunan Abu Dāwud

Book of Sales

Chapter: Regarding Muzābanah; Ḥadīth no. 3361.

Jāmi' At-Tirmidhi

Book of Sales as reported from the Prophet (PBUH)

Chapter: What was reported on 'Arāya and the concession given in this regard; Ḥadīth no. 1300.

Sunan An-Nasā'i

Book of Sales

Chapter: Selling fresh dates for dry dates; Ḥadīth no. 4533.

Sunan Ibn Mājah

Book of Trade

Chapter: Muzābanah and Muḥāqalah; Ḥadīth no. 2265.

Chapter: The one who sells date-palms bearing fruits.

Ibn 'Umar (may Allah be pleased with him) reported: "I heard the Messenger of Allah (may Allah's peace and blessings be upon him) say: "Whoever buys date-palms after they have been pollinated, their fruits belong to the seller unless the buyer stipulates otherwise. And whoever buys a slave who owns some property, the property belongs to the one who sold him unless the buyer stipulates otherwise."

Saḥīḥ Al-BukhāriBook of Musāqāh (Irrigation of land for a specific return)Chapter: A man having right of passage in an orchard or right of water share in a date-palm grove; Ḥadīth no. 2379.Saḥīḥ MuslimBook of SalesChapter: The one who sells date-palms bearing fruits; Ḥadīth no. 1543.Sunan Abu DāwudBook of Sales - Chapters on Ijārah (Lease)Chapter: Regarding a slave who is sold while he has property; Ḥadīth no. 3433Jāmi' At-TirmidhiBook of Sales as reported from the Prophet (PBUH)Chapter: What is reported on buying date-palms that have been pollinated and a slave who has property; Ḥadīth no. 1244.Sunan An-Nasā'iBook of SalesChapter: Selling date-palms but not its fruits; Ḥadīth no. 4635.Sunan Ibn MājahBook of TradeChapter: What is reported on selling pollinated date-palms or a slave who has property; Ḥadīth no. 2210.

Book of Musāqāh (Irrigation of land for a specific return)

Chapter: A man having right of passage in an orchard or right of water share in a date-palm grove; Ḥadīth no. 2379.

Saḥīḥ Muslim

Book of Sales

Chapter: The one who sells date-palms bearing fruits; Hadīth no. 1543.

Sunan Abu Dāwud

Book of Sales - Chapters on Ijārah (Lease)

Chapter: Regarding a slave who is sold while he has property; Hadīth no. 3433

Jāmi' At-Tirmidhi

Book of Sales as reported from the Prophet (PBUH)

Chapter: What is reported on buying date-palms that have been pollinated and a slave who has property; Hadīth no. 1244.

Sunan An-Nasā'i

Book of Sales

Chapter: Selling date-palms but not its fruits; Hadīth no. 4635.

Sunan Ibn Mājah

Book of Trade

Chapter: What is reported on selling pollinated date-palms or a slave who has property; Hadīth no. 2210.

Chapter: Forbiddance of Muhāqalah, Muzābanah, Mukhābarah, selling fruits before they are evidently in a good state, and Mu'āwamah sale which means to sell for many years ahead.

Jābir ibn 'Abdullāh (may Allah be pleased with him) reported: "The Prophet (may Allah's peace and blessings be upon him) forbade the sales called Mukhābarah, Muhāqalah, Muzābanah, and the selling of fruits until they are evidently in a good state. He also forbade the selling of fruits but for money, except in the case of 'Arāya."

Sahīh Al-BukhāriBook of Musāqāh (Irrigation of land for a specific return)Chapter: A man having a passage way in a garden or a share in a date-palm grove; Hadīth no. 2381.Sahīh MuslimBook of SalesChapter: Forbiddance of Muhāqalah, Muzābanah, Mukhābarah, selling fruits before they are evidently in a good state, and Mu'āwamah sale which means to sell for many years ahead; Hadīth no. 1536.Sunan Abu DāwudBook of SalesChapter: About Mukhābarah; Hadīth no. 3405.Jāmi' At-TirmidhiBook of Sales as reported from the Prophet (PBUH)Chapter: What is reported on the forbiddance of making exceptions; Hadīth no. 1290.Sunan An-Nasā'iBook of SalesChapter: Selling fruits before they are evidently in a good state; Hadīth no. 4523.Sunan Ibn MājahBook of TradeChapter: Muzābanah and Muhāqalah; Hadīth no. 2266.

Book of Musāqāh (Irrigation of land for a specific return)

Chapter: A man having a passage way in a garden or a share in a date-palm grove; Hadīth no. 2381.

Sahīh Muslim

Book of Sales

Chapter: Forbiddance of Muhāqalah, Muzābanah, Mukhābarah, selling fruits before they are evidently in a good state, and Mu'āwamah sale which means to sell for many years ahead; Hadīth no. 1536.

Sunan Abu Dāwud

Book of Sales

Chapter: About Mukhābarah; Hadīth no. 3405.

Jāmi' At-Tirmidhi

Book of Sales as reported from the Prophet (PBUH)

Chapter: What is reported on the forbiddance of making exceptions; Hadīth no. 1290.

Sunan An-Nasā'i

Book of Sales

Chapter: Selling fruits before they are evidently in a good state; Hadīth no. 4523.

Sunan Ibn Mājah

Book of Trade

Chapter: Muzābanah and Muhāqalah; Hadīth no. 2266.

Chapter: Land lending.

Ibn 'Abbās (may Allah be pleased with him) reported that the Prophet (may Allah's peace and blessings be upon him) did not forbid it, but rather stated: "That one of you lends to his brother a piece of land is better for him than taking from him a fixed rental fee."

Sahīh Al-BukhāriBook of Cultivation and SharecroppingChapter: Hadīth no. 2330.Sahīh MuslimBook of SalesChapter: Land lending.Sunan Abu DāwudBook of SalesChapter: Regarding sharecropping; Hadīth no. 3389.Jāmi' At-TirmidhiBook of Rulings as reported from the Prophet (PBUH)Chapter: On sharecropping; Hadīth no. 1385.Sunan An-Nasā'iBook of SharecroppingChapter: Mentioning the differing Hadīths regarding the forbiddance of leasing out land in return for one third or one quarter of the harvest and the different wordings reported by the narrators; Hadīth no. 3873.Sunan Ibn MājahBook of MortgagesChapter: Concession of leasing uncultivated land in return for gold and silver; Hadīth no. 2457.

Book of Cultivation and Sharecropping

Chapter: Hadīth no. 2330.

Sahīh Muslim

Book of Sales

Chapter: Land lending.

Sunan Abu Dāwud

Book of Sales

Chapter: Regarding sharecropping; Hadīth no. 3389.

Jāmi' At-Tirmidhi

Book of Rulings as reported from the Prophet (PBUH)

Chapter: On sharecropping; Hadīth no. 1385.

Sunan An-Nasā'i

Book of Sharecropping

Chapter: Mentioning the differing Hadīths regarding the forbiddance of leasing out land in return for one third or one quarter of the harvest and the different wordings reported by the narrators; Hadīth no. 3873.

Sunan Ibn Mājah

Book of Mortgages

Chapter: Concession of leasing uncultivated land in return for gold and silver; Hadīth no. 2457.

Book of Musāqāh (Irrigation of land for a specific return)

Chapter: Musāqāh and contracting to utilize the land in return for a share of the fruits and crops.

'Abdullah ibn 'Umar (may Allah be pleased with him) reported that the Prophet (PBUH) concluded a contract with the people of Khaybar to utilize the land on the condition that half its harvest of fruits or crops would be their share. The Prophet (PBUH) used to give his wives one hundred Wasqs; eighty Wasqs of dates and twenty Wasqs of barley. When 'Umar became Caliph, he gave the wives of the Prophet (PBUH) the option of either having part of the land and water as their shares or carrying on the previous practice. Some of them chose the land and some chose the Wasqs, and 'Ā'ishah chose the land.

Sahīh Al-BukhāriBook of SharecroppingChapter: Sharecropping by the half and the like; Hadīth no. 2328.Sahīh MuslimBook of MusāqāhChapter: Musāqāh and contracting to utilize the land in return for a share of the fruits and crops; Hadīth no. 1551.Sunan Abu DāwudBook of Kharāj (Tax on agrarian land owned by non-Muslims), Rulership, and Spoils of WarChapter: What is reported on the judgment on the land of Khaybar; Hadīth no. 3008.Jāmi' At-TirmidhiBook of Rulings as reported from the Prophet (PBUH)Chapter: What is reported on share-cropping; Hadīth no. 1383.Sunan An-Nasā'iBook of SharecroppingChapter: Mentioning the difference in the reported wordings on sharecropping; Hadīth no. 3929.Sunan Ibn MājahBook of MortgagesChapter: Contracts on date-palms and fresh grapes; Hadīth no. 2467.

Book of Sharecropping

Chapter: Sharecropping by the half and the like; Hadīth no. 2328.

Sahīh Muslim

Book of Musāqāh

Chapter: Musāqāh and contracting to utilize the land in return for a share of the fruits and crops; Hadīth no. 1551.

Sunan Abu Dāwud

Book of Kharāj (Tax on agrarian land owned by non-Muslims), Rulership, and Spoils of War

Chapter: What is reported on the judgment on the land of Khaybar; Hadīth no. 3008.

Jāmi' At-Tirmidhi

Book of Rulings as reported from the Prophet (PBUH)

Chapter: What is reported on share-cropping; Hadīth no. 1383.

Sunan An-Nasā'i

Book of Sharecropping

Chapter: Mentioning the difference in the reported wordings on sharecropping; Hadīth no. 3929.

Sunan Ibn Mājah

Book of Mortgages

Chapter: Contracts on date-palms and fresh grapes; Hadīth no. 2467.

Chapter: Whoever finds an item he sold with the buyer who went bankrupt is entitled to rescind the sale.

Abu Hurayrah (may Allah be pleased with him) reported: "The Messenger of Allah (may Allah's peace and blessings be upon him) said [or he said that he heard the Messenger of Allah (may Allah's peace and blessings be upon him) say]: 'Whoever finds his property intact with a man or person who went bankrupt is the worthiest of everyone else to take it back.'"

Sahīh Al-BukhāriBook of Loans, Payment of Loans, Freezing of Property, and BankruptcyChapter: If someone finds his property with a bankrupt person in cases of sale, loan, or deposit, he is the the worthiest to take it back; Hadīth no. 2402.Sahīh MuslimBook of MusāqāhChapter: Whoever finds an item he sold to a person who went bankrupt, he is entitled to take it back; Hadīth no. 1559.Sunan Abu DāwudBook of Sales - Chapters on Ijārah (Lease)Chapter: A man goes bankrupt, then another finds his property intact with him; Hadīth no. 3519.Jāmi' At-TirmidhiBook of Sales as reported from the Prophet (PBUH)Chapter: What is reported on: When a man in debt becomes bankrupt and the debtor finds his property with him; Hadīth no. 1262.Sunan An-Nasā'iBook of SalesChapter: A man buys something then becomes bankrupt, then what he bought is found intact with him; Hadīth no. 4676.Sunan Ibn MājahBook of RulingsChapter: Whoever finds his exact property with a man who went bankrupt; Hadīth no. 2358.

Book of Loans, Payment of Loans, Freezing of Property, and Bankruptcy

Chapter: If someone finds his property with a bankrupt person in cases of sale, loan, or deposit, he is the the worthiest to take it back; Hadīth no. 2402.

Sahīh Muslim

Book of Musāqāh

Chapter: Whoever finds an item he sold to a person who went bankrupt, he is entitled to take it back; Hadīth no. 1559.

Sunan Abu Dāwud

Book of Sales - Chapters on Ijārah (Lease)

Chapter: A man goes bankrupt, then another finds his property intact with him; Hadīth no. 3519.

Jāmi' At-Tirmidhi

Book of Sales as reported from the Prophet (PBUH)

Chapter: What is reported on: When a man in debt becomes bankrupt and the debtor finds his property with him; Hadīth no. 1262.

Sunan An-Nasā'i

Book of Sales

Chapter: A man buys something then becomes bankrupt, then what he bought is found intact with him; Hadīth no. 4676.

Sunan Ibn Mājah

Book of Rulings

Chapter: Whoever finds his exact property with a man who went bankrupt; Hadīth no. 2358.

Chapter: Prohibition of procrastination in paying off debts by a rich man and the validity of Hawālah (transference of debts)

and the desirability of accepting it if the debts are transferred to a rich man.

Abu Hurayrah (may Allah be pleased with him) reported that the Messenger of Allah (may Allah's peace and blessings be upon him) said: "Procrastination in paying debts by a wealthy person is injustice. So, if your debt is transferred from your debtor to a rich debtor, you should agree."

Sahīh Al-BukhāriBook of Hawālah (transference of debts from a person to another)Chapter: Hawālah and whether it could be rescinded; Hadīth no. 2287.Sahīh MuslimBook of Musāqāh (Irrigation of land for a specific return)Chapter: Prohibition of procrastination in paying off debts by a rich man and the validity of Hawālah (transference of debts) and the desirability of accepting it if the debt is transferred to a rich man; Hadīth no. 1564.Sunan Abu DāwudBook of SalesChapter: Regarding procrastination in paying off debts; Hadīth no. 3345.Jāmi' At-TirmidhiBook of Transactions as reported from the Messenger of Allah (PBUH)Chapter: What is reported on procrastination in paying off debts by a rich man; Hadīth no. 1308.Sunan An-Nasā'iBook of SalesChapter: Procrastination in paying off debts by a rich man; Hadīth no. 4688.Sunan Ibn MājahBook of CharityChapter: Hawālah (transference of debts from a person to another); Hadīth no. 2403.

Book of Hawālah (transference of debts from a person to another)

Chapter: Hawālah and whether it could be rescinded; Hadīth no. 2287.

Sahīh Muslim

Book of Musāqāh (Irrigation of land for a specific return)

Chapter: Prohibition of procrastination in paying off debts by a rich man and the validity of Hawālah (transference of debts) and the desirability of accepting it if the debt is transferred to a rich man; Hadīth no. 1564.

Sunan Abu Dāwud

Book of Sales

Chapter: Regarding procrastination in paying off debts; Hadīth no. 3345.

Jāmi' At-Tirmidhi

Book of Transactions as reported from the Messenger of Allah (PBUH)

Chapter: What is reported on procrastination in paying off debts by a rich man; Hadīth no. 1308.

Sunan An-Nasā'i

Book of Sales

Chapter: Procrastination in paying off debts by a rich man; Hadīth no. 4688.

Sunan Ibn Mājah

Book of Charity

Chapter: Hawālah (transference of debts from a person to another); Hadīth no. 2403.

Chapter: Prohibition of a dog's price, the fees given to a soothsayer, and the earnings of a prostitute, and the forbiddance of selling a cat.

Abu Mas'ūd al-Ansāri (may Allah be pleased with him) reported: "The Messenger of Allah (may Allah's peace and blessings be upon him) forbade the price of a dog, the earning of a prostitute, and the money paid to a soothsayer."

Sahīh Al-BukhāriBook of SalesChapter: The price of a dog; Hadīth no. 2237.Sahīh MuslimBook of MusāqāhChapter: Prohibition of a dog's price, the fees given to a soothsayer, and the earnings of a prostitute, and the forbiddance of selling a cat; Hadīth no. 1567.Sunan Abu DāwudBook of Sales - Chapters on IjārahChapter: Regarding the fees given to a soothsayer; Hadīth no. 3428.Jāmi' At-TirmidhiBook of Marriage as Reported from the Messenger of Allah (PBUH)Chapter: What is reported on the dislike of the earnings of a prostitute; Hadīth no. 1133.Sunan An-Nasā'iBook of Hunting and SlaughteringChapter: Forbiddance of the price of a dog; Hadīth no. 4292.Sunan Ibn MājahBook of TradeChapter: Forbiddance of a dog's price, the earnings of a prostitute, the fees given to a soothsayer, and money paid for services of a stud stallion; Hadīth no. 2159.

Book of Sales

Chapter: The price of a dog; Hadīth no. 2237.

Sahīh Muslim

Book of Musāqāh

Chapter: Prohibition of a dog's price, the fees given to a soothsayer, and the earnings of a prostitute, and the forbiddance of selling a cat; Hadīth no. 1567.

Sunan Abu Dāwud

Book of Sales - Chapters on Ijārah

Chapter: Regarding the fees given to a soothsayer; Hadīth no. 3428.

Jāmi' At-Tirmidhi

Book of Marriage as Reported from the Messenger of Allah (PBUH)

Chapter: What is reported on the dislike of the earnings of a prostitute; Hadīth no. 1133.

Sunan An-Nasā'i

Book of Hunting and Slaughtering

Chapter: Forbiddance of the price of a dog; Hadīth no. 4292.

Sunan Ibn Mājah

Book of Trade

Chapter: Forbiddance of a dog's price, the earnings of a prostitute, the fees given to a soothsayer, and money paid for services of a stud stallion; Hadīth no. 2159.

Chapter: The command to kill dogs and its abrogation and the prohibition of keeping them except for the purposes of hunting or guarding land or cattle and the like.

Abu Hurayrah (may Allah be pleased with him) reported that the Messenger of Allah (may Allah's peace and blessings be upon him) said: "Whoever keeps a dog, one Qīrāt of the reward of his good deeds is deducted daily, unless the dog is used for guarding a farm or cattle."

Sahīh Al-Bukhārī Book of the Beginning of Creation Chapter: If a fly falls into the drink of any one of you, he should dip it (in the drink then remove it) for in one of its wings there is a disease and in the other there is cure; Hadīth no. 3324. Sahīh Muslim Book of Musāqāh Chapter: The command to kill dogs and its abrogation and the prohibition of keeping them except for the purpose of hunting or guarding land or cattle and the like; Hadīth no. 1575. Sunan Abu Dāwud Book of Hunting Chapter: Keeping a dog for hunting and other purposes; Hadīth no. 2844. Jāmi' At-Tirmidhi Book of Hunting as reported from the Messenger of Allah (PBUH) Chapter: What is reported on how much the rewards of good deeds of whoever keeps a dog decrease; Hadīth no. 1490. Sunan An-Nasā'i Book of Hunting and Slaughtering Chapter: Concession for keeping a dog for farming purposes; Hadīth no. 4289. Sunan Ibn Mājah Book of Hunting Chapter: Forbiddance of keeping a dog except for hunting or guarding farms or cattle; Hadīth no. 3204.

Book of the Beginning of Creation

Chapter: If a fly falls into the drink of any one of you, he should dip it (in the drink then remove it) for in one of its wings there is a disease and in the other there is cure; Hadīth no. 3324.

Sahīh Muslim

Book of Musāqāh

Chapter: The command to kill dogs and its abrogation and the prohibition of keeping them except for the purpose of hunting or guarding land or cattle and the like; Hadīth no. 1575.

Sunan Abu Dāwud

Book of Hunting

Chapter: Keeping a dog for hunting and other purposes; Hadīth no. 2844.

Jāmi' At-Tirmidhi

Book of Hunting as reported from the Messenger of Allah (PBUH)

Chapter: What is reported on how much the rewards of good deeds of whoever keeps a dog decrease; Hadīth no. 1490.

Sunan An-Nasā'i

Book of Hunting and Slaughtering

Chapter: Concession for keeping a dog for farming purposes; Hadīth no. 4289.

Sunan Ibn Mājah

Book of Hunting

Chapter: Forbiddance of keeping a dog except for hunting or guarding farms or cattle; Hadīth no. 3204.

Chapter: Prohibition of selling alcohol, dead animals, swine and idols.

Jābir ibn 'Abdullāh (may Allah be pleased with him) reported that he heard the Messenger of Allah (may Allah's peace and blessings be upon him) in the year of the Conquest, when he was in Makkah, say: "Indeed, Allah and His Messenger prohibited selling alcohol, dead animals, swine, and idols." It was said: "O Messenger of Allah, what about the fat of the dead animals that is used for coating boats and hides, and people use it for lighting purposes?" He said: "No, it is prohibited." Then the Messenger of Allah (may Allah's peace and blessings be upon him) said: "May Allah destroy the Jews. When Allah prohibited the fat (of dead animals) to them, they melted it then sold it and consumed its price."

Sahīh Al-Bukhārī Book of Sales Chapter: Selling dead animals and idols; Hadīth no. 2236. Sahīh Muslim Book of Musāqāh Chapter: Prohibition of selling alcohol, dead animals, swine, and idols; Hadīth no. 1581. Sunan Abu Dāwud Book of Sales - Chapters on Ijārah (Lease) Chapter: The price of alcohol and dead animals; Hadīth no. 3486.Jāmi' At-TirmidhiBook of Transactions as reported from the Messenger of Allah (PBUH)Chapter: What is reported on selling hides of dead animals and idols; Hadīth no. 1297.Sunan An-Nasā'iBook of Fara' and 'AtīrahChapter: Forbiddance of making use of the fat of dead animals; Hadīth no. 4256.Sunan Ibn MājahBook of TradeChapter: What is unlawful to sell; Hadīth no. 2167.

Book of Sales

Chapter: Selling dead animals and idols; Hadīth no. 2236.

Sahīh Muslim

Book of Musāqāh

Chapter: Prohibition of selling alcohol, dead animals, swine, and idols; Hadīth no. 1581.

Sunan Abu Dāwud

Book of Sales - Chapters on Ijārah (Lease)

Chapter: The price of alcohol and dead animals; Hadīth no. 3486.

Jāmi' At-Tirmidhi

Book of Transactions as reported from the Messenger of Allah (PBUH)

Chapter: What is reported on selling hides of dead animals and idols; Hadīth no. 1297.

Sunan An-Nasā'i

Book of Fara' and 'Atīrah

Chapter: Forbiddance of making use of the fat of dead animals; Hadīth no. 4256.

Sunan Ibn Mājah

Book of Trade

Chapter: What is unlawful to sell; Hadīth no. 2167.

Chapter: Doing what is lawful and refraining from what is doubtful.

An-Nu'mān ibn Bashīr (may Allah be pleased with him) reported that he heard the Prophet (may Allah's peace and blessings be upon him) say: "Verily, the lawful is clear and unlawful is clear, and between them are doubtful matters which many people do not know. Whoever avoids doubtful matters clears his liability regarding his religion and his honor, and whoever falls into doubtful matters will fall into the unlawful, just like the shepherd who grazes his animals in the vicinity of a pasture declared prohibited (by the king) and is, thus, likely to let them graze in a prohibited area (and be punished for that). Verily, every king has a protected area and the protected area of Allah is His prohibitions. Verily, in the body there is a piece of flesh which if it becomes upright then the entire body will be upright, and if it becomes corrupt the entire body will be corrupt. Verily, it is the heart."

Sahīh Al-BukhāriBook of FaithChapter: Merit of the one who clears his liability regarding his religion; Hadīth no. 52.Sahih MuslimBook of Musāqāh (Irrigation of land for a specific return)Chapter: Doing what is lawful and refraining from what is doubtful; Hadīth no. 1599.Sunan Abu DāwudBook of SalesChapter: Avoiding doubtful matters; Hadīth no. 3330.Jāmi' At-TirmidhiBook of Transactions as reported from the Messenger of Allah (PBUH)Chapter: What is reported on refraining from doubtful matters; Hadīth no. 1205.Sunan An-Nasā'iBook of SalesChapter: Avoiding doubtful matters in sources of earning; Hadīth no. 4453.Sunan Ibn MājahBook of TribulationsChapter: Refraining from doubtful matters; Hadīth no. 3984.

Book of Faith

Chapter: Merit of the one who clears his liability regarding his religion; Hadīth no. 52.

Sahih Muslim

Book of Musāqāh (Irrigation of land for a specific return)

Chapter: Doing what is lawful and refraining from what is doubtful; Hadīth no. 1599.

Sunan Abu Dāwud

Book of Sales

Chapter: Avoiding doubtful matters; Hadīth no. 3330.

Jāmi' At-Tirmidhi

Book of Transactions as reported from the Messenger of Allah (PBUH)

Chapter: What is reported on refraining from doubtful matters; Hadīth no. 1205.

Sunan An-Nasā'i

Book of Sales

Chapter: Avoiding doubtful matters in sources of earning; Hadīth no. 4453.

Sunan Ibn Mājah

Book of Tribulations

Chapter: Refraining from doubtful matters; Hadīth no. 3984.

Chapter: Selling a camel and stipulating riding it.

Jābir (may Allah be pleased with him) reported that he was riding a tired camel. The Prophet (may Allah's peace and blessings be upon him) passed by and struck it and invoked Allah's blessings for it. The camel became so fast like it had never been before. The Prophet (may Allah's peace and blessings be upon him) then said: "Sell it to me for one 'ūqiyyah (of gold)." I said: "no." He again said: "Sell it to me for one 'ūqiyyah (of gold)." I sold it and stipulated that I should ride it to my home. When we arrived (in Madinah), I took the camel to the Prophet (may Allah's peace and blessings be upon him) and he gave me its price. I returned home but he sent for me (and when I went to him) he said: "I would not take your camel. Take your camel as a gift for you."

Sahīh Al-BukhāriBook of ConditionsChapter: It is permissible for the seller to stipulate that he rides the (sold) animal to a certain place; Hadīth no. 2718.Sahīh MuslimBook of MusāqāhChapter: Selling a camel and stipulating riding it; Hadīth no. 715.Sunan Abu DāwudBook of Sales - Chapters on Ijārah (Lease)Chapter: Stipulating a condition in a sale transaction; Hadīth no. 3505.Jāmi' At-TirmidhiBook of Transactions as reported from the Messenger of Allah (PBUH)Chapter: What is reported on stipulating a condition to ride the sold animal; Hadīth no. 1253.Sunan An-Nasā'iBook of SalesChapter: A sale that involves a condition and both the sale and the condition are valid; Hadīth no. 4637.Sunan Ibn MājahBook of TradeChapter: Bidding up; Hadīth no. 2205.

Book of Conditions

Chapter: It is permissible for the seller to stipulate that he rides the (sold) animal to a certain place; Hadīth no. 2718.

Sahīh Muslim

Book of Musāqāh

Chapter: Selling a camel and stipulating riding it; Hadīth no. 715.

Sunan Abu Dāwud

Book of Sales - Chapters on Ijārah (Lease)

Chapter: Stipulating a condition in a sale transaction; Hadīth no. 3505.

Jāmi' At-Tirmidhi

Book of Transactions as reported from the Messenger of Allah (PBUH)

Chapter: What is reported on stipulating a condition to ride the sold animal; Hadīth no. 1253.

Sunan An-Nasā'i

Book of Sales

Chapter: A sale that involves a condition and both the sale and the condition are valid; Hadīth no. 4637.

Sunan Ibn Mājah

Book of Trade

Chapter: Bidding up; Hadīth no. 2205.

Chapter: Salam sale (a sale in which a price is paid for goods to be delivered later).

Ibn 'Abbās (may Allah be pleased with him) reported: "The Prophet (may Allah 's peace and blessings be upon him) came to Madinah when its people used to pay in advance the price of dates to be delivered within two or three years. He said (to them): 'Whoever pays in advance the price of a thing to be delivered later should pay it for a specified measure, a specified weight, and a fixed term.'"

Sahīh Al-BukhāriBook of Salam Sale (a sale in which a price is paid for goods to be delivered later)Chapter: Salam sale of a definite known weight; Hadīth no. 2240.Sahīh MuslimBook of MusāqāhChapter: Salam sale; Hadīth no. 1604.Sunan Abu DāwudBook of Sales - Chapters on IjārahChapter: Regarding advance payment; Hadīth no. 3463.Jāmi' At-TirmidhiBook of Transactions as reported from the Messenger of Allah (PBUH)Chapter: What is reported on advance payment in foodstuff and dates; Hadīth no. 1311.Sunan An-Nasā'iBook of SalesChapter: Advance payment in fruits; Hadīth no. 4616.Sunan Ibn MājahBook of TradeChapter: Advance payment for a specified measure and weight with a specified fixed time; Hadīth no. 2280.

Book of Salam Sale (a sale in which a price is paid for goods to be delivered later)

Chapter: Salam sale of a definite known weight; Hadīth no. 2240.

Sahīh Muslim

Book of Musāqāh

Chapter: Salam sale; Hadīth no. 1604.

Sunan Abu Dāwud

Book of Sales - Chapters on Ijārah

Chapter: Regarding advance payment; Hadīth no. 3463.

Jāmi' At-Tirmidhi

Book of Transactions as reported from the Messenger of Allah (PBUH)

Chapter: What is reported on advance payment in foodstuff and dates; Hadīth no. 1311.

Sunan An-Nasā'i

Book of Sales

Chapter: Advance payment in fruits; Hadīth no. 4616.

Sunan Ibn Mājah

Book of Trade

Chapter: Advance payment for a specified measure and weight with a specified fixed time; Hadīth no. 2280.

Chapter: Pre-emption.

Jābir ibn 'Abdullāh (may Allah be pleased with him) reported: "The Prophet (may Allah's peace and blessings be upon him) decreed for partners the right of pre-emption in property which had not been divided up. But if the boundaries are demarcated and the roads are fixed, then there is no right of pre-emption."

Sahīh Al-BukhāriBook of Pre-emptionChapter: Pre-emption is in what has not been divided, but if the boundaries are demarcated then there is no right of pre-emption; Hadīth no. 2257.Sahīh MuslimBook of MusāqāhChapter: Pre-emption; Hadīth no. 1608.Sunan Abu DāwudBook of Sales - Chapters on IjārahChapter: Regarding pre-emption; Hadīth no. 3514.Jāmi' At-TirmidhiBook of Rulings as reported from the Messenger of Allah (PBUH)Chapter: If boundaries are demarcated and roads are laid down, then there is no right of pre-emption; Hadīth no. 1370.Sunan An-Nasā'iBook of SalesChapter: Selling a shared property; Hadīth no. 4646.Sunan Ibn MājahBook of Pre-emptionBook: If boundaries are demarcated, then there is no right of pre-emption; Hadīth no. 2499.

Book of Pre-emption

Chapter: Pre-emption is in what has not been divided, but if the boundaries are demarcated then there is no right of pre-emption; Hadīth no. 2257.

Sahīh Muslim

Book of Musāqāh

Chapter: Pre-emption; Hadīth no. 1608.

Sunan Abu Dāwud

Book of Sales - Chapters on Ijārah

Chapter: Regarding pre-emption; Hadīth no. 3514.

Jāmi' At-Tirmidhi

Book of Rulings as reported from the Messenger of Allah (PBUH)

Chapter: If boundaries are demarcated and roads are laid down, then there is no right of pre-emption; Hadīth no. 1370.

Sunan An-Nasā'i

Book of Sales

Chapter: Selling a shared property; Hadīth no. 4646.

Sunan Ibn Mājah

Book of Pre-emption

Book: If boundaries are demarcated, then there is no right of pre-emption; Hadīth no. 2499.

Book of the Law of Inheritance

Chapter: Inheritance of one who leaves behind neither ascendants nor descendants as heirs.

Jābir ibn 'Abdullāh (may Allah be pleased with him) reported: "Once I fell ill. The Prophet (may Allah's peace and blessings be upon him) and Abu Bakr came walking to pay me a visit and found me unconscious. The Prophet (may Allah's peace and blessings be upon him) performed ablution and then poured the remaining water upon me so I came to my senses and saw the Prophet. I said: 'O Messenger of Allah, what shall I do with my property? How shall I distribute my property?' He did not reply till the verse of inheritance was revealed."

Sahīh Al-BukhāriBook of PatientsChapter: Visiting the unconscious; Hadīth no. 5651.Sahīh MuslimBook of the Law of InheritanceChapter: Inheritance of one who leaves behind neither ascendants nor descendants as heirs; Hadīth no. 1616.Sunan Abu DāwudBook of the Law of InheritanceChapter: Regarding one who leaves behind neither ascendants nor descendants as heirs; Hadīth no. 2886.Jāmi' At-TirmidhiBook of the Law of Inheritance as reported from the Messenger of Allah (PBUH)Chapter: Inheritance of sisters; Hadīth no. 2097.Sunan An-Nasā'iBook of PurificationChapter: Making use of the water left over from ablution; Hadīth no. 138.Sunan Ibn MājahBook of the Law of InheritanceChapter: Inheritance of one who leaves behind neither ascendants nor descendants as heirs; Hadīth no. 2728.

Book of Patients

Chapter: Visiting the unconscious; Hadīth no. 5651.

Sahīh Muslim

Book of the Law of Inheritance

Chapter: Inheritance of one who leaves behind neither ascendants nor descendants as heirs; Hadīth no. 1616.

Sunan Abu Dāwud

Book of the Law of Inheritance

Chapter: Regarding one who leaves behind neither ascendants nor descendants as heirs; Hadīth no. 2886.

Jāmi' At-Tirmidhi

Book of the Law of Inheritance as reported from the Messenger of Allah (PBUH)

Chapter: Inheritance of sisters; Hadīth no. 2097.

Sunan An-Nasā'i

Book of Purification

Chapter: Making use of the water left over from ablution; Hadīth no. 138.

Sunan Ibn Mājah

Book of the Law of Inheritance

Chapter: Inheritance of one who leaves behind neither ascendants nor descendants as heirs; Hadīth no. 2728.

Chapter : Whoever leaves behind a property, then it is for his heirs.

Abu Hurayrah (may Allah be pleased with him) reported that whenever a dead man in debt was brought to Allah's Messenger (may Allah's peace and blessings be upon him) he would ask: "Has he left anything to repay his debt?" If he was informed that he had left something to repay his debts, he would perform the funeral prayer over him; otherwise he would order the Muslims to perform the funeral prayer over him. When Allah made the Prophet (may Allah's peace and blessings be upon him) wealthy through conquests, he said: "I am more entitled to be the guardian of the believers than themselves, so if a Muslim dies while in debt, I am responsible for the repayment of his debt, and whoever leaves wealth (after his death) it is for his heirs."

Sahīh Al-BukhāriBook of Kafālah (Guarantee)Chapter: The one who undertakes to repay the debts of a dead person does not have the right to withdraw his word; Hadīth no. 2298.Sahīh MuslimBook of the Law of InheritanceChapter: Whoever leaves behind property, then it is for his heirs; Hadīth no. 1619.Sunan Abu DāwudBook of Kharāj (Tax on agrarian land owned by non-Muslims), Rulership, and Spoils of War.Chapter: Providing for the offspring; Hadīth no. 2955.Jāmi' At-TirmidhiBook of FuneralsChapter: What is reported on offering the funeral prayer for an indebted person; Hadīth no. 1070.Sunan An-Nasā'iBook of FuneralsChapter: Offering the funeral prayer for a deceased who owes a debt; Hadīth no. 1963.Sunan Ibn MājahBook of CharityChapter: Whoever leaves an unpaid debt or dependents, then it is Allah and His Messenger who take charge of them; Hadīth no. 2415.

Book of Kafālah (Guarantee)

Chapter: The one who undertakes to repay the debts of a dead person does not have the right to withdraw his word; Hadīth no. 2298.

Sahīh Muslim

Book of the Law of Inheritance

Chapter: Whoever leaves behind property, then it is for his heirs; Hadīth no. 1619.

Sunan Abu Dāwud

Book of Kharāj (Tax on agrarian land owned by non-Muslims), Rulership, and Spoils of War.

Chapter: Providing for the offspring; Hadīth no. 2955.

Jāmi' At-Tirmidhi

Book of Funerals

Chapter: What is reported on offering the funeral prayer for an indebted person; Hadīth no. 1070.

Sunan An-Nasā'i

Book of Funerals

Chapter: Offering the funeral prayer for a deceased who owes a debt; Hadīth no. 1963.

Sunan Ibn Mājah

Book of Charity

Chapter: Whoever leaves an unpaid debt or dependents, then it is Allah and His Messenger who take charge of them; Hadīth no. 2415.

Book of Gifts

Chapter: The dislike for a person to buy what he has given as charity from the one to whom he gave it.

'Umar (may Allah be pleased with him) reported: "I donated a horse for Jihād (fighting in the cause of Allah). The man who had the horse neglected it, so I wanted to buy it back, thinking that he would sell it for a cheap price. I asked the Prophet (may Allah's peace and blessings be upon him) about this and he said: 'Do not buy it back and do not take back your charity, even if he gives it to you for one dirham, for the one who takes back his charity is like the one who takes back his vomit.'"

Sahīh Al-BukhāriBook of ZakahChapter: Can one buy something which he has given in charity?; Hadīth no. 1409.Sahīh MuslimBook of GiftsChapter: It is disliked for a person to buy what he has given as charity from the one to whom he gave it; Hadīth no. 1620.Sunan Abu DāwudBook of ZakahChapter: A man buying what he has given as charity; Hadīth no. 1593.Jāmi' At-TirmidhiBook of Zakah as reported from the Messenger of Allah (PBUH)Chapter: What is reported on the dislike of taking back ones' charity; Hadīth no. 668.Sunan An-Nasā'iBook of ZakahChapter: Buying the charity; Hadīth no. 2615.Sunan Ibn MājahBook of CharityChapter: If one gives something in charity then finds it offered for sale, may he buy it?; Hadīth no. 2392.

Book of Zakah

Chapter: Can one buy something which he has given in charity?; Hadīth no. 1409.

Sahīh Muslim

Book of Gifts

Chapter: It is disliked for a person to buy what he has given as charity from the one to whom he gave it; Hadīth no. 1620.

Sunan Abu Dāwud

Book of Zakah

Chapter: A man buying what he has given as charity; Hadīth no. 1593.

Jāmi' At-Tirmidhi

Book of Zakah as reported from the Messenger of Allah (PBUH)

Chapter: What is reported on the dislike of taking back ones' charity; Hadīth no. 668.

Sunan An-Nasā'i

Book of Zakah

Chapter: Buying the charity; Hadīth no. 2615.

Sunan Ibn Mājah

Book of Charity

Chapter: If one gives something in charity then finds it offered for sale, may he buy it?; Hadīth no. 2392.

Chapter: Prohibition of taking back the charity and gift after they have been received, except what one gives to his children down to all levels.

Ibn 'Abbās (may Allah be pleased with him) reported that the Messenger of Allah (may Allah's peace and blessings be upon him) said: "He who takes back his gift is like a dog that vomits then licks its vomit."

Sahīh Al-BukhāriBook of Giving Gifts and its Merit and Encouraging ItChapter: Husband and wife giving gifts to each other; Hadīth no. 2589.Sahīh MuslimBook of GiftsChapter: Prohibition of taking back charity and gifts after they have been received except what one gives to his children down to all levels; Hadīth no. 1622.Sunan Abu DāwudBook of IjārahChapter: Taking back a gift; Hadīth no. 3538.Jāmi' At-TirmidhiBook of Sales as reported from the Messenger of Allah (PBUH)Chapter: What is reported on taking back a gift; Hadīth no. 1298.Sunan An-Nasā'iBook of GiftsChapter: A parent taking back what he gave to his child, and mentioning the different reports of the narrators in this regard; Hadīth no. 3691.Sunan Ibn MājahBook of GiftsChapter: Taking back a gift; Hadīth no. 2385.

Book of Giving Gifts and its Merit and Encouraging It

Chapter: Husband and wife giving gifts to each other; Hadīth no. 2589.

Sahīh Muslim

Book of Gifts

Chapter: Prohibition of taking back charity and gifts after they have been received except what one gives to his children down to all levels; Hadīth no. 1622.

Sunan Abu Dāwud

Book of Ijārah

Chapter: Taking back a gift; Hadīth no. 3538.

Jāmi' At-Tirmidhi

Book of Sales as reported from the Messenger of Allah (PBUH)

Chapter: What is reported on taking back a gift; Hadīth no. 1298.

Sunan An-Nasā'i

Book of Gifts

Chapter: A parent taking back what he gave to his child, and mentioning the different reports of the narrators in this regard; Hadīth no. 3691.

Sunan Ibn Mājah

Book of Gifts

Chapter: Taking back a gift; Hadīth no. 2385.

Chapter: Dislike of favoring some children over the others in gifts.

An-Nu'mān ibn Bashīr (may Allah be pleased with him) said while he was on the pulpit: "My father gave me a gift. 'Amrah bint Rawāhah (his mother) said: 'I would not agree to it unless you make Allah's Messenger (PBUH) a witness to it.' My father went to Allah's Messenger (PBUH) and said: 'I have given a gift to my son from 'Amrah bint Rawāhah, but she ordered me to make you, O Allah's Messenger, a witness to it.' Allah's Messenger (PBUH) asked: 'Have you given (the like of it) to all of your children?' He replied in the negative. Allah's Messenger (PBUH) said: 'Then fear Allah and treat your children equally.' My father then returned and took back his gift."

Sahīh Al-BukhāriBook of Gifts, Its Merit and Encouraging ItChapter: Taking witnesses for gift-giving; Hadīth no. 2587.Sahīh MuslimBook of GiftsChapter: Dislike of favoring some children over the others in gifts; Hadīth no. 1623.Sunan Abu DāwudBook of IjārahChapter: A man favoring some of his children in gift-giving; Hadīth no. 3542.Jāmi' At-TirmidhiBook of Rulings as reported from the Messenger of Allah (PBUH)Chapter: What was reported on gift-giving and treating children equally (in this regard); Hadīth no. 1367.Sunan An-Nasā'iBook of GiftsChapter: The different versions of the report of An-Nu'mān ibn Bashīr regarding gifts; Hadīth no. 3681.Sunan Ibn MājahBook of GiftsChapter: A man giving a gift to one of his children; Hadīth no. 2376.

Book of Gifts, Its Merit and Encouraging It

Chapter: Taking witnesses for gift-giving; Hadīth no. 2587.

Sahīh Muslim

Book of Gifts

Chapter: Dislike of favoring some children over the others in gifts; Hadīth no. 1623.

Sunan Abu Dāwud

Book of Ijārah

Chapter: A man favoring some of his children in gift-giving; Hadīth no. 3542.

Jāmi' At-Tirmidhi

Book of Rulings as reported from the Messenger of Allah (PBUH)

Chapter: What was reported on gift-giving and treating children equally (in this regard); Hadīth no. 1367.

Sunan An-Nasā'i

Book of Gifts

Chapter: The different versions of the report of An-Nu'mān ibn Bashīr regarding gifts; Hadīth no. 3681.

Sunan Ibn Mājah

Book of Gifts

Chapter: A man giving a gift to one of his children; Hadīth no. 2376.

Chapter: 'Umra (gift without condition, where property is transferred to beneficiary following death of donor).

Jābir (may Allah be pleased with him) reported: "'Umra gift is for the one upon whom it is bestowed."

Sahīh Al-BukhāriBook of Gift-giving, Its Merit, and Encouraging ItChapter: What is reported on 'Umra and Ruqba; Hadīth no. 2625.Sahīh MuslimBook of GiftsChapter: 'Umra gift; Hadīth no. 1625.Sunan Abu DāwudBook of IjārahChapter: Regarding 'Umra gift; Hadīth no. 3550.Jāmi' At-TirmidhiBook of Rulings as reported from the Messenger of Allah (PBUH)Chapter: What is reported on 'Umra and Ruqba gifts; Hadīth no. 1350.Sunan An-Nasā'iBook of 'Umra GiftChapter: Mentioning the difference between the report of Yahya ibn Abi Kathīr and Muhammad ibn 'Amr and that of Abu Salamah in this regard; Hadīth no. 3751.Sunan Ibn MājahBook of GiftsChapter: 'Umra gift; Hadīth no. 2380.

Book of Gift-giving, Its Merit, and Encouraging It

Chapter: What is reported on 'Umra and Ruqba; Hadīth no. 2625.

Sahīh Muslim

Book of Gifts

Chapter: 'Umra gift; Hadīth no. 1625.

Sunan Abu Dāwud

Book of Ijārah

Chapter: Regarding 'Umra gift; Hadīth no. 3550.

Jāmi' At-Tirmidhi

Book of Rulings as reported from the Messenger of Allah (PBUH)

Chapter: What is reported on 'Umra and Ruqba gifts; Hadīth no. 1350.

Sunan An-Nasā'i

Book of 'Umra Gift

Chapter: Mentioning the difference between the report of Yahya ibn Abi Kathīr and Muhammad ibn 'Amr and that of Abu Salamah in this regard; Hadīth no. 3751.

Sunan Ibn Mājah

Book of Gifts

Chapter: 'Umra gift; Hadīth no. 2380.

Book of Wills and Testaments

'Abdullāh ibn 'Umar (may Allah be pleased with him) reported that the Messenger of Allah (may Allah's peace and blessings be upon him) said: "It is the duty of a Muslim who has something to be given as a bequest not to spend two nights without having his will written about it."

Sahīh Al-BukhāriBook of Wills and TestamentsChapter: Wills and testaments; Hadīth no. 2738.Sahīh MuslimBook of Wills and TestamentsHadīth no. 1627.Sunan Abu DāwudBook of Wills and TestamentsChapter: What is reported on what is commanded about wills; Hadīth no. 2862.Jāmi' At-TirmidhiBook of FuneralsChapter: What is reported on encouraging to make a will; Hadīth no. 974.Sunan An-Nasā'iBook of Wills and TestamentsChapter: It is disliked to delay the will; Hadīth no. 3615.Sunan Ibn MājahBook of Wills and TestamentsChapter: Encouraging to make a will; Hadīth no. 2699.

Book of Wills and Testaments

Chapter: Wills and testaments; Hadīth no. 2738.

Sahīh Muslim

Book of Wills and Testaments

Hadīth no. 1627.

Sunan Abu Dāwud

Book of Wills and Testaments

Chapter: What is reported on what is commanded about wills; Hadīth no. 2862.

Jāmi' At-Tirmidhi

Book of Funerals

Chapter: What is reported on encouraging to make a will; Hadīth no. 974.

Sunan An-Nasā'i

Book of Wills and Testaments

Chapter: It is disliked to delay the will; Hadīth no. 3615.

Sunan Ibn Mājah

Book of Wills and Testaments

Chapter: Encouraging to make a will; Hadīth no. 2699.

Chapter: Making a will for one third (of the estate).

Sa'd ibn Abi Waqqās (may Allah be pleased with him) reported: "The Messenger of Allah (may Allah's peace and blessings be upon him) came to visit me in the year of the Farewell Hajj as I was very ill. I said to him: 'O Messenger of Allah, you can see how ill I am. I have wealth and no one will inherit me except a daughter. Shall I give two thirds of my wealth in charity?' He said: 'no.' I said: 'Then shall I give one half?' He said: 'no.' Then he said: '(Give) one third, and one third is a lot. Indeed, leaving your heirs rich is better than leaving them poor begging from people. You never spend anything seeking thereby the pleasure of Allah but you are rewarded for it, even what you put in your wife's mouth.' I said: 'O Messenger of Allah, will I be left here in Makkah after my companions have departed to Madinah?' He said: 'If you are left behind and do good deeds whereby you seek Allah's pleasure, you will be raised a degree and your status will be elevated on account of them. Perhaps you would be left behind so that some people might benefit by you and others might be harmed by you. O Allah, complete for my Companions their Hijrah (immigration to Madinah), and do not turn them back on their heels. The unfortunate one, however, is Sa'd ibn Khawlah.' (The Messenger of Allah (may Allah's peace and blessings be upon him) felt sorry for him as he had died in Makkah)."

Sahīh Al-BukhāriBook of FuneralsChapter: The Prophet (PBUH) pities Sa'd ibn Khawlah; Hadīth no. 1295.Sahīh MuslimBook of Wills and TestamentsChapter: Making a will for one third of the estate; Hadīth no. 1628.Sunan Abu DāwudBook of Wills and TestamentsChapter: What is reported on what is not allowed for a testator to give from his wealth; Hadīth no. 2864.Jāmi' At-TirmidhiBook of Wills and Testaments as reported from the Messenger of Allah (PBUH)Chapter: What is reported on making a will for one third (of the estate); Hadīth no. 2116.Sunan An-Nasā'iBook of Wills and TestamentsChapter: Making a will for one third (of the estate); Hadīth no. 3629.Sunan Ibn MājahBook of Wills and TestamentsChapter: Making a will for one third of the estate; Hadīth no. 2708.

Book of Funerals

Chapter: The Prophet (PBUH) pities Sa'd ibn Khawlah; Hadīth no. 1295.

Sahīh Muslim

Book of Wills and Testaments

Chapter: Making a will for one third of the estate; Hadīth no. 1628.

Sunan Abu Dāwud

Book of Wills and Testaments

Chapter: What is reported on what is not allowed for a testator to give from his wealth; Hadīth no. 2864.

Jāmi' At-Tirmidhi

Book of Wills and Testaments as reported from the Messenger of Allah (PBUH)

Chapter: What is reported on making a will for one third (of the estate); Hadīth no. 2116.

Sunan An-Nasā'i

Book of Wills and Testaments

Chapter: Making a will for one third (of the estate); Hadīth no. 3629.

Sunan Ibn Mājah

Book of Wills and Testaments

Chapter: Making a will for one third of the estate; Hadīth no. 2708.

Chapter: Waqf (endowment).

Ibn 'Umar (may Allah be pleased with him) reported that (his father) 'Umar ibn al-Khattāb acquired a piece of land in Khaybar, so he came to the Prophet (may Allah's peace and blessings be upon him) to seek his orders on what he should do with it. He said: "O Messenger of Allah, I have acquired a piece of land in Khaybar, and I have never acquired a property more precious to me than it. What do you command me to do with it?" He (the Prophet, may Allah's peace and blessings be upon him) said: "If you wish, you can keep it as an endowment and give its yields in charity." So, 'Umar gave the land in charity on condition that it would neither be sold nor given as a gift nor bequeathed as inheritance. He gave its yields as charity to the poor, the relatives, for emancipation of slaves, in Allah's cause, and for the wayfarers and guests. It was permissible for its administrator to eat from it in a reasonable just manner and feed others without seeking to be wealthy by means of it. Ibn Sīrīn said: "... without storing the yields with the purpose of becoming rich."

Sahīh Al-BukhāriBook of ConditionsChapter: Stipulating conditions in an endowment; Hadīth no. 2737.Sahīh MuslimBook of Wills and TestamentsChapter: Waqf (endowment); Hadīth no. 1632.Sunan Abu DāwudBook of Wills and TestamentsChapter: What is reported on a man making an endowment; Hadīth no. 2878.Jāmi' At-TirmidhiBook of Rulings as reported from the Messenger of Allah (PBUH)Chapter: Regarding Waqf (endowment); Hadīth no. 1375.Sunan An-Nasā'iBook of EndowmentsChapter: Endowments. How an endowment is to be recorded, and mentioning the differences cited about Ibn 'Awn's version of Ibn 'Umar's report in this regard; Hadīth no. 3599.Sunan Ibn MājahBook of CharityChapter: Whoever makes an endowment; Hadīth no. 2396.

Book of Conditions

Chapter: Stipulating conditions in an endowment; Hadīth no. 2737.

Sahīh Muslim

Book of Wills and Testaments

Chapter: Waqf (endowment); Hadīth no. 1632.

Sunan Abu Dāwud

Book of Wills and Testaments

Chapter: What is reported on a man making an endowment; Hadīth no. 2878.

Jāmi' At-Tirmidhi

Book of Rulings as reported from the Messenger of Allah (PBUH)

Chapter: Regarding Waqf (endowment); Hadīth no. 1375.

Sunan An-Nasā'i

Book of Endowments

Chapter: Endowments. How an endowment is to be recorded, and mentioning the differences cited about Ibn 'Awn's version of Ibn 'Umar's report in this regard; Hadīth no. 3599.

Sunan Ibn Mājah

Book of Charity

Chapter: Whoever makes an endowment; Hadīth no. 2396.

Book of Vows

Chapter: The command to fulfill vows.

'Abdullāh ibn 'Abbās (may Allah be pleased with him) reported that Sa'd ibn 'Ubādah al-Ansāri (may Allah be pleased with him) asked the Prophet (may Allah 's peace and blessings be upon him) about a vow that had been due upon his mother who died before fulfilling it. So, he (the Prophet, may Allah 's peace and blessings be upon him) told him to fulfill it on her behalf, and this became the followed practice in this regard since then.

Sahīh Al-BukhāriBook of Oaths and VowsChapter: The one who dies without fulfilling a vow; Hadīth no. 6698.Sahīh MuslimBook of VowsChapter: The command to fulfill vows; Hadīth no. 1638.Sunan Abu DāwudBook of Oaths and VowsChapter: Fulfilling a vow on behalf of a deceased person; Hadīth no. 3307.Jāmi' At-TirmidhiBook of Vows and Oaths as reported from the Messenger of Allah (PBUH)Chapter: What is reported on fulfilling a vow on behalf of a deceased person; Hadīth no. 1546.Sunan An-Nasā'iBook of Wills and TestamentsChapter: The merit of giving charity on behalf of a deceased person; Hadīth no. 3657.Sunan Ibn MājahBook of ExpiationsChapter: The one who dies without fulfulling a vow; Hadīth no. 2132.

Book of Oaths and Vows

Chapter: The one who dies without fulfulling a vow; Hadīth no. 6698.

Sahīh Muslim

Book of Vows

Chapter: The command to fulfill vows; Hadīth no. 1638.

Sunan Abu Dāwud

Book of Oaths and Vows

Chapter: Fulfilling a vow on behalf of a deceased person; Hadīth no. 3307.

Jāmi' At-Tirmidhi

Book of Vows and Oaths as reported from the Messenger of Allah (PBUH)

Chapter: What is reported on fulfilling a vow on behalf of a deceased person; Hadīth no. 1546.

Sunan An-Nasā'i

Book of Wills and Testaments

Chapter: The merit of giving charity on behalf of a deceased person; Hadīth no. 3657.

Sunan Ibn Mājah

Book of Expiations

Chapter: The one who dies without fulfulling a vow; Hadīth no. 2132.

Chapter: The forbiddance of making a vow and that it repels nothing.

Abu Hurayrah (may Allah be pleased with him) reported that the Prophet (may Allah's peace and blessings be upon him) said: "A vow does not bring for the son of Adam anything that is not decreed for him, but his vow may coincide with what has been decreed for him, and thereby Allah extracts deeds from the miser. So, he gives (in charity) for the fulfillment of what has been decreed for him what he would not give before were it not for his vow."

Sahīh Al-BukhāriBook of Oaths and VowsChapter: Fulfilling vows; Hadīth no. 6694.Sahīh MuslimBook of VowsChapter: Forbiddance of making a vow and that it repels nothing; Hadīth no. 1640.Sunan Abu DāwudBook of Oaths and VowsChapter: Forbidding vows; Hadīth no. 3288.Jāmi' At-TirmidhiBook of Vows and Oaths as reported from the Messenger of Allah (PBUH)Chapter: The dislike of vows; Hadīth no. 1538.Sunan An-Nasā'iBook of Oaths and VowsChapter: A vow does not advance anything or delay it; Hadīth no. 3804.Sunan Ibn MājahBook of ExpiationsChapter: Forbidding vows; Hadīth no. 2123.

Book of Oaths and Vows

Chapter: Fulfilling vows; Hadīth no. 6694.

Sahīh Muslim

Book of Vows

Chapter: Forbiddance of making a vow and that it repels nothing; Hadīth no. 1640.

Sunan Abu Dāwud

Book of Oaths and Vows

Chapter: Forbidding vows; Hadīth no. 3288.

Jāmi' At-Tirmidhi

Book of Vows and Oaths as reported from the Messenger of Allah (PBUH)

Chapter: The dislike of vows; Hadīth no. 1538.

Sunan An-Nasā'i

Book of Oaths and Vows

Chapter: A vow does not advance anything or delay it; Hadīth no. 3804.

Sunan Ibn Mājah

Book of Expiations

Chapter: Forbidding vows; Hadīth no. 2123.

Book of Oaths

Chapter: Forbiddance to swear by other than Allah Almighty.

'Abdullāh ibn 'Umar (may Allah be pleased with him) reported: "The Messenger of Allah (may Allah's peace and blessings be upon him) found 'Umar ibn al-Khattāb amongst the riders and he was swearing by his father, so he said: 'Indeed, Allah forbids you from swearing by your fathers. He who has to swear should swear by Allah or remain silent.'"

Sahīh Al-BukhāriBook of Oaths and VowsChapter: Do not swear by your fathers; Hadīth no. 6646.Sahīh MuslimBook of OathsChapter: Forbiddance to swear by other than Allah Almighty; Hadīth no. 1646.Sunan Abu DāwudBook of Oaths and VowsChapter: The dislike of swearing by one's fathers; Hadīth no. 3249.Jāmi' At-TirmidhiBook of Vows and Oaths as reported from the Messenger of Allah (PBUH)Chapter: What is reported on the dislike of swearing by other than Allah; Hadīth no. 1534.Sunan An-Nasā'iBook of Oaths and VowsChapter: Swearing by one's fathers; Hadīth no. 3766.Sunan Ibn MājahBook of ExpiationsChapter: Forbiddance to swear by other than Allah; Hadīth no. 2094.

Book of Oaths and Vows

Chapter: Do not swear by your fathers; Hadīth no. 6646.

Sahīh Muslim

Book of Oaths

Chapter: Forbiddance to swear by other than Allah Almighty; Hadīth no. 1646.

Sunan Abu Dāwud

Book of Oaths and Vows

Chapter: The dislike of swearing by one's fathers; Hadīth no. 3249.

Jāmi' At-Tirmidhi

Book of Vows and Oaths as reported from the Messenger of Allah (PBUH)

Chapter: What is reported on the dislike of swearing by other than Allah; Hadīth no. 1534.

Sunan An-Nasā'i

Book of Oaths and Vows

Chapter: Swearing by one's fathers; Hadīth no. 3766.

Sunan Ibn Mājah

Book of Expiations

Chapter: Forbiddance to swear by other than Allah; Hadīth no. 2094.

Chapter: The one who swears by Al-Lāt. and Al-'Uzza should say: La ilāha illa-Allah (There is no true god except Allah).

Abu Hurayrah (may Allah be pleased with him) reported that the Messenger of Allah (may Allah's peace and blessings be upon him) said: "Whoever swears by Al-Lāt and Al-'Uzza (pagan idols) should say: 'La ilāha illa-Allah (There is no true god except Allah)'. And whoever says to his companion: 'Come and gamble with me', should give charity."

Sahīh Al-BukhāriBook of Interpretation of the Qur'anChapter: Allah's saying: {So have you considered Al-Lāt and Al-'Uzza?}; Hadīth no. 4860.Sahīh MuslimBook of OathsChapter: Whoever swears by Al-Lāt and Al-'Uzza (pagan idols) should say: La ilāha illa-Allah (There is no true god but Allah); Hadīth no. 1647.Sunan Abu DāwudBook of Oaths and VowsChapter: Swearing by other than Allah; Hadīth no. 3247.Jāmi' At-TirmidhiBook of Vows and Oaths as reported from the Messenger of Allah (PBUH)Chapter: Hadīth no. 1545.Sunan An-Nasā'iBook of Oaths and VowsChapter: Swearing by Al-Lāt (pagan idol); Hadīth no. 3775.Sunan Ibn MājahBook of ExpiationsChapter: Forbiddance to swear by other than Allah; Hadīth no. 2096.

Book of Interpretation of the Qur'an

Chapter: Allah's saying: {So have you considered Al-Lāt and Al-'Uzza?}; Hadīth no. 4860.

Sahīh Muslim

Book of Oaths

Chapter: Whoever swears by Al-Lāt and Al-'Uzza (pagan idols) should say: La ilāha illa-Allah (There is no true god but Allah); Hadīth no. 1647.

Sunan Abu Dāwud

Book of Oaths and Vows

Chapter: Swearing by other than Allah; Hadīth no. 3247.

Jāmi' At-Tirmidhi

Book of Vows and Oaths as reported from the Messenger of Allah (PBUH)

Chapter: Hadīth no. 1545.

Sunan An-Nasā'i

Book of Oaths and Vows

Chapter: Swearing by Al-Lāt (pagan idol); Hadīth no. 3775.

Sunan Ibn Mājah

Book of Expiations

Chapter: Forbiddance to swear by other than Allah; Hadīth no. 2096.

Chapter: It is recommended for one who takes an oath (to do something) then finds another choice to be better, to go for the better choice and expiate his (first) oath.

Zahdam reported: "Once we were in the house of Abu Mūsa and he offered a cooked rooster. A man from the tribe of Banu Taym-illāh with red complexion as if he were from the Byzantine war prisoners was present. Abu Mūsa invited him to share the meal but he said (apologizing): 'I saw it eating something (dirty) so I developed an aversion to eating it, and I swore that I would not eat (it).' Abu Mūsa said: 'Come along, I will tell you about this matter (i.e. how to cancel one's oath). I went to the Prophet (may Allah's peace and blessings be upon him) in the company of a group of Ash'ariyyūn, asking him to provide us with riding animals. He said: 'By Allah, I will not provide you with any riding animals, and I have nothing to make you ride on.' Then some camels as booty were brought to Allah's Messenger (may Allah's peace and blessings be upon him) and he asked for us, saying: 'Where are the group of Ash'ariyyūn?' Then he ordered that we be given five white-hump camels. When we set out we said: 'What have we done? We will never be blessed (with what we have been given).' So we returned to him and said: 'We asked you to provide us with riding animals but you swore that you would not provide us with any riding animals. Have you forgotten?' He replied: 'It was not me who provided you with riding animals. It was Allah who provided you with them, and, by Allah, Allah willing, if I ever swear to do something then I find that it is better to do something else, I will do the thing which is better and make expiation for my (broken) oath.'"

Sahīh Al-BukhāriBook of the Obligation of Khumus (One Fifth of the Booty)Chapter: Evidence that Khumus is meant for the needs of Muslims; Hadīth no. 3133.Sahīh MuslimBook of OathsChapter: It is recommended for one who swears to do something then finds another choice to be better, to go for the better choice and expiate his oath; Hadīth no. 1649.Sunan Abu DāwudBook of Oaths and VowsChapter: A man expiates for his oath before breaking it; Hadīth no. 3276.Jāmi' At-TirmidhiBook of Foods as reported from the Messenger of Allah (PBUH)Chapter: What is reported on eating chicken; Hadīth no. 1826.Sunan An-Nasā'iBook of Oaths and VowsChapter: Expiating for the oath before breaking it; Hadīth no. 3780.Sunan Ibn MājahBook of ExpiationsChapter: The one who swears to do something then finds another choice to be better; Hadīth no. 2107.

Book of the Obligation of Khumus (One Fifth of the Booty)

Chapter: Evidence that Khumus is meant for the needs of Muslims; Hadīth no. 3133.

Sahīh Muslim

Book of Oaths

Chapter: It is recommended for one who swears to do something then finds another choice to be better, to go for the better choice and expiate his oath; Hadīth no. 1649.

Sunan Abu Dāwud

Book of Oaths and Vows

Chapter: A man expiates for his oath before breaking it; Hadīth no. 3276.

Jāmi' At-Tirmidhi

Book of Foods as reported from the Messenger of Allah (PBUH)

Chapter: What is reported on eating chicken; Hadīth no. 1826.

Sunan An-Nasā'i

Book of Oaths and Vows

Chapter: Expiating for the oath before breaking it; Hadīth no. 3780.

Sunan Ibn Mājah

Book of Expiations

Chapter: The one who swears to do something then finds another choice to be better; Hadīth no. 2107.

Chapter: The vow of a disbeliever and what he should do regarding it if he embraces Islam.

'Abdullāh ibn 'Umar (may Allah be pleased with him) reported that 'Umar ibn al-khattāb (may Allah be pleased with him) said: "O Messenger of Allah, I made a vow before embracing Islam to observe I'tikāf for one night in the Sacred Mosque." Thereupon, the Prophet (may Allah's peace and blessings be upon him) said to him: "Fulfill your vow." So he observed I'tikāf for one night.

Sahīh Al-BukhāriBook of I'tikāfChapter: Observing I'tikāf without fasting; Hadīth no. 2042.Sahīh MuslimBook of OathsChapter: The vow of a disbeliever and what he should do regarding it if he embraces Islam; Hadīth no. 1656.Sunan Abu DāwudBook of Oaths and VowsChapter: If someone made a vow before embracing Islam; Hadīth no. 3325.Jāmi' At-TirmidhiBook of Oaths and Vows as reported from the Messenger of Allah (PBUH)Chapter: What is reported on fulfilling vows; Hadīth no. 1539.Sunan An-Nasā'iBook of Oaths and VowsChapter: If someone makes a vow then embraces Islam before fulfilling it; Hadīth no. 3820.Sunan Ibn MājahBook of FastingChapter: Observing I'tikāf for one day or one night; Hadīth no. 1772.

Book of I'tikāf

Chapter: Observing I'tikāf without fasting; Hadīth no. 2042.

Sahīh Muslim

Book of Oaths

Chapter: The vow of a disbeliever and what he should do regarding it if he embraces Islam; Hadīth no. 1656.

Sunan Abu Dāwud

Book of Oaths and Vows

Chapter: If someone made a vow before embracing Islam; Hadīth no. 3325.

Jāmi' At-Tirmidhi

Book of Oaths and Vows as reported from the Messenger of Allah (PBUH)

Chapter: What is reported on fulfilling vows; Hadīth no. 1539.

Sunan An-Nasā'i

Book of Oaths and Vows

Chapter: If someone makes a vow then embraces Islam before fulfilling it; Hadīth no. 3820.

Sunan Ibn Mājah

Book of Fasting

Chapter: Observing I'tikāf for one day or one night; Hadīth no. 1772.

Chapter: Permissibility of selling a Mudabbar (a slave who is promised to be manumitted after his master's death).

Jābir (may Allah be pleased with him) said: "A man from the Ansār made his slave a Mudabbar (promised him manumission after his master's death) and he had no property other than him. When the

Prophet (may Allah's peace and blessings be upon him) heard of this, he said (to his Companions): 'Who wants to buy him (the slave) from me?' So Nu'aym ibn an-Nahhām bought him for eight-hundred dirhams." I (the sub-narrator) heard Jābir say: "That was a coptic slave who died in the same year."

Sahīh Al-BukhāriBook of Expiations for Unfulfilled OathsChapter: The manumission of the Mudabbar, Umm al-Walad, and the Mukātab as expiation, and the manumission of a bastard child; Hadīth no. 6716.Sahīh MuslimBook of OathsChapter: Permissibility of selling a Mudabbar slave; Hadīth no. 997.Sunan Abu DāwudBook of Manumission of SlavesChapter: Regarding selling a Mudabbar slave; Hadīth no. 3957.Jāmi' At-TirmidhiBook of Sales as reported from the Messenger of Allah (PBUH)Chapter: What is reported on selling a Mudabbar slave; Hadīth no. 1219.Sunan An-Nasā'iBook of ZakahChapter: Which charity is best?; Hadīth no. 2546.Sunan Ibn MājahBook of Manumission of SlavesChapter: The Mudabbar slave; Hadīth no. 2513.

Book of Expiations for Unfulfilled Oaths

Chapter: The manumission of the Mudabbar, Umm al-Walad, and the Mukātab as expiation, and the manumission of a bastard child; Hadīth no. 6716.

Sahīh Muslim

Book of Oaths

Chapter: Permissibility of selling a Mudabbar slave; Hadīth no. 997.

Sunan Abu Dāwud

Book of Manumission of Slaves

Chapter: Regarding selling a Mudabbar slave; Hadīth no. 3957.

Jāmi' At-Tirmidhi

Book of Sales as reported from the Messenger of Allah (PBUH)

Chapter: What is reported on selling a Mudabbar slave; Hadīth no. 1219.

Sunan An-Nasā'i

Book of Zakah

Chapter: Which charity is best?; Hadīth no. 2546.

Sunan Ibn Mājah

Book of Manumission of Slaves

Chapter: The Mudabbar slave; Hadīth no. 2513.

Book of Qasāmah (Compurgation), Muhāribīn (Rebels), Qasās (Retribution), and Diyyah (blood money)

Chapter: Qasāmah

Bushayr ibn Yasār, the freed slave of the Ansār, reported that Rāfi' ibn Khadīj and Sahl ibn Abi Hathmah narrated to him that: "'Abdullāh ibn Sahl and Muhayyisah ibn Mas'ūd went to Khaybar and they dispersed in the gardens of the date-palm trees. 'Abdullah ibn Sahl was murdered. Then 'Abdur-Rahmān ibn Sahl, Huwayyisah and Muhayyisah, the two sons of Mas'ūd, came to the Prophet (PBUH) and spoke about the case of their (murdered) friend. 'Abdur-Rahmān, who was the youngest of them all, started talking. The Prophet (PBUH) said: 'Let the older (among you) speak first.' So they spoke about the case of their (murdered) friend. The Prophet (PBUH) said: 'Will fifty of you take an oath whereby you will have the right to receive the blood money of your murdered man (or he said: your companion)'. They said: 'O Allah's Messenger, it is an incident that we did not witness.' The Prophet (PBUH) said: 'Then the Jews will release you from the oath if fifty of them (the Jews) should take an oath to contradict your claim.' They said: 'O Allah's Messenger, they are disbelievers (and they will take a false oath).' Then Allah's Messenger (PBUH) himself paid the Diyyah (blood money) to them. Sahl said: 'I was there when one of those she-camels kicked me as she entered a fold of theirs.'"

Sahīh Al-BukhāriBook of Good MannersChapter: Honoring the elders, and the eldest should be the first to speak; Hadīth no. 6142, 6143.Sahīh MuslimBook of Qasāmah (Compurgation), Muhāribīn (Rebels), Qasās (Retribution), and Diyyah (blood money)Chapter: Qasāmah; Hadīth no. 1669.Sunan Abu DāwudBook of Blood MoneyChapter: Killing on the basis of Qasāmah; Hadīth no. 4520.Jāmi' At-TirmidhiBook of Blood Money as reported from the Messenger of Allah (PBUH)Chapter: What is reported on Qasāmah; Hadīth no. 1422.Sunan An-Nasā'iBook of QasāmahChapter: Mentioning the different versions of the narrators of Sahl's report in this regard; Hadīth no. 4712.Sunan Ibn MājahBook of Blood MoneyChapter: Qasāmah; Hadīth no. 2677.

Book of Good Manners

Chapter: Honoring the elders, and the eldest should be the first to speak; Hadīth no. 6142, 6143.

Sahīh Muslim

Book of Qasāmah (Compurgation), Muhāribīn (Rebels), Qasās (Retribution), and Diyyah (blood money)

Chapter: Qasāmah; Hadīth no. 1669.

Sunan Abu Dāwud

Book of Blood Money

Chapter: Killing on the basis of Qasāmah; Hadīth no. 4520.

Jāmi' At-Tirmidhi

Book of Blood Money as reported from the Messenger of Allah (PBUH)

Chapter: What is reported on Qasāmah; Hadīth no. 1422.

Sunan An-Nasā'i

Book of Qasāmah

Chapter: Mentioning the different versions of the narrators of Sahl's report in this regard; Hadīth no. 4712.

Sunan Ibn Mājah

Book of Blood Money

Chapter: Qasāmah; Hadīth no. 2677.

Chapter: Ruling concerning Rebels and Apostates.

Anas (may Allah be pleased with him) reported: "Some people from 'Ukl or 'Uraynah came to Madinah, and the climate of Madinah did not suit them so they became ill. The Prophet (PBUH) ordered them to go to the milch camels and drink from their urine and milk as medicine. They went there and when they recovered from their illness, they killed the herdsman of the Prophet (PBUH) and drove off the camels. The news about them reached the Prophet (PBUH) early in the morning, so he sent people in pursuit of them, and they were captured and brought to him around noon. He ordered that their hands and feet be cut off and their eyes be branded with iron, and they were thrown out to Al-Harrah. They begged for water but were not given any." Abu Qilābah said: "Those men stole, killed, apostatized after embracing faith, and waged war against Allah and his Messenger."

Sahīh Al-BukhāriBook of AblutionChapter: Urine of camels, sheep, and other animals, and their folds; Hadīth no. 233.Sahīh MuslimBook of Qasāmah (Compurgation), Muhāribīn (Rebels), Qasās (Retribution), and Diyyah (blood money)Chapter: Ruling on Rebels and Apostates; Hadīth no. 1671.Sunan Abu DāwudBook of Prescribed PunishmentsChapter: What is reported on Rebellion, Hadīth no. 4364.Jāmi' At-TirmidhiBook of Foods as reported from the Messenger of Allah (PBUH)Chapter: What is reported on drinking the urine of camels; Hadīth no. 1845.Sunan An-Nasā'iBook of PurificationChapter: Urine of edible animals; Hadīth no. 306.Sunan Ibn MājahBook of MedicineChapter: Urine of camels; Hadīth no. 3503.

Book of Ablution

Chapter: Urine of camels, sheep, and other animals, and their folds; Hadīth no. 233.

Sahīh Muslim

Book of Qasāmah (Compurgation), Muhāribīn (Rebels), Qasās (Retribution), and Diyyah (blood money)

Chapter: Ruling on Rebels and Apostates; Hadīth no. 1671.

Sunan Abu Dāwud

Book of Prescribed Punishments

Chapter: What is reported on Rebellion, Hadīth no. 4364.

Jāmi' At-Tirmidhi

Book of Foods as reported from the Messenger of Allah (PBUH)

Chapter: What is reported on drinking the urine of camels; Hadīth no. 1845.

Sunan An-Nasā'i

Book of Purification

Chapter: Urine of edible animals; Hadīth no. 306.

Sunan Ibn Mājah

Book of Medicine

Chapter: Urine of camels; Hadīth no. 3503.

Chapter: Confirmation of retribution in the case of killing with a stone or other sharp or heavy objects, and killing a man in retaliation for a woman.

Anas ibn Mālik (may Allah be pleased with him) reported: "A girl wearing silver accessories went out in Madinah and a Jew struck her with a stone. She was brought to the Prophet (may Allah's peace and blessings be upon him) before taking her last breath. He asked her: 'Did so-and-so kill you?' She raised her head (denying that). He asked again: 'Did so- and-so kill you?' She raised her head (denying that). He asked her the third time: 'Did so-and-so kill you?' She lowered her head (agreeing). The Messenger of Allah (may Allah's peace and blessings be upon him) sent for the killer and killed him between two stones."

Sahīh Al-BukhāriBook of Blood MoneyChapter: If someone kills with a stone or a stick; Hadīth no. 6877.Sahih MuslimBook of Qasāmah (Compurgation), Muhāribīn (Rebels), Qasās (Retribution), and Diyyah (blood money)Chapter: Confirmation of retribution in cases of killing by a stone or by other sharp or heavy objects, and killing a man in retaliation for a woman; Hadīth no. 1672.Sunan Abu DāwudBook of Blood MoneyChapter: A killer is to be killed on the basis of retribution; Hadīth no. 4529.Jāmi' At-TirmidhiBook of Blood Money as reported from the Messenger of Allah (PBUH)Chapter: What is reported on someone whose head was crushed by a rock; Hadīth no. 1394.Sunan An-Nasā'iBook of

QasāmahChapter: Killing a man in retaliation for a woman; Hadīth no. 4742.Sunan Ibn MājahBook of Blood MoneyChapter: A killer is to be killed in the same way he killed; Hadīth no. 2666.

Book of Blood Money

Chapter: If someone kills with a stone or a stick; Hadīth no. 6877.

Sahih Muslim

Book of Qasāmah (Compurgation), Muhāribīn (Rebels), Qasās (Retribution), and Diyyah (blood money)

Chapter: Confirmation of retribution in cases of killing by a stone or by other sharp or heavy objects, and killing a man in retaliation for a woman; Hadīth no. 1672.

Sunan Abu Dāwud

Book of Blood Money

Chapter: A killer is to be killed on the basis of retribution; Hadīth no. 4529.

Jāmi' At-Tirmidhi

Book of Blood Money as reported from the Messenger of Allah (PBUH)

Chapter: What is reported on someone whose head was crushed by a rock; Hadīth no. 1394.

Sunan An-Nasā'i

Book of Qasāmah

Chapter: Killing a man in retaliation for a woman; Hadīth no. 4742.

Sunan Ibn Mājah

Book of Blood Money

Chapter: A killer is to be killed in the same way he killed; Hadīth no. 2666.

Chapter: What makes killing a Muslim lawful.

'Abdullāh ibn Mas'ūd (may Allah be pleased with him) reported that the Messenger of Allah (may Allah's peace and blessings be upon him) said: "It is unlawful to spill the blood of a Muslim who testifies that there is no true god except Allah and that I am the Messenger of Allah except in three cases: a life for a life, a previously-married person who commits adultery, and the one who forsakes his religion and separates from the Muslim community (i.e. the apostate)."

Sahīh Al-BukhāriBook of Blood MoneyChapter: The statement of Allah Almighty: {And We ordained for them therein a life for a life, an eye for an eye, a nose for a nose, an ear for an ear, a tooth for a tooth, and for wounds is legal retribution. But whoever gives [up his right as] charity, it is an expiation for him. And whoever does not judge by what Allah has revealed – it is those who are the unjust}; Hadīth no. 6878.Sahīh MuslimBook of Qasāmah (Compurgation), Muhāribīn (Rebels), Qasās (Retribution), and Diyyah (blood money)Chapter: What makes shedding the blood of a Muslim lawful; Hadīth no. 1676.Sunan Abu DāwudBook of Prescribed PunishmentsChapter: Ruling on the one who commits apostasy; Hadīth no. 4352.Jāmi' At-TirmidhiBook of Blood Money as reported from the Messenger of Allah (PBUH)Chapter: What is reported on: It is not lawful to shed the blood of a Muslim except in three cases; Hadīth no. 1402.Sunan An-Nasā'iBook of Prohibition of BloodshedChapter: Mentioning what makes shedding the blood of a Muslim lawful; Hadīth no. 4016.Sunan Ibn MājahBook of Prescribed PunishmentsChapter: It is unlawful to shed the blood of a Muslim except in three cases; Hadīth no. 2534.

Book of Blood Money

Chapter: The statement of Allah Almighty: {And We ordained for them therein a life for a life, an eye for an eye, a nose for a nose, an ear for an ear, a tooth for a tooth, and for wounds is legal retribution. But whoever gives [up his right as] charity, it is an expiation for him. And whoever does not judge by what Allah has revealed – it is those who are the unjust}; Hadīth no. 6878.

Sahīh Muslim

Book of Qasāmah (Compurgation), Muhāribīn (Rebels), Qasās (Retribution), and Diyyah (blood money)

Chapter: What makes shedding the blood of a Muslim lawful; Hadīth no. 1676.

Sunan Abu Dāwud

Book of Prescribed Punishments

Chapter: Ruling on the one who commits apostasy; Hadīth no. 4352.

Jāmi' At-Tirmidhi

Book of Blood Money as reported from the Messenger of Allah (PBUH)

Chapter: What is reported on: It is not lawful to shed the blood of a Muslim except in three cases; Hadīth no. 1402.

Sunan An-Nasā'i

Book of Prohibition of Bloodshed

Chapter: Mentioning what makes shedding the blood of a Muslim lawful; Hadīth no. 4016.

Sunan Ibn Mājah

Book of Prescribed Punishments

Chapter: It is unlawful to shed the blood of a Muslim except in three cases; Hadīth no. 2534.

Chapter: Blood money of a fetus, the obligation to pay blood money in case of manslaughter

and semi-intentional murder is on the perpetrator's male relatives.

Abu Hurayrah (may Allah be pleased with him) reported: "The Messenger of Allah (PBUH) judged between two women from the Hudhayl tribe who fought each other and one of them threw a stone at the other that hit her belly and she was pregnant, killing the child in her womb. They filed their case with the Prophet (PBUH) and he judged that the blood money for what was in her womb was a male or female slave. The guardian of the woman who was fined said : 'O Allah's Messenger! Shall I be fined for a creature that has neither drunk nor eaten, neither spoke nor cried?There should be no blood money for a case like that.' Upon that, the Prophet (PBUH) said: 'Verily, this is a brother of soothsayers (as he spoke in rhymed prose like them).'"

Sahīh Al-BukhāriBook of MedicineChapter: Soothsaying; Hadīth no. 5758.Sahīh MuslimBook of Qasāmah (Compurgation), Muhāribīn (Rebels), Qasās (Retribution), and Diyyah (blood money)Chapter: Blood money of a fetus, the obligation on the perpetrator's male relatives to pay blood money in case of manslaughter and semi-intentional murder; Hadīth no. 1681.Sunan Abu DāwudBook of Blood MoneyChapter: Blood money of a fetus; Hadīth no. 4577.Jāmi' At-TirmidhiBook of Blood Money as reported from the Messenger of Allah (PBUH)Chapter: What is reported on the blood money of a fetus; Hadīth no. 1410.Sunan An-Nasā'iBook of QasāmahChapter: Blood money of a woman's fetus; Hadīth no. 4818.Sunan Ibn MājahBook of Blood MoneyChapter: Blood money of a fetus; Hadīth no. 2639.

Book of Medicine

Chapter: Soothsaying; Hadīth no. 5758.

Sahīh Muslim

Book of Qasāmah (Compurgation), Muhāribīn (Rebels), Qasās (Retribution), and Diyyah (blood money)

Chapter: Blood money of a fetus, the obligation on the perpetrator's male relatives to pay blood money in case of manslaughter and semi-intentional murder; Hadīth no. 1681.

Sunan Abu Dāwud

Book of Blood Money

Chapter: Blood money of a fetus; Hadīth no. 4577.

Jāmi' At-Tirmidhi

Book of Blood Money as reported from the Messenger of Allah (PBUH)

Chapter: What is reported on the blood money of a fetus; Hadīth no. 1410.

Sunan An-Nasā'i

Book of Qasāmah

Chapter: Blood money of a woman's fetus; Hadīth no. 4818.

Sunan Ibn Mājah

Book of Blood Money

Chapter: Blood money of a fetus; Hadīth no. 2639.

Al-Mughīrah ibn Shu'bah (may Allah be pleased with him) reported that 'Umar (may Allah be pleased with him) consulted them concerning the case of causing a woman to lose her fetus. Al-Mughīrah said: "The Prophet (may Allah's peace and blessings be upon him) ruled that its blood money is a male or female slave." Muhammad ibn Maslamah testified that he witnessed the Prophet (may Allah's peace and blessings be upon him) give that judgment."

Sahīh Al-BukhāriBook of Blood MoneyChapter: A woman's fetus; Hadīth no. 6905, 6906.Sahīh MuslimBook of Qasāmah (Compurgation), Muhāribīn (Rebels), Qasās (Retaliation), and Diyyah (blood money)Chapter: Blood money of a fetus, the obligation on the perpetrator's male relatives to pay blood money in case of manslaughter and semi-intentional murder; Hadīth no. 1682.Sunan Abu DāwudBook of Blood MoneyChapter: Blood money of a fetus; Hadīth no. 4569.Jāmi' At-TirmidhiBook of Blood Money as reported from the Messenger of Allah (PBUH)Chapter: What is reported on the blood money of a fetus; Hadīth no. 1411.Sunan An-Nasā'iBook of QasāmahChapter: Blood money of a woman's fetus; Hadīth no. 4821.Sunan Ibn MājahBook of Blood MoneyChapter: Blood money of a fetus; Hadīth no. 2633.

Book of Blood Money

Chapter: A woman's fetus; Hadīth no. 6905, 6906.

Sahīh Muslim

Book of Qasāmah (Compurgation), Muhāribīn (Rebels), Qasās (Retaliation), and Diyyah (blood money)

Chapter: Blood money of a fetus, the obligation on the perpetrator's male relatives to pay blood money in case of manslaughter and semi-intentional murder; Hadīth no. 1682.

Sunan Abu Dāwud

Book of Blood Money

Chapter: Blood money of a fetus; Hadīth no. 4569.

Jāmi' At-Tirmidhi

Book of Blood Money as reported from the Messenger of Allah (PBUH)

Chapter: What is reported on the blood money of a fetus; Hadīth no. 1411.

Sunan An-Nasā'i

Book of Qasāmah

Chapter: Blood money of a woman's fetus; Hadīth no. 4821.

Sunan Ibn Mājah

Book of Blood Money

Chapter: Blood money of a fetus; Hadīth no. 2633.

Book of Prescribed Punishments

Chapter: Prescribed punishment for theft and the amount that makes it due.

'Ā'ishah (may Allah be pleased with her) reported that the Prophet (may Allah's peace and blessings be upon him) said: "The hand of a thief is to be cut off for a quarter of a dinar or more."

Sahīh Al-BukhāriBook of Prescribed PunishmentsChapter: Statement of Allah Almighty: {As for the thief, the male and female, amputate their hands...} and the amount that makes amputation due; Hadīth no. 6789.Sahīh MuslimBook of Prescribed PunishmentsChapter: The prescribed punishment for theft and the amount that makes it due; Hadīth no. 1684.Sunan Abu DāwudBook of Prescribed PunishmentsChapter: Amount of theft that makes amputation (of the thief's hand) due; Hadīth no. 4383.Jāmi' At-TirmidhiBook of Prescribed Punishments as reported from the Messenger of Allah (PBUH)Chapter: What is reported on the amount of theft that makes amputation of the thief's hand due; Hadīth no. 1445.Sunan An-Nasā'iBook of Amputation of Thief's HandChapter: Mentioning the different versions of Az-Zuhri's report; Hadīth no. 4914.Sunan Ibn MājahBook of Prescribed PunishmentsChapter: Prescribed punishment of a theif; Hadīth no. 2585.

Book of Prescribed Punishments

Chapter: Statement of Allah Almighty: {As for the thief, the male and female, amputate their hands...} and the amount that makes amputation due; Hadīth no. 6789.

Sahīh Muslim

Book of Prescribed Punishments

Chapter: The prescribed punishment for theft and the amount that makes it due; Hadīth no. 1684.

Sunan Abu Dāwud

Book of Prescribed Punishments

Chapter: Amount of theft that makes amputation (of the thief's hand) due; Hadīth no. 4383.

Jāmi' At-Tirmidhi

Book of Prescribed Punishments as reported from the Messenger of Allah (PBUH)

Chapter: What is reported on the amount of theft that makes amputation of the thief's hand due; Hadīth no. 1445.

Sunan An-Nasā'i

Book of Amputation of Thief's Hand

Chapter: Mentioning the different versions of Az-Zuhri's report; Hadīth no. 4914.

Sunan Ibn Mājah

Book of Prescribed Punishments

Chapter: Prescribed punishment of a theif; Hadīth no. 2585.

'Abdullāh ibn 'Umar (may Allah be pleased with him) reported: "The Prophet (may Allah's peace and blessings be upon him) cut off the hand of a thief for stealing a shield whose price was three dirhams."

Sahīh Al-BukhāriBook of Prescribed PunishmentsChapter: Statement of Allah Almighty: {As for the thief, the male and female, amputate their hands...} and the amount that makes amputation due; Hadīth no. 6798.Sahīh MuslimBook of Prescribed PunishmentsChapter: The prescribed punishment for theft and the amount that makes it due; Hadīth no. 1686.Sunan Abu DāwudBook of Prescribed PunishmentsChapter: Amount of theft that makes amputation (of the thief's hand) due; Hadīth no. 4385.Jāmi' At-TirmidhiBook of Prescribed Punishments as reported from the Messenger of Allah (PBUH)Chapter: What is reported on the amount of theft that makes amputation of the thief's hand due; Hadīth no. 1446.Sunan An-Nasā'iBook of Amputation of Thief's HandChapter: The amount of theft that makes amputation of the thief's hand due; Hadīth no. 4907.Sunan Ibn MājahBook of Prescribed PunishmentsChapter: Prescribed punishment of a theif; Hadīth no. 2584.

Book of Prescribed Punishments

Chapter: Statement of Allah Almighty: {As for the thief, the male and female, amputate their hands...} and the amount that makes amputation due; Hadīth no. 6798.

Sahīh Muslim

Book of Prescribed Punishments

Chapter: The prescribed punishment for theft and the amount that makes it due; Hadīth no. 1686.

Sunan Abu Dāwud

Book of Prescribed Punishments

Chapter: Amount of theft that makes amputation (of the thief's hand) due; Hadīth no. 4385.

Jāmi' At-Tirmidhi

Book of Prescribed Punishments as reported from the Messenger of Allah (PBUH)

Chapter: What is reported on the amount of theft that makes amputation of the thief's hand due; Hadīth no. 1446.

Sunan An-Nasā'i

Book of Amputation of Thief's Hand

Chapter: The amount of theft that makes amputation of the thief's hand due; Hadīth no. 4907.

Sunan Ibn Mājah

Book of Prescribed Punishments

Chapter: Prescribed punishment of a theif; Hadīth no. 2584.

Chapter: Amputating the hand of a thief of noble descent or otherwise

and forbiddance of interceding to waive a prescribed punishment.

'Ā'ishah (may Allah be pleased with her) reported: "The Quraysh (tribe) were greatly concerned about the case of the Makhzūmi woman who had committed theft. They wondered who should intercede for her with the Messenger of Allah (may Allah's peace and blessings be upon him). Some said: 'Only Osāmah ibn Zayd, the Prophet's beloved one, would dare do so.' So Osāmah spoke to him about it and his answer was: 'Do you intercede regarding one of the punishments prescribed by Allah?' Then, he got up and addressed the people saying: 'The people before you were ruined because if a noble person among them committed theft, they would leave him unpunished, but if a weak person among them committed theft, they would inflict the legal punishment upon him. By Allah, if Fātimah, the daughter of Muhammad, were to commit theft, I would cut off her hand.'"

Sahīh Al-BukhāriBook of the Hadīths on the ProphetsChapter: Hadīth no. 3475.Sahīh MuslimBook of Prescribed PunishmentsChapter: Amputating the hand of a thief of noble descent or otherwise, and forbiddance of interceding to waive a prescribed punishment; Hadīth no. 1688.Sunan Abu DāwudBook of Prescribed PunishmentsChapter: Intercession concerning waiving a prescribed punishment; Hadīth no. 4373.Jāmi' At-TirmidhiBook of Prescribed Punishments as reported from the Messenger of Allah (PBUH)Chapter: What is reported on the dislike of intercession to waive prescribed punishments; Hadīth no. 1430.Sunan An-Nasā'iBook of Amputation of the Thief's HandChapter: Mentioning the different wordings of the narrators of Az-Zuhri's report concerning the Makhzūmi woman who committed theft; Hadīth no. 4894.Sunan Ibn MājahBook of Prescribed PunishmentsChapter: Intercession to waive prescribed punishments; Hadīth no. 2547.

Book of the Hadīths on the Prophets

Chapter: Hadīth no. 3475.

Sahīh Muslim

Book of Prescribed Punishments

Chapter: Amputating the hand of a thief of noble descent or otherwise, and forbiddance of interceding to waive a prescribed punishment; Hadīth no. 1688.

Sunan Abu Dāwud

Book of Prescribed Punishments

Chapter: Intercession concerning waiving a prescribed punishment; Hadīth no. 4373.

Jāmi' At-Tirmidhi

Book of Prescribed Punishments as reported from the Messenger of Allah (PBUH)

Chapter: What is reported on the dislike of intercession to waive prescribed punishments; Hadīth no. 1430.

Sunan An-Nasā'i

Book of Amputation of the Thief's Hand

Chapter: Mentioning the different wordings of the narrators of Az-Zuhri's report concerning the Makhzūmi woman who committed theft; Hadīth no. 4894.

Sunan Ibn Mājah

Book of Prescribed Punishments

Chapter: Intercession to waive prescribed punishments; Hadīth no. 2547.

Chapter: The one who admits committing Zina (unlawful sexual intercourse)

Abu Hurayrah and Zayd ibn Khālid al-Juhani (may Allah be pleased with them) reported: "Two Bedouin men came to the Messenger of Allah (PBUH), so one of them said: 'O Messenger of Allah, I adjure you, by Allah, to judge in my case according to the Book of Allah.' The other disputant – who had more knowledge than him – said: 'Yes, judge between us according to the Book of Allah, and give me permission to speak first.' The Messenger of Allah (PBUH) said: 'Speak.' He said: 'My son was employed by this man, and he committed adultery with his wife. I was told that the punishment for my son would be stoning but that he could be ransomed for one hundred sheep and their offspring. I asked the people of knowledge and they told me that the punishment for my son would be one hundred lashes and exile for one year and that this man's wife would be stoned.' The Messenger of Allah (PBUH) said: 'By the One in Whose hand my soul is, I will judge between you according to the Book of Allah. The offspring and sheep will be returned, and your son is to be given one hundred lashes and exiled for one year. O Unays, go to that man's wife in the morning and if she admits, then stone her.' So he went to her the next day and she admitted it, and the Messenger of Allah (PBUH) gave the order that she be stoned."

Sahīh Al-BukhāriBook of ConditionsChapter: The conditions that are not permissible in prescribed punishments; Hadith no. 2724, 2725.Sahīh MuslimBook of Prescribed PunishmentsChapter: Confessing to committing Zina; Hadith no. 1697, 1698.Sunan Abu DāwudBook of Prescribed PunishmentsChapter: The woman from Juhaynah tribe whom the Prophet (PBUH) ordered that she be stoned; Hadīth no. 4445.Jāmi' At-TirmidhiBook of Prescribed Punishments as reported from the Messenger of Allah (PBUH)Chapter: What is reported on stoning a married person who commits unlawful sexual intercourse; Hadīth no. 1433.Sunan An-Nasā'iBook of the Code of Conduct of JudgesChapter: Sparing women the need to attend the judgment session; Hadīth no. 5410.Sunan Ibn MājahBook of Prescribed PunishmentsChapter: Prescribed punishment for unlawful sexual intercourse; Hadīth no. 2549.

Book of Conditions

Chapter: The conditions that are not permissible in prescribed punishments; Hadith no. 2724, 2725.

Sahīh Muslim

Book of Prescribed Punishments

Chapter: Confessing to committing Zina; Hadith no. 1697, 1698.

Sunan Abu Dāwud

Book of Prescribed Punishments

Chapter: The woman from Juhaynah tribe whom the Prophet (PBUH) ordered that she be stoned; Hadith no. 4445.

Jāmi' At-Tirmidhi

Book of Prescribed Punishments as reported from the Messenger of Allah (PBUH)

Chapter: What is reported on stoning a married person who commits unlawful sexual intercourse; Hadīth no. 1433.

Sunan An-Nasā'i

Book of the Code of Conduct of Judges

Chapter: Sparing women the need to attend the judgment session; Hadīth no. 5410.

Sunan Ibn Mājah

Book of Prescribed Punishments

Chapter: Prescribed punishment for unlawful sexual intercourse; Hadīth no. 2549.

Chapter: No compensation is due for an injury caused by an animal, mine, or well.

Abu Hurayrah (may Allah be pleased with him) reported that the Messenger of Allah (may Allah's peace and blessings be upon him) said: "There is no compensation for one killed or wounded by an animal or by falling into a well or because of working in a mine; and one fifth is due on the buried treasure."

Saḥīḥ Al-BukhāriBook of ZakahChapter: One fifth is due on the buried treasure; Hadīth no. 1499.Saḥīḥ MuslimBook of Prescribed PunishmentsChapter: No compensation is due for an injury caused by an animal, mine, or well; Hadīth no. 1710.Sunan Abu DāwudBook of Blood MoneyChapter: No compensation is due for an injury caused by an animal, mine, or well; Hadīth no. 4593.Jāmi' At-TirmidhiBook of Zakah as reported from the Messenger of Allah (PBUH)Chapter: What was reported on: No compensation is due for an injury caused by an animal and that a fifth is due on the buried treasure; Hadīth no. 642.Sunan An-Nasā'iBook of ZakahChapter: Mines; Hadīth no. 2495.Sunan Ibn MājahBook of Blood MoneyChapter: Cases where no compensation is due; Hadīth no. 2673.

Book of Zakah

Chapter: One fifth is due on the buried treasure; Hadīth no. 1499.

Saḥīḥ Muslim

Book of Prescribed Punishments

Chapter: No compensation is due for an injury caused by an animal, mine, or well; Hadīth no. 1710.

Sunan Abu Dāwud

Book of Blood Money

Chapter: No compensation is due for an injury caused by an animal, mine, or well; Hadīth no. 4593.

Jāmi' At-Tirmidhi

Book of Zakah as reported from the Messenger of Allah (PBUH)

Chapter: What was reported on: No compensation is due for an injury caused by an animal and that a fifth is due on the buried treasure; Hadīth no. 642.

Sunan An-Nasā'i

Book of Zakah

Chapter: Mines; Hadīth no. 2495.

Sunan Ibn Mājah

Book of Blood Money

Chapter: Cases where no compensation is due; Hadīth no. 2673.

Book of Legal Judgments

Chapter: The oath is due on the defendant.

Abu Mulaykah reported: "I wrote to Ibn 'Abbās (may Allah be pleased with him) and he wrote back to me that the Prophet (may Allah's peace and blessings be upon him) ruled that the oath is due on the defendant (the one against whom the claim is made)."

Saḥīḥ Al-BukhāriBook of MortgageChapter: If a dispute arises between the mortgagor (borrower) and mortgagee (lender), providing proof is the responsibility of the plaintiff and taking an oath is due on the defendant; Hadīth no. 2514.Saḥīḥ MuslimBook of Legal JudgmentsChapter: The oath is due on the defendant; Hadīth no. 1711.Sunan Abu DāwudBook of Legal JudgmentsChapter: The oath is due on the defendant; Hadīth no. 3619.Jāmi' At-TirmidhiBook of Rulings as reported from the Messenger of Allah (PBUH)Chapter: What is reported on: Providing proof is due on the plaintiff, and taking an oath is due on the defendant; Hadīth no. 1342.Sunan An-Nasā'iBook of the Code of Conduct of

JudgesChapter: The judge advising disputants to take an oath; Hadīth no. 5425.Sunan Ibn MājahBook of RulingsChapter: Providing proof is the responsibility of the plaintiff, and taking an oath is due on the defendant; Hadīth no. 2321.

Book of Mortgage

Chapter: If a dispute arises between the mortgagor (borrower) and mortgagee (lender), providing proof is the responsibility of the plaintiff and taking an oath is due on the defendant; Hadīth no. 2514.

Sahīh Muslim

Book of Legal Judgments

Chapter: The oath is due on the defendant; Hadīth no. 1711.

Sunan Abu Dāwud

Book of Legal Judgments

Chapter: The oath is due on the defendant; Hadīth no. 3619.

Jāmi' At-Tirmidhi

Book of Rulings as reported from the Messenger of Allah (PBUH)

Chapter: What is reported on: Providing proof is due on the plaintiff, and taking an oath is due on the defendant; Hadīth no. 1342.

Sunan An-Nasā'i

Book of the Code of Conduct of Judges

Chapter: The judge advising disputants to take an oath; Hadīth no. 5425.

Sunan Ibn Mājah

Book of Rulings

Chapter: Providing proof is the responsibility of the plaintiff, and taking an oath is due on the defendant; Hadīth no. 2321.

Chapter: Issuing a judgment based on what is apparent and the plaintiff's eloquent presentation of his case.

Umm Salamah (may Allah be pleased with her) reported: "The Messenger of Allah (may Allah's peace and blessings be upon him) heard voices arguing at the door of his chamber, so he went out to them and said: 'I am only a human being, and you refer your disputes to me. Perhaps some of you are more eloquent than others, so I deem him truthful and rule in his favor. He whom I, by my judgment, give an undue share of a Muslim's right, then it is indeed a portion of fire, so let him burden himself with it or abandon it.'"

Sahīh Al-BukhāriBook of RulingsChapter: Whoever is given the right of his brother through a judge's decision should refrain from taking it, for the judge's decision does not render the unlawful lawful or the lawful unlawful; Hadīth no. 7181Sahīh MuslimBook of Legal JudgmentsChapter: Issuing a judgment based on what is apparent and the plaintiff's eloquent presentation of his case; Hadīth no. 1713.Sunan Abu DāwudBook of Legal JudgmentsChapter: A judge issuing an incorrect judgment; Hadīth no. 3583.Jāmi' At-TirmidhiBook of Rulings as reported from the Messenger of Allah (PBUH)Chapter: What is reported on the severe threat for one who is awarded a judgment for something that he is not entitled to take; Hadīth no. 1339.Sunan An-Nasā'iBook of the Code of Conduct of JudgesChapter: Giving judgment based on what is apparent; Hadīth no. 5401.Sunan Ibn MājahBook of RulingsChapter: A judge's decision does not render the unlawful lawful or the lawful unlawful; Hadīth no. 2317.

Book of Rulings

Chapter: Whoever is given the right of his brother through a judge's decision should refrain from taking it, for the judge's decision does not render the unlawful lawful or the lawful unlawful; Hadīth no. 7181

Sahīh Muslim

Book of Legal Judgments

Chapter: Issuing a judgment based on what is apparent and the plaintiff's eloquent presentation of his case; Hadīth no. 1713.

Sunan Abu Dāwud

Book of Legal Judgments

Chapter: A judge issuing an incorrect judgment; Hadīth no. 3583.

Jāmi' At-Tirmidhi

Book of Rulings as reported from the Messenger of Allah (PBUH)

Chapter: What is reported on the severe threat for one who is awarded a judgment for something that he is not entitled to take; Hadīth no. 1339.

Sunan An-Nasā'i

Book of the Code of Conduct of Judges

Chapter: Giving judgment based on what is apparent; Hadīth no. 5401.

Sunan Ibn Mājah

Book of Rulings

Chapter: A judge's decision does not render the unlawful lawful or the lawful unlawful; Hadīth no. 2317.

Chapter: Dislike of issuing verdict by judge when he is angry.

'Abdur Rahmān ibn Abi Bakrah (may Allah be pleased with him) reported: "Abu Bakrah wrote to his son who was in Sijistān: Do not judge between two persons when you are angry, for I heard the Prophet (may Allah's peace and blessings be upon him) saying: 'A judge should not judge between two persons while he is in a state of anger.'"

Sahih Al-BukhāriBook of RulingsChapter: Should judge issue judgment or give Fatwa while in a state of anger?; Hadīth no. 7158.Sahīh MuslimBook of Legal JudgmentsChapter: Dislike that a judge issues verdict while in state of anger; Hadīth no. 1717.Sunan Abu DāwudBook of Legal JudgmentsChapter: A judge issuing verdict while in state of anger; Hadīth no. 3589.Jāmi' At-TirmidhiBook of Rulings as reported from the Messenger of Allah (PBUH)Chapter: What is reported on: A judge should not issue verdict while in a state of anger; Hadīth no. 1334.Sunan An-Nasā'iBook of the Code of Conduct of JudgesChapter: What a judge should avoid; Hadīth no. 5406.Sunan Ibn MājahBook of RulingsChapter: A judge should not issue verdict while in a state of anger; Hadīth no. 2316.

Book of Rulings

Chapter: Should judge issue judgment or give Fatwa while in a state of anger?; Hadīth no. 7158.

Sahīh Muslim

Book of Legal Judgments

Chapter: Dislike that a judge issues verdict while in state of anger; Hadīth no. 1717.

Sunan Abu Dāwud

Book of Legal Judgments

Chapter: A judge issuing verdict while in state of anger; Hadīth no. 3589.

Jāmi' At-Tirmidhi

Book of Rulings as reported from the Messenger of Allah (PBUH)

Chapter: What is reported on: A judge should not issue verdict while in a state of anger; Hadīth no. 1334.

Sunan An-Nasā'i

Book of the Code of Conduct of Judges

Chapter: What a judge should avoid; Hadīth no. 5406.

Sunan Ibn Mājah

Book of Rulings

Chapter: A judge should not issue verdict while in a state of anger; Hadīth no. 2316.

Book of Rulership

Chapter: Obligation to obey rulers in whatever does not involve sin, and prohibition to obey them in whatever involves sin.

'Abdullāh ibn 'Umar (may Allah be pleased with him) reported that the Prophet (may Allah's peace and blessings be upon him) said: "Listening and obeying are due on a Muslim regarding what he likes or dislikes so long as he is not commanded to commit a sin. If he is commanded to commit a sin, then there is neither listening nor obeying (due on him)."

Sahīh Al-BukhāriBook of RulingsChapter: Listening and obeying are due to the ruler unless he commands committing a sin; Hadīth no. 7144.Sahīh MuslimBook of RulershipChapter: Obligation to obey the rulers in whatever does not involve sin and prohibition to obey them in whatever involves sin; Hadīth no. 1839.Sunan Abu DāwudBook of JihādChapter: Regarding obedience; Hadīth no. 2626.Jāmi' At-TirmidhiBook of Jihād as reported from the Messenger of Allah (PBUH)Chapter: What is reported on: No obedience is due to a created being in what involves disobedience to the Creator; Hadīth no. 1707.Sunan An-Nasā'iBook of Bay'ahChapter: Punishment of whoever is commanded to commit a sin and he obeys; Hadīth no. 4206.Sunan Ibn MājahBook of JihādChapter: No obedience is due when it involves disobeying Allah; Hadīth no. 2864.

Book of Rulings

Chapter: Listening and obeying are due to the ruler unless he commands committing a sin; Hadīth no. 7144.

Sahīh Muslim

Book of Rulership

Chapter: Obligation to obey the rulers in whatever does not involve sin and prohibition to obey them in whatever involves sin; Hadīth no. 1839.

Sunan Abu Dāwud

Book of Jihād

Chapter: Regarding obedience; Hadīth no. 2626.

Jāmi' At-Tirmidhi

Book of Jihād as reported from the Messenger of Allah (PBUH)

Chapter: What is reported on: No obedience is due to a created being in what involves disobedience to the Creator; Hadīth no. 1707.

Sunan An-Nasā'i

Book of Bay'ah

Chapter: Punishment of whoever is commanded to commit a sin and he obeys; Hadīth no. 4206.

Sunan Ibn Mājah

Book of Jihād

Chapter: No obedience is due when it involves disobeying Allah; Hadīth no. 2864.

Chapter: Pledging after the Conquest of Makkah to adhere to Islam,

engage in Jihād, and do good; and explaining the meaning of: No Hijrah (emigration) is due after the Conquest.

'Abdullah ibn 'Abbās (may Allah be pleased with him) reported: "On the day of the Conquest of Makkah, the Messenger of Allah (may Allah's peace and blessings be upon him) said: 'There is no Hijrah (emigration) after the Conquest (of Makkah), but there is Jihād and (good) intention, and whenever you are called for Jihād, you should immediately respond to the call. Verily, Allah has made this city sacred since the day He created the heavens and earth. It is a sanctuary by Allah's decree until the Day of Judgment. Fighting in it was not permissible for anyone before me, and it was made permissible for me for only an hour of a day. It is sacred by the sacredness granted by Allah until the Day of Judgment. Its thorns should not be cut off, its game should not be chased, and any lost item found therein should not be picked up except by one who would announce it publicly (to find its owner), and its green grass should not be cut off.' Al-'Abbās said: 'O Messenger of Allah, except for Idhkhir (lemongrass), for it is used by their blacksmiths and for their domestic purposes.' So, the Prophet (may Allah's peace and blessings be upon him) said: 'Except for Idhkhir.'"

Sahīh Al-BukhāriBook of the Penalty of Hunting (while in state of Ihrām)Chapter: It is unlawful to fight in Makkah; Hadīth no. 1834.Sahīh MuslimBook of RulershipChapter: Pledging after the Conquest of Makkah to adhere to Islam, engage in Jihād, and do good; and explaining the meaning of: No Hijrah (emigration) is due after the Conquest; Hadīth no. 1353.Sunan Abu DāwudBook of RitualsChapter: Sanctity of the precincts of Makkah; Hadīth no. 2017.Jāmi' At-TirmidhiBook of Military Expeditions as reported from the Messenger of Allah (PBUH)Chapter: What is reported on Hijrah (emigration); Hadīth no. 1590.Sunan An-Nasā'iBook of Rituals of HajjChapter: Sanctity of Makkah; Hadīth no. 2874.Sunan Ibn MājahBook of JihādChapter: Setting out when call for Jihād is announced; Hadīth no. 2773.

Book of the Penalty of Hunting (while in state of Ihrām)

Chapter: It is unlawful to fight in Makkah; Hadīth no. 1834.

Sahīh Muslim

Book of Rulership

Chapter: Pledging after the Conquest of Makkah to adhere to Islam, engage in Jihād, and do good; and explaining the meaning of: No Hijrah (emigration) is due after the Conquest; Hadīth no. 1353.

Sunan Abu Dāwud

Book of Rituals

Chapter: Sanctity of the precincts of Makkah; Hadīth no. 2017.

Jāmi' At-Tirmidhī

Book of Military Expeditions as reported from the Messenger of Allah (PBUH)

Chapter: What is reported on Hijrah (emigration); Hadīth no. 1590.

Sunan An-Nasā'i

Book of Rituals of Hajj

Chapter: Sanctity of Makkah; Hadīth no. 2874.

Sunan Ibn Mājah

Book of Jihād

Chapter: Setting out when call for Jihād is announced; Hadīth no. 2773.

Chapter: Defining the age of puberty.

Ibn 'Umar (may Allah be pleased with him) reported: "The Messenger of Allah (may Allah's peace and blessings be upon him) called me to present myself in front of him on the eve of the battle of Uhud, while I was fourteen years old at that time, and he did not allow me to take part in that battle, but he called me to present myself in front of him on the eve of the battle of the Trench when I was fifteen years old, and he allowed me (to join the battle)." Nāfi' reported: "I went to 'Umar ibn 'Abdul 'Azīz who was caliph at that time and related the above narration to him, and he said: 'This age (fifteen) is the limit between the child and adult,' and wrote to his governors to give salaries to those who reached the age of fifteen.'"

Sahīh Al-BukhāriBook of WitnessesChapter: Boys attaining the age of puberty and their testimony; Hadīth no. 2664.Sahīh MuslimBook of RulershipChapter: Defining the age of puberty; Hadīth no. 1868.Sunan Abu DāwudBook of Kharāj (Tax on agrarian land owned by non-Muslims), Rulership, and Spoils of War.Chapter: The age at which a man is entitled to a share due to taking part in battle; Hadīth no. 2957.Jāmi' At-TirmidhiBook of Rulings as reported from the Messenger of Allah (PBUH)Chapter: What is reported on the age of puberty of men and women; Hadīth no. 1361.Sunan An-Nasā'iBook of DivorceChapter: When does the divorce of a boy count; Hadīth no. 3431.Sunan Ibn MājahBook of Prescribed PunishmentsChapter: Those on whom prescribed punishment is not due; Hadīth no. 2543.

Book of Witnesses

Chapter: Boys attaining the age of puberty and their testimony; Hadīth no. 2664.

Sahīh Muslim

Book of Rulership

Chapter: Defining the age of puberty; Hadīth no. 1868.

Sunan Abu Dāwud

Book of Kharāj (Tax on agrarian land owned by non-Muslims), Rulership, and Spoils of War.

Chapter: The age at which a man is entitled to a share due to taking part in battle; Hadīth no. 2957.

Jāmi' At-Tirmidhī

Book of Rulings as reported from the Messenger of Allah (PBUH)

Chapter: What is reported on the age of puberty of men and women; Hadīth no. 1361.

Sunan An-Nasā'i

Book of Divorce

Chapter: When does the divorce of a boy count; Hadīth no. 3431.

Sunan Ibn Mājah

Book of Prescribed Punishments

Chapter: Those on whom prescribed punishment is not due; Hadīth no. 2543.

Chapter: Horse racing and making them lean (for that purpose).

Ibn 'Umar (may Allah be pleased with him) reported: "The Messenger of Allah (may Allah's peace and blessings be upon him) held a horse race, with horses that had been made lean by training, from Hafyā' to Thaniyyat al-Wadā'." (I asked Musa: "What was the distance between those two places?" He replied: "Six miles or seven.") "And he held a race from Thaniyyat al-Wadā' to the mosque of Banu Zurayq between the horses which had not undergone such training." (I asked: "What was the distance between those two places?" He replied: "One mile or so.") Ibn 'Umar was amongst those who participated in those races.

Sahīh Al-BukhāriBook of Jihād and Military ExpeditionsChapter: Maximum distance of race for horses made lean by training; Hadīth no. 2870.Sahīh MuslimBook of RulershipChapter: Horse racing and training horses to make them lean; Hadīth no. 1870.Sunan Abu DāwudBook of JihādChapter: Regarding racing; Hadīth no. 2575.Jāmi' At-TirmidhiBook of Jihād as reported from the Messenger of Allah (PBUH)Chapter: What is reported on contests and racing; Hadīth no. 1699.Sunan An-Nasā'iBook of horsesChapter: Making horses lean for racing; Hadīth no. 3584.Sunan Ibn MājahBook of JihādChapter: Racing and contests; Hadīth no. 2877.

Book of Jihād and Military Expeditions

Chapter: Maximum distance of race for horses made lean by training; Hadīth no. 2870.

Sahīh Muslim

Book of Rulership

Chapter: Horse racing and training horses to make them lean; Hadīth no. 1870.

Sunan Abu Dāwud

Book of Jihād

Chapter: Regarding racing; Hadīth no. 2575.

Jāmi' At-Tirmidhi

Book of Jihād as reported from the Messenger of Allah (PBUH)

Chapter: What is reported on contests and racing; Hadīth no. 1699.

Sunan An-Nasā'i

Book of horses

Chapter: Making horses lean for racing; Hadīth no. 3584.

Sunan Ibn Mājah

Book of Jihād

Chapter: Racing and contests; Hadīth no. 2877.

Chapter: Merit of Jihād and Ribāt.

Abu Sa'īd al-Khudri (may Allah be pleased with him) reported: "Someone asked: 'O Messenger of Allah, who is the best among the people?' The Messenger of Allah (may Allah's peace and blessings be upon him) said: 'A believer who strives in Allah's cause with his life and wealth.' They asked: 'Who is next?' He replied: 'A believer in one of the mountain passes, fearing Allah and sparing the people his evil.'"

Sahīh Al-BukhāriBook of Jihād and Military ExpeditionsChapter: The best of people is a believer who strives in Allah's cause with his life and wealth; Hadīth no. 2786.Sahīh MuslimBook of RulershipChapter: Merit of Jihād and Ribāt; Hadīth no. 1888.Sunan Abu DāwudBook of JihādChapter: Regarding the reward of Jihād; Hadīth no. 2485.Jāmi' At-TirmidhiBook of the merits of Jihād as reported from the Messenger of Allah (PBUH)Chapter: What is reported on: Who is the best among the people?; Hadīth no. 1660.Sunan An-Nasā'iBook of JihādChapter: Merit of the one who strives in Allah's cause by his life and wealth; Hadīth no. 3105.Sunan Ibn MājahBook of TribulationsChapter: Seclusion; Hadīth no. 3978.

Book of Jihād and Military Expeditions

Chapter: The best of people is a believer who strives in Allah's cause with his life and wealth; Hadīth no. 2786.

Sahīh Muslim

Book of Rulership

Chapter: Merit of Jihād and Ribāt; Hadīth no. 1888.

Sunan Abu Dāwud

Book of Jihād

Chapter: Regarding the reward of Jihād; Hadīth no. 2485.

Jāmi' At-Tirmidhi

Book of the merits of Jihād as reported from the Messenger of Allah (PBUH)

Chapter: What is reported on: Who is the best among the people?; Hadīth no. 1660.

Sunan An-Nasā'i

Book of Jihād

Chapter: Merit of the one who strives in Allah's cause by his life and wealth; Hadīth no. 3105.

Sunan Ibn Mājah

Book of Tribulations

Chapter: Seclusion; Hadīth no. 3978.

Chapter: Merit of supplying the one who fights in the cause of Allah

with a riding mount or anything else and taking good care of his family in his absence.

Zayd ibn Khālid al-Juhani (may Allah be pleased with him) reported that the Messenger of Allah (may Allah's peace and blessings be upon him) said: "Whoever equips a fighter in the cause of Allah has indeed taken part in the fight himself; and whoever looks after the dependents of a fighter in his absence properly has indeed taken part in the fight himself."

Sahīh Al-BukhāriBook of Jihād and Military ExpeditionsChapter: Merit of the one who equips a fighter in the cause of Allah or looks after his dependents in his absence; Hadīth no. 2843.Sahīh MuslimBook of RulershipChapter: Merit of supplying the one who fights in the cause of Allah with a riding mount or anything else and taking good care of his family in his absence; Hadīth no. 1895.Sunan Abu

DāwudBook of JihādChapter: What is considered as participation in battle; Hadīth no. 2509.Jāmi' At-TirmidhiBook of the merits of Jihād as reported from the Messenger of Allah (PBUH)Chapter: What is reported on the merit of the one who equips a fighter in the cause of Allah; Hadīth no. 1628.Sunan An-Nasā'iBook of JihādChapter: Merit of the one who equips a fighter in the cause of Allah; Hadīth no. 3180.Sunan Ibn MājahBook of JihādChapter: The one who equips a fighter in the cause of Allah; Hadīth no. 2759

Book of Jihād and Military Expeditions

Chapter: Merit of the one who equips a fighter in the cause of Allah or looks after his dependents in his absence; Hadīth no. 2843.

Sahīh Muslim

Book of Rulership

Chapter: Merit of supplying the one who fights in the cause of Allah with a riding mount or anything else and taking good care of his family in his absence; Hadīth no. 1895.

Sunan Abu Dāwud

Book of Jihād

Chapter: What is considered as participation in battle; Hadīth no. 2509.

Jāmi' At-Tirmidhi

Book of the merits of Jihād as reported from the Messenger of Allah (PBUH)

Chapter: What is reported on the merit of the one who equips a fighter in the cause of Allah; Hadīth no. 1628.

Sunan An-Nasā'i

Book of Jihād

Chapter: Merit of the one who equips a fighter in the cause of Allah; Hadīth no. 3180.

Sunan Ibn Mājah

Book of Jihād

Chapter: The one who equips a fighter in the cause of Allah; Hadīth no. 2759

Chapter: The one who fights so that Allah's word be superior, then his fight is in the cause of Allah.

Abu Mūsa al-Ash'ari (may Allah be pleased with him) reported: "A man came to the Prophet (may Allah's peace and blessings be upon him) and said: 'O Messenger of Allah, what kind of fighting is in Allah's cause? (I ask this) for some of us fight because of being enraged and angry and some out of zealotry.' The Prophet (may Allah's peace and blessings be upon him) raised his head (as the questioner was standing) and said: 'Whoever fights so that the word of Allah be the uppermost, then he fights in Allah's cause.'"

Sahīh Al-BukhāriBook of KnowledgeChapter: Asking while standing a scholar who is sitting; Hadīth no.123.Sahīh MuslimBook of RulershipChapter: Whoever fights so that the word of Allah be the uppermost is fighting in the cause of Allah; Hadīth no.1904.Sunan Abu DāwudBook of JihādChapter: Whoever fights so that the word of Allah be the uppermost is fighting in the cause of Allah; Hadīth no. 2517.Jāmi' At-TirmidhiBook of the merits of Jihād as reported from the Messenger of Allah (PBUH)Chapter: What is reported on the one who fights out of ostentation and in pursuit of worldly gains; Hadīth no. 1646.Sunan An-Nasā'iBook of JihādChapter: Whoever fights so that the word of Allah be the uppermost is fighting in the cause of Allah; Hadīth no. 3136.Sunan Ibn MājahBook of JihādChapter: The intention in fighting; Hadīth no. 2783.

Book of Knowledge

Chapter: Asking while standing a scholar who is sitting; Hadīth no.123.

Sahīh Muslim

Book of Rulership

Chapter: Whoever fights so that the word of Allah be the uppermost is fighting in the cause of Allah; Hadīth no.1904.

Sunan Abu Dāwud

Book of Jihād

Chapter: Whoever fights so that the word of Allah be the uppermost is fighting in the cause of Allah; Hadīth no. 2517.

Jāmi' At-Tirmidhi

Book of the merits of Jihād as reported from the Messenger of Allah (PBUH)

Chapter: What is reported on the one who fights out of ostentation and in pursuit of worldly gains; Hadīth no. 1646.

Sunan An-Nasā'i

Book of Jihād

Chapter: Whoever fights so that the word of Allah be the uppermost is fighting in the cause of Allah; Hadīth no. 3136.

Sunan Ibn Mājah

Book of Jihād

Chapter: The intention in fighting; Hadīth no. 2783.

Chapter: The statement of Allah's Messenger (PBUH): "Indeed, deeds are judged based on the intention" and that fighting in Allah's cause and other deeds are included in it.

'Umar ibn al-Khattāb (may Allah be pleased with him) reported: "I heard the Messenger of Allah (may Allah's peace and blessings be upon him) say: 'Verily, the reward of deeds depends on the intention behind them, and each person will be rewarded according to what he has intended. So, he whose migration is for the sake of Allah and His Messenger, then his migration is for the sake of Allah and His Messenger, and he whose migration is to achieve some worldly gain or to take some woman in marriage, then his migration is for that for which he migrated.'"

Sahīh Al-BukhāriBook of Oaths and VowsChapter: The intention in oaths; Hadīth no. 6689.Sahīh MuslimBook of RulershipChapter: The statement of Allah's Messenger (PBUH): "Indeed, deeds are judged based on the intention" and that fighting in Allah's cause and other deeds are included in it; Hadīth no. 1907.Sunan Abu DāwudBook of DivorceChapter: Statements that imply divorce, and intentions; Hadīth no. 2201.Jāmi' At-TirmidhiBook of the merits of Jihād as reported from the Messenger of Allah (PBUH)Chapter: What is reported on the one who fights out of ostentation and in pursuit of worldly gains; Hadīth no. 1647.Sunan An-Nasā'iBook of PurificationChapter: The intention in ablution; Hadīth no. 75.Sunan Ibn MājahBook of AsceticismChapter: The intention; Hadīth no. 4227.

Book of Oaths and Vows

Chapter: The intention in oaths; Hadīth no. 6689.

Sahīh Muslim

Book of Rulership

Chapter: The statement of Allah's Messenger (PBUH): "Indeed, deeds are judged based on the intention" and that fighting in Allah's cause and other deeds are included in it; Hadīth no. 1907.

Sunan Abu Dāwud

Book of Divorce

Chapter: Statements that imply divorce, and intentions; Hadīth no. 2201.

Jāmi' At-Tirmidhi

Book of the merits of Jihād as reported from the Messenger of Allah (PBUH)

Chapter: What is reported on the one who fights out of ostentation and in pursuit of worldly gains; Hadīth no. 1647.

Sunan An-Nasā'i

Book of Purification

Chapter: The intention in ablution; Hadīth no. 75.

Sunan Ibn Mājah

Book of Ascetism

Chapter: The intention; Hadīth no. 4227.

Chapter: Merit of military campaigning by sea.

Anas ibn Mālik (may Allah be pleased with him) reported: "The Messenger of Allah (PBUH) used to visit Umm Harām bint Milhān, who would offer him meals. Umm Harām was the wife of 'Ubādah ibn as-Sāmit. Allah's Messenger (PBUH) once visited her and she fed him then inspected his head for lice. Allah's Messenger (PBUH) fell asleep then woke up smiling. Umm Harām asked: 'What makes you smile, O Allah's Messenger?' He said: 'Some of my followers were presented before me as fighters in Allah's cause on board a ship in the sea; they were kings on the thrones (or like kings on the thrones).' (Is'hāq, a sub-narrator was not sure as to which wording the Prophet used) Umm Harām said: 'O Allah's Messenger, invoke Allah that He makes me one of them.' Allah's Messenger (PBUH) invoked Allah for her and fell asleep again then woke up smiling. Once again Umm Harām asked: 'What makes you smile, O Allah's Messenger?' He replied: 'Some of my followers were presented to me as fighters in Allah's Cause,' repeating the same dream. Umm Harām said: 'O Allah's Messenger, invoke Allah that He makes me one of them.' He said: 'You are amongst the first ones.' Later, she did board a ship on the sea during the caliphate of Mu'āwiyah ibn Abi Sufyān, and after she disembarked, she fell off her riding animal and died."

Sahīh Al-BukhāriBook of Jihād and Military ExpeditionsChapter: Invoking Allah in favor of men and women to be among those who engage in Jihād and attain martyrdom; Hadīth no. 2788, 2789.Sahīh MuslimBook of RulershipChapter: Merit of military campaigning by sea; Hadīth no. 1912.Sunan Abu DāwudBook of JihādChapter: Merit of military campaigning by sea; Hadīth no. 2490.Jāmi' At-TirmidhiBook of the merits of Jihād as reported from the Messenger of Allah (PBUH)Chapter: What is reported on military campaigning by sea battling; Hadīth no. 1645.Sunan An-Nasā'iBook of JihādChapter: Merit of military campaigning by sea; Hadīth no. 3171.Sunan Ibn MājahBook of JihādChapter: Merit of military campaigning by sea; Hadīth no. 2776.

Book of Jihād and Military Expeditions

Chapter: Invoking Allah in favor of men and women to be among those who engage in Jihād and attain martyrdom; Hadīth no. 2788, 2789.

Sahīh Muslim

Book of Rulership

Chapter: Merit of military campaigning by sea; Hadīth no. 1912.

Sunan Abu Dāwud

Book of Jihād

Chapter: Merit of military campaigning by sea; Hadīth no. 2490.

Jāmi' At-Tirmidhi

Book of the merits of Jihād as reported from the Messenger of Allah (PBUH)

Chapter: What is reported on military campaigning by sea battling; Hadīth no. 1645.

Sunan An-Nasā'i

Book of Jihād

Chapter: Merit of military campaigning by sea; Hadīth no. 3171.

Sunan Ibn Mājah

Book of Jihād

Chapter: Merit of military campaigning by sea; Hadīth no. 2776.

Book of Hunting and Slaughtering, and Animals that are Lawful to Eat

Chapter: Hunting by trained hounds.

'Adiyy ibn Hātim (may Allah be pleased with him) reported: "I asked the Prophet (may Allah's peace and blessings be upon him) about the game killed by a Mi'rād (a sharp-edged piece of wood or a piece of wood fitted with a sharp piece of iron used for hunting). He said: 'If the game is killed with the sharp edge, eat it, but if it is killed with the broad side, then it was beaten to death (thus unlawful to eat).' I asked him about the game killed by a trained hound. He said: 'If the hound catches the game for you, eat it, for killing the game by the hound is like its slaughtering. But if you see with your hound or hounds another one, and you are afraid that it might have shared in hunting the game with your hound and killed it, then you should not eat of it, because you have mentioned Allah's name on (sending) your hound only, but you have not mentioned it on the other hound.'"

Sahīh Al-BukhāriBook of Slaughtering and HuntingChapter: Mentioning Allah's name when hunting; Hadīth no. 5475.Sahīh MuslimBook of Hunting, Slaughtering and Animals Lawful to EatChapter: Hunting by trained hounds; Hadīth no. 1929.Sunan Abu DāwudBook of HuntingChapter: Regarding hunting; Hadīth no. 2847.Jāmi' At-TirmidhiBook of Hunting as reported from the Messenger of Allah (PBUH)Chapter: What is reported on what may be eaten of animals caught by a hound and what may not be eaten; Hadīth no. 1465.Sunan An-Nasā'iBook of Hunting and SlaughteringChapter: The command to mention Allah's name when hunting; Hadīth no. 4263.Sunan Ibn MājahBook of HuntingChapter: Game caught by a hound; Hadīth no. 3208.

Book of Slaughtering and Hunting

Chapter: Mentioning Allah's name when hunting; Hadīth no. 5475.

Sahīh Muslim

Book of Hunting, Slaughtering and Animals Lawful to Eat

Chapter: Hunting by trained hounds; Hadīth no. 1929.

Sunan Abu Dāwud

Book of Hunting

Chapter: Regarding hunting; Hadīth no. 2847.

Jāmi' At-Tirmidhi

Book of Hunting as reported from the Messenger of Allah (PBUH)

Chapter: What is reported on what may be eaten of animals caught by a hound and what may not be eaten; Hadīth no. 1465.

Sunan An-Nasā'i

Book of Hunting and Slaughtering

Chapter: The command to mention Allah's name when hunting; Hadīth no. 4263.

Sunan Ibn Mājah

Book of Hunting

Chapter: Game caught by a hound; Hadīth no. 3208.

Abu Tha'labah al-Khushani (may Allah be pleased with him) reported: "I said: 'O Prophet of Allah, we live in the land of the People of the Book; can we eat in their utensils? It is also a land of game and I hunt the game with my bow, with my untrained hound, and with my trained hound. What is lawful for me to eat?' He said: 'As for what you mentioned about the utensils of the People of the Book, if you can find other utensils, do not use theirs, but if you cannot find (other than theirs), wash their utensils and eat in them. If you hunt an animal with your bow after mentioning Allah's name, eat it. If you hunt something with your trained hound after mentioning Allah's name, eat it. If you hunt something with your untrained hound and manage to slaughter it (before it dies), eat it.'"

Sahīh Al-BukhāriBook of Slaughtering and HuntingChapter: Hunting with a bow; Hadīth no. 5478.Sahīh MuslimBook of Hunting, Slaughtering and Animals Lawful to EatChapter: Hunting by trained hounds; Hadīth no. 1930.Sunan Abu DāwudBook of HuntingChapter: Hunting; Hadīth no. 2855.Jāmi' At-TirmidhiBook of Foods as reported from the Messenger of Allah (PBUH)Chapter: What is reported on eating in the disbelievers' utensils; Hadīth no. 1797.Sunan An-Nasā'iBook of Hunting and SlaughteringChapter: If the hunted game becomes rotten; Hadīth no. 4303.Sunan Ibn MājahBook of JihādChapter: Eating in the disbelievers' utensils; Hadīth no. 2831.

Book of Slaughtering and Hunting

Chapter: Hunting with a bow; Hadīth no. 5478.

Sahīh Muslim

Book of Hunting, Slaughtering and Animals Lawful to Eat

Chapter: Hunting by trained hounds; Hadīth no. 1930.

Sunan Abu Dāwud

Book of Hunting

Chapter: Hunting; Hadīth no. 2855.

Jāmi' At-Tirmidhi

Book of Foods as reported from the Messenger of Allah (PBUH)

Chapter: What is reported on eating in the disbelievers' utensils; Hadīth no. 1797.

Sunan An-Nasā'i

Book of Hunting and Slaughtering

Chapter: If the hunted game becomes rotten; Hadīth no. 4303.

Sunan Ibn Mājah

Book of Jihād

Chapter: Eating in the disbelievers' utensils; Hadīth no. 2831.

Chapter: The prohibition of eating beasts of prey with fangs
and birds with talons.

Abu Tha'labah (may Allah be pleased with him) reported that the Messenger of Allah (may Allah's peace and blessings be upon him) prohibited eating any fanged beast of prey.

Sahīh Al-BukhāriBook of Slaughtering and HuntingChapter: Eating fanged beasts of prey; Hadīth no. 5530.Sahīh MuslimBook of Hunting, Slaughtering and Animals Lawful to EatChapter: The prohibition of eating beasts of prey with fangs and birds with talons; Hadīth no. 1932.Sunan Abu DāwudBook of FoodsChapter: The prohibition of eating beasts of prey; Hadīth no. 3802.Jāmi' At-TirmidhiBook of Foods as reported from the Messenger of Allah (PBUH)Chapter: What is reported on the dislike of eating all animals with fangs and all birds with talons; Hadīth no. 1477.Sunan An-Nasā'iBook of Hunting and SlaughteringChapter: The prohibition of eating beasts of prey; Hadīth no. 4325.Sunan Ibn MājahBook of JihādChapter: Eating fanged beasts of prey; Hadīth no. 3232.

Book of Slaughtering and Hunting

Chapter: Eating fanged beasts of prey; Hadīth no. 5530.

Sahīh Muslim

Book of Hunting, Slaughtering and Animals Lawful to Eat

Chapter: The prohibition of eating beasts of prey with fangs and birds with talons; Hadīth no. 1932.

Sunan Abu Dāwud

Book of Foods

Chapter: The prohibition of eating beasts of prey; Hadīth no. 3802.

Jāmi' At-Tirmidhi

Book of Foods as reported from the Messenger of Allah (PBUH)

Chapter: What is reported on the dislike of eating all animals with fangs and all birds with talons; Hadīth no. 1477.

Sunan An-Nasā'i

Book of Hunting and Slaughtering

Chapter: The prohibition of eating beasts of prey; Hadīth no. 4325.

Sunan Ibn Mājah

Book of Jihād

Chapter: Eating fanged beasts of prey; Hadīth no. 3232.

Chapter: The permissibility of eating dead animals of the sea.

Jābir (may Allah be pleased with him) reported: "We set out in the army of Al-Khabat and Abu 'Ubaydah was the commander of the troops. We were struck with severe hunger and the sea threw out a dead whale the like of which we had never seen. It was called Al-'Anbar (sperm whale). We ate of it for half a month. Abu 'Ubaydah took (and fixed) one of its bones and a rider passed underneath it (without touching it). (Jābir added:) Abu 'Ubaydah said (to us): 'Eat (of that fish).' When we arrived at Madinah, we informed the Prophet (may Allah's peace and blessings be upon him) about that, and he said: 'Eat, for it is provision that Allah brought out for you. Feed us if you have some of it.' So, some of them gave him (of that fish) and he ate it."

Sahīh Al-BukhāriBook of Military ExpeditionsChapter: Battle of the sea-coast, when they were lying in wait for the caravans of Quraysh and their commander was Abu 'Ubaydah ibn al-Jarrāh (may Allah be pleased with him); Hadīth no. 4362.Sahīh MuslimBook of Hunting, Slaughtering and Animals Lawful to EatChapter: The permissibility of eating dead animals of the sea; Hadīth no. 1935.Sunan Abu DāwudBook of FoodsChapter: Regarding sea animals; Hadīth no. 3840.Jāmi' At-TirmidhiChapter: Description of the Day of Judgment, Raqā'iq (heart-softening reports), and religious prudence as reported from the Messenger of Allah (PBUH)Chapter: Hadīth no. 2475.Sunan An-Nasā'iBook of Hunting and SlaughteringChapter: The dead animals of the sea; Hadīth no. 4353Sunan Ibn MājahBook of AscetismChapter: Lifestyle of the Companions of the Prophet (PBUH); Hadīth no. 4159.

Book of Military Expeditions

Chapter: Battle of the sea-coast, when they were lying in wait for the caravans of Quraysh and their commander was Abu 'Ubaydah ibn al-Jarrāh (may Allah be pleased with him); Hadīth no. 4362.

Sahīh Muslim

Book of Hunting, Slaughtering and Animals Lawful to Eat

Chapter: The permissibility of eating dead animals of the sea; Hadīth no. 1935.

Sunan Abu Dāwud

Book of Foods

Chapter: Regarding sea animals; Hadīth no. 3840.

Jāmi' At-Tirmidhi

Chapter: Description of the Day of Judgment, Raqā'iq (heart-softening reports), and religious prudence as reported from the Messenger of Allah (PBUH)

Chapter: Hadīth no. 2475.

Sunan An-Nasā'i

Book of Hunting and Slaughtering

Chapter: The dead animals of the sea; Hadīth no. 4353

Sunan Ibn Mājah

Book of Ascetism

Chapter: Lifestyle of the Companions of the Prophet (PBUH); Hadīth no. 4159.

Chapter: Regarding eating horse meat.

Jābir ibn 'Abdullāh (may Allah be pleased with him) reported: "The Prophet (may Allah's peace and blessings be upon him) forbade eating the flesh of donkeys and permitted eating the flesh of horses on the Day of Khaybar."

Sahīh Al-BukhāriBook of Slaughtering and HuntingChapter: Horse meat; Hadīth no. 5520.Sahīh MuslimBook of Hunting, Slaughtering and Animals Lawful to EatChapter: Regarding eating horse meat; Hadīth no. 1941.Sunan Abu DāwudBook of FoodsChapter: Regarding eating horse meat; Hadīth no. 3788.Jāmi' At-TirmidhiBook of Foods as reported from the Messenger of Allah (PBUH)Chapter: What is reported on eating horse meat; Hadīth no. 1793.Sunan An-Nasā'iBook of Hunting and SlaughteringChapter: Permission given for eating horse meat; Hadīth no. 4327.Sunan Ibn MājahBook of SlaughteringChapter: Horse meat; Hadīth no. 3191.

Book of Slaughtering and Hunting

Chapter: Horse meat; Hadīth no. 5520.

Sahīh Muslim

Book of Hunting, Slaughtering and Animals Lawful to Eat

Chapter: Regarding eating horse meat; Hadīth no. 1941.

Sunan Abu Dāwud

Book of Foods

Chapter: Regarding eating horse meat; Hadīth no. 3788.

Jāmi' At-Tirmidhi

Book of Foods as reported from the Messenger of Allah (PBUH)

Chapter: What is reported on eating horse meat; Hadīth no. 1793.

Sunan An-Nasā'i

Book of Hunting and Slaughtering

Chapter: Permission given for eating horse meat; Hadīth no. 4327.

Sunan Ibn Mājah

Book of Slaughtering

Chapter: Horse meat; Hadīth no. 3191.

Chapter: The permissibility of eating rabbits.

Anas (may Allah be pleased with him) reported: "We provoked a rabbit at Marr Azh-Zhahrān. My companions chased it till they got tired. But I alone ran after it and caught it and brought it to Abu Talhah. He slaughtered it and sent its hip or two thighs to Allah's Messenger (may Allah's peace and blessings be upon him). (The narrator confirms that he sent two thighs), and he accepted it." The sub-narrator asked Anas: "And he ate from it?" Anas replied: "And he ate from it." Then he said: "He accepted it."

Sahīh Al-BukhāriBook of Gift-giving, its Merit, and Encouraging itChapter: Accepting the gift of game; Hadīth no. 2572.Sahīh MuslimBook of Hunting, Slaughtering and Animals Lawful to EatChapter: The permissibility of eating rabbits; Hadīth no. 1953.Sunan Abu DāwudBook of FoodsChapter: Regarding eating rabbits; Hadīth no. 3791.Jāmi' At-TirmidhiBook of Foods as reported from the Messenger of Allah (PBUH)Chapter: What is reported on eating rabbits; Hadīth no. 1789.Sunan An-Nasā'iBook of Hunting and SlaughteringChapter: Rabbits; Hadīth no. 4312.Sunan Ibn MājahBook of HuntingChapter: Rabbits; Hadīth no. 3243.

Book of Gift-giving, its Merit, and Encouraging it

Chapter: Accepting the gift of game; Hadīth no. 2572.

Sahīh Muslim

Book of Hunting, Slaughtering and Animals Lawful to Eat

Chapter: The permissibility of eating rabbits; Hadīth no. 1953.

Sunan Abu Dāwud

Book of Foods

Chapter: Regarding eating rabbits; Hadīth no. 3791.

Jāmi' At-Tirmidhi

Book of Foods as reported from the Messenger of Allah (PBUH)

Chapter: What is reported on eating rabbits; Hadīth no. 1789.

Sunan An-Nasā'i

Book of Hunting and Slaughtering

Chapter: Rabbits; Hadīth no. 4312.

Sunan Ibn Mājah

Book of Hunting

Chapter: Rabbits; Hadīth no. 3243.

Book of Udhiyahs (Sacrifices)

Chapter: It is recommended to offer Udhiyah, and slaughter it directly without delegation, and it is recommended to mention Allah's name on it and recite Takbīr

Anas ibn Mālik (may Allah be pleased with him) reported: "The Prophet (may Allah's peace and blessings be upon him) sacrificed two black and white horned rams, which he slaughtered with his own hand. He said: 'Bismillah (in the name of Allah), Allahu Akbar (Allah is the Greatest)' and put his foot on their necks."

Sahīh Al-BukhāriBook of Sacrificial AnimalsChapter: Reciting Takbīr upon slaughtering. Hadīth no.5565.Sahīh MuslimBook of Sacrificial AnimalsChapter: It is recommended to offer Udhiyah (sacrificial animal), to slaughter it directly without delegation, to mention Allah's name and recite Takbīr on it; Hadīth no. 1966.Sunan Abu DāwudBook of Sacrificial AnimalsChapter: What is recommended of sacrificial animals; Hadīth no. 2794.Jāmi' At-TirmidhiBook of Sacrificial Animals as reported from the Messenger of Allah (PBUH)Chapter: What is reported on sacrificing two rams; Hadīth no. 1494.Sunan An-Nasā'iBook of Sacrificial AnimalsChapter: Rams; Hadīth no. 4387.Sunan Ibn MājahBook of Sacrificial AnimalsChapter: The Udhiyahs (sacrificial animals) of the Messenger of Allah (PBUH); Hadīth no. 3120.

Book of Sacrificial Animals

Chapter: Reciting Takbīr upon slaughtering. Hadīth no.5565.

Sahīh Muslim

Book of Sacrificial Animals

Chapter: It is recommended to offer Udhiyah (sacrificial animal), to slaughter it directly without delegation, to mention Allah's name and recite Takbīr on it; Hadīth no. 1966.

Sunan Abu Dāwud

Book of Sacrificial Animals

Chapter: What is recommended of sacrificial animals; Hadīth no. 2794.

Jāmi' At-Tirmidhi

Book of Sacrificial Animals as reported from the Messenger of Allah (PBUH)

Chapter: What is reported on sacrificing two rams; Hadīth no. 1494.

Sunan An-Nasā'i

Book of Sacrificial Animals

Chapter: Rams; Hadīth no. 4387.

Sunan Ibn Mājah

Book of Sacrificial Animals

Chapter: The Udhiyahs (sacrificial animals) of the Messenger of Allah (PBUH); Hadīth no. 3120.

Chapter: The permissibility of slaughtering by any tool that causes blood to flow

except for a tooth, nail, and all other bones.

Rāfi' ibn Khadīj (may Allah be pleased with him) reported: "We were with the Prophet (PBUH) in Dhul-Hulayfah when the people were stricken by hunger. They got camels and sheep as war booty." He added: "The Prophet (PBUH) was behind the people. They hurried and slaughtered the animals and put their meat in pots and started cooking it. (When the Prophet came) he ordered the pots to be overturned then he distributed the animals (of the booty), regarding ten sheep as equal to one camel. One of the camels fled and the people ran after it till they were exhausted. There were only a few horses with them. A man threw an arrow at the camel, and Allah stopped the camel with it. The Prophet (PBUH) said: 'Some of these animals are like wild animals, so if you lose control over one of these animals, treat it in this way.' Before distributing them among the soldiers, my grandfather said: 'We may meet the enemy soon and we have no knives; can we slaughter the animals with reeds?' The Prophet (PBUH) said: 'Use whatever causes blood to flow, and eat the animals if the name of Allah has been mentioned before slaughtering them. Do not slaughter with teeth or claws and I will tell you why: It is because teeth are bones and claws are the knives of Abyssinians.'"

Sahīh Al-BukhāriBook of PartnershipChapter: Distributing sheep; Hadīth no. 2488.Sahīh MuslimBook of Sacrificial AnimalsChapter: The permissibility of slaughtering by any tool that causes blood to flow, except for a tooth, nail, and all other bones; Hadīth no. 1968.Sunan Abu DāwudBook of Sacrificial AnimalsChapter: Slaughtering with Marwah (a sharp-edged white stone); Hadīth no. 2821.Jāmi' At-TirmidhiBook of Rulings and Lessons as reported from the Messenger of Allah (PBUH)Chapter: What is reported on slaughtering by reeds and other things; Hadīth no. 1491.Sunan An-Nasā'iBook of Hunting and SlaughteringChapter: Domesticated animals that turn wild; Hadīth no. 4297.Sunan Ibn MājahBook of Sacrificial AnimalsChapter: How many sheep are equivalent to one camel; Hadīth no. 3137.

Book of Partnership

Chapter: Distributing sheep; Hadīth no. 2488.

Sahīh Muslim

Book of Sacrificial Animals

Chapter: The permissibility of slaughtering by any tool that causes blood to flow, except for a tooth, nail, and all other bones; Hadīth no. 1968.

Sunan Abu Dāwud

Book of Sacrificial Animals

Chapter: Slaughtering with Marwah (a sharp-edged white stone); Hadīth no. 2821.

Jāmi' At-Tirmidhi

Book of Rulings and Lessons as reported from the Messenger of Allah (PBUH)

Chapter: What is reported on slaughtering by reeds and other things; Hadīth no. 1491.

Sunan An-Nasā'i

Book of Hunting and Slaughtering

Chapter: Domesticated animals that turn wild; Hadīth no. 4297.

Sunan Ibn Mājah

Book of Sacrificial Animals

Chapter: How many sheep are equivalent to one camel; Hadīth no. 3137.

Book of Fara' and 'Atīrah (Sacrificial animals dedicated to idols)

Abu Hurayrah (may Allah be pleased with him) reported that the Prophet (may Allah's peace and blessings be upon him) said: "Neither Fara' nor 'Atīrah (is permissible)." Fara' was the first offspring (of an animal) which the pagans used to offer (as a sacrifice) to their idols. 'Atīrah was (an animal which was to be slaughtered) during the month of Rajab.

Sahīh Al-BukhāriBook of 'Aqīqah (Sacrificial Animal Offered for the Occasion of Birth)Chapter: Fara'; Hadīth no. 5473.Sahīh MuslimBook of Sacrificial AnimalsChapter: Fara' and 'Atīrah; Hadīth no. 1976.Sunan Abu DāwudBook of Sacrificial AnimalsChapter: Regarding 'Atīrah; Hadīth no. 2831.Jāmi' At-TirmidhiBook of Sacrificial Animals as reported from the Messenger of Allah (PBUH)Chapter: What is reported on Fara' and 'Atīrah; Hadīth no. 1512.Sunan An-Nasā'iBook of Fara' and 'Atīrah;Hadīth no. 4222.Sunan Ibn MājahBook of SlaughteringChapter: Fara' and 'Atīrah; Hadīth no. 3168.

Book of 'Aqīqah (Sacrificial Animal Offered for the Occasion of Birth)

Chapter: Fara'; Hadīth no. 5473.

Sahīh Muslim

Book of Sacrificial Animals

Chapter: Fara' and 'Atīrah; Hadīth no. 1976.

Sunan Abu Dāwud

Book of Sacrificial Animals

Chapter: Regarding 'Atīrah; Hadīth no. 2831.

Jāmi' At-Tirmidhi

Book of Sacrificial Animals as reported from the Messenger of Allah (PBUH)

Chapter: What is reported on Fara' and 'Atīrah; Hadīth no. 1512.

Sunan An-Nasā'i

Book of Fara' and 'Atīrah;

Hadīth no. 4222.

Sunan Ibn Mājah

Book of Slaughtering

Chapter: Fara' and 'Atīrah; Hadīth no. 3168.

Book of Drinks

Chapter: The dislike of soaking dates and raisins together.

Jābir (may Allah be pleased with him) reported: "The Prophet (may Allah's peace and blessings be upon him) forbade (drinks prepared from) raisins, dates, unripe dates, and fresh ripe dates."

Sahīh Al-BukhāriBook of DrinksChapter: Those who held that unripe-date drink and ripe-date drink should not be mixed if it causes intoxication, and should not be cooked together; Hadīth no. 5601.Sahīh MuslimBook of DrinksChapter: The dislike of soaking dates and raisins together; Hadīth no. 1986.Sunan Abu DāwudBook of DrinksChapter: Regarding mixing the two items; Hadīth no. 3703.Jāmi' At-TirmidhiBook of Drinks as reported from the Messenger of Allah (PBUH)Chapter: What is reported on mixing unripe dates with ripe fresh dates (in one drink); Hadīth no. 1876.Sunan An-Nasā'iBook of DrinksChapter: Mixing unripe dates with ripe fresh dates (in one drink); Hadīth no. 5554.Sunan Ibn MājahBook of DrinksChapter: Forbidding mixing the two items (in one drink); Hadīth no. 3395.

Book of Drinks

Chapter: Those who held that unripe-date drink and ripe-date drink should not be mixed if it causes intoxication, and should not be cooked together; Hadīth no. 5601.

Sahīh Muslim

Book of Drinks

Chapter: The dislike of soaking dates and raisins together; Hadīth no. 1986.

Sunan Abu Dāwud

Book of Drinks

Chapter: Regarding mixing the two items; Hadīth no. 3703.

Jāmi' At-Tirmidhi

Book of Drinks as reported from the Messenger of Allah (PBUH)

Chapter: What is reported on mixing unripe dates with ripe fresh dates (in one drink); Hadīth no. 1876.

Sunan An-Nasā'i

Book of Drinks

Chapter: Mixing unripe dates with ripe fresh dates (in one drink); Hadīth no. 5554.

Sunan Ibn Mājah

Book of Drinks

Chapter: Forbidding mixing the two items (in one drink); Hadīth no. 3395.

Chapter: Stating that every intoxicant is an alcoholic drink and every alcoholic drink is unlawful.

'Ā'ishah (may Allah be pleased with her) reported: "The Messenger of Allah (may Allah's peace and blessings be upon him) was asked about Bit', which is a drink prepared from honey that the people of Yemen used to drink. The Messenger of Allah (may Allah's peace and blessings be upon him) said: 'Any drink that intoxicates is unlawful.'"

Sahīh Al-BukhāriBook of DrinksChapter: Alcoholic drink prepared from honey, known as Bit'; Hadīth no. 5586.Sahīh MuslimBook of DrinksChapter: Stating that every intoxicant is an alcoholic drink and every alcoholic drink is unlawful; Hadīth no. 2001.Sunan Abu DāwudBook of DrinksChapter: Forbidding intoxicants; Hadīth no. 3682.Jāmi' At-TirmidhiBook of Drinks as reported from the Messenger of Allah (PBUH)Chapter: What is reported on: Every intoxicant is unlawful; Hadīth no. 1863.Sunan An-Nasā'iBook of DrinksChapter: The prohibition of every drink that causes intoxication; Hadīth no. 5592.Sunan Ibn MājahBook of DrinksChapter: Every intoxicant is unlawful; Hadīth no. 3386.

Book of Drinks

Chapter: Alcoholic drink prepared from honey, known as Bit'; Hadīth no. 5586.

Sahīh Muslim

Book of Drinks

Chapter: Stating that every intoxicant is an alcoholic drink and every alcoholic drink is unlawful; Hadīth no. 2001.

Sunan Abu Dāwud

Book of Drinks

Chapter: Forbidding intoxicants; Hadīth no. 3682.

Jāmi' At-Tirmidhi

Book of Drinks as reported from the Messenger of Allah (PBUH)

Chapter: What is reported on: Every intoxicant is unlawful; Hadīth no. 1863.

Sunan An-Nasā'i

Book of Drinks

Chapter: The prohibition of every drink that causes intoxication; Hadīth no. 5592.

Sunan Ibn Mājah

Book of Drinks

Chapter: Every intoxicant is unlawful; Hadīth no. 3386.

'Abdullah ibn 'Umar (may Allah be pleased with him) reported that the Messenger of Allah (may Allah's peace and blessings be upon him) said: "Whoever drinks alcohol in the life of this world and does not repent thereof will be deprived of it in the Hereafter."

Sahīh Al-BukhāriBook of DrinksChapter: The statement of Allah Almighty: {indeed, intoxicants, gambling, [sacrificing on] stone altars [to other than Allah], and divining arrows are but defilement from the work of Satan, so avoid it that you may be successful.}; Hadīth no. 5575.Sahīh MuslimBook of DrinksChapter: Stating that every intoxicant is an alcoholic drink and every alcoholic drink is unlawful; Hadīth no. 2003.Sunan Abu DāwudBook of DrinksChapter: Forbidding intoxicants; Hadīth no. 3679.Jāmi' At-TirmidhiBook of Drinks as reported from the Messenger of Allah (PBUH)Chapter: What is reported on the one who drinks alcohol; Hadīth no. 1861.Sunan An-Nasā'iBook of DrinksChapter: Repentance of one who drinks alcohol; Hadīth no .5671.Sunan Ibn MājahBook of DrinksChapter: Whoever drinks alcohol in the life of this world will not drink it in the Hereafter; Hadīth no. 3373.

Book of Drinks

Chapter: The statement of Allah Almighty: {indeed, intoxicants, gambling, [sacrificing on] stone altars [to other than Allah], and divining arrows are but defilement from the work of Satan, so avoid it that you may be successful.}; Hadīth no. 5575.

Sahīh Muslim

Book of Drinks

Chapter: Stating that every intoxicant is an alcoholic drink and every alcoholic drink is unlawful; Hadīth no. 2003.

Sunan Abu Dāwud

Book of Drinks

Chapter: Forbidding intoxicants; Hadīth no. 3679.

Jāmi' At-Tirmidhi

Book of Drinks as reported from the Messenger of Allah (PBUH)

Chapter: What is reported on the one who drinks alcohol; Hadīth no. 1861.

Sunan An-Nasā'i

Book of Drinks

Chapter: Repentance of one who drinks alcohol; Hadīth no .5671.

Sunan Ibn Mājah

Book of Drinks

Chapter: Whoever drinks alcohol in the life of this world will not drink it in the Hereafter; Hadīth no. 3373.

Book of Dress and Adornment

Chapter: The prohibition of using utensils made of gold and silver for both men and woman, the prohibition of wearing a gold ring or silk clothes for men and their permissibility for women, and the permissibility for a man to wear clothes that have silk strips as long as they do not exceed the width of four fingers.

'Abdur-Rahmān ibn Abi Layla reported that they once were with Hudhayfah who asked for water and a Magian brought him water. When he put the cup in his hand, he threw it at him and said: "Had I not forbidden him to do so more than once or twice," as if wanting to say: "I would not have done so," adding, "but I heard the Prophet (may Allah's peace and blessings be upon him) saying: 'Do not wear silk or brocade, and do not drink in vessels of gold and silver, and do not eat in plates made of them, for these are for them (the disbelievers) in this world and for us in the Hereafter.'"

Sahīh Al-BukhāriBook of FoodsChapter: Eating in utensils decorated with silver; Hadīth no. 5426.Sahīh MuslimBook of Dress and AdornmentChapter: The prohibition of using utensils made of gold and silver for both men and woman, the prohibition of wearing a gold ring or silk clothes for men and their permissibility for women, and the permissibility for a man to wear clothes that have silk strips as long as they do not exceed the width of four fingers; Hadīth no. 2067.Sunan Abu DāwudBook of DrinksChapter: Drinking in utensils made of gold and silver; Hadīth no. 3723.Jāmi' At-TirmidhiBook of Drinks as reported from the Messenger of Allah (PBUH)Chapter: What is reported on the dislike of drinking in utensils made of gold and silver; Hadīth no. 1878.Sunan An-Nasā'iBook of AdornmentChapter: Mentioning the forbiddance of wearing brocade; Hadīth no. 5301.Sunan Ibn MājahBook of DrinksChapter: Drinking in utensils made of silver; Hadīth no. 3414.

Book of Foods

Chapter: Eating in utensils decorated with silver; Hadīth no. 5426.

Sahīh Muslim

Book of Dress and Adornment

Chapter: The prohibition of using utensils made of gold and silver for both men and woman, the prohibition of wearing a gold ring or silk clothes for men and their permissibility for women, and the permissibility for a man to wear clothes that have silk strips as long as they do not exceed the width of four fingers; Hadīth no. 2067.

Sunan Abu Dāwud

Book of Drinks

Chapter: Drinking in utensils made of gold and silver; Hadīth no. 3723.

Jāmi' At-Tirmidhī

Book of Drinks as reported from the Messenger of Allah (PBUH)

Chapter: What is reported on the dislike of drinking in utensils made of gold and silver; Hadīth no. 1878.

Sunan An-Nasā'i

Book of Adornment

Chapter: Mentioning the forbiddance of wearing brocade; Hadīth no. 5301.

Sunan Ibn Mājah

Book of Drinks

Chapter: Drinking in utensils made of silver; Hadīth no. 3414.

Abu 'Uthmān an-Nahdi (may Allah have mercy upon him) said: "A letter from 'Umar came to us while we were in Azerbaijān in the company of 'Utbah ibn Farqad. It stated that Allah's Messenger (may Allah's peace and blessings be upon him) forbade (wearing) silk but to the extent of these two fingers (joining his index and middle fingers). We at once understood by these words that he meant (silk) patterns (on the cloth)."

Sahīh Al-BukhāriBook of ClothingChapter: Wearing silk for men and using it as a spread for sitting and how much of it is permissible; Hadīth no. 5828.Sahīh MuslimBook of Dress and AdornmentChapter: Prohibition of using utensils made of gold and silver for both men and woman, the prohibition of wearing a gold ring or silk clothes for men and their permissibility for women, and the permissibility for a man to wear clothes that have silk strips as long as they do not exceed the width of four fingers; Hadīth no. 2069.Sunan Abu DāwudBook of ClothingChapter: What is reported on wearing silk; Hadīth no. 4042.Jāmi' At-TirmidhīBook of Clothing as reported from the Messenger of Allah (PBUH)Chapter: What is reported on silk and gold; Hadīth no. 1721.Sunan An-Nasā'iBook of AdornmentChapter: Concession to wear silk; Hadīth no. 5312.Sunan Ibn MājahBook of JihādChapter: Wearing silk and brocade in battle; Hadīth no. 2820.

Book of Clothing

Chapter: Wearing silk for men and using it as a spread for sitting and how much of it is permissible; Hadīth no. 5828.

Sahīh Muslim

Book of Dress and Adornment

Chapter: Prohibition of using utensils made of gold and silver for both men and woman, the prohibition of wearing a gold ring or silk clothes for men and their permissibility for women, and the permissibility for a man to wear clothes that have silk strips as long as they do not exceed the width of four fingers; Hadīth no. 2069.

Sunan Abu Dāwud

Book of Clothing

Chapter: What is reported on wearing silk; Hadīth no. 4042.

Jāmi' At-Tirmidhī

Book of Clothing as reported from the Messenger of Allah (PBUH)

Chapter: What is reported on silk and gold; Hadīth no. 1721.

Sunan An-Nasā'ī

Book of Adornment

Chapter: Concession to wear silk; Hadīth no. 5312.

Sunan Ibn Mājah

Book of Jihād

Chapter: Wearing silk and brocade in battle; Hadīth no. 2820.

Chapter: Permissibility of wearing silk for a man who suffers itchy skin or the like.

Anas (may Allah be pleased with him) reported that the Prophet (may Allah's peace and blessings be upon him) allowed 'Abdur-Rahmān ibn 'Awf and Az-Zubayr to wear silk shirts because of an itch that they suffered.Sahīh Al-BukhāriBook of Jihād and Military ExpeditionsChapter: Wearing silk in battle; Hadīth no. 2919.Sahīh MuslimBook of Dress and AdornmentChapter: Permissibility of wearing silk for a man who suffers itchy skin or the like; Hadīth no. 2076.Sunan Abu DāwudBook of ClothingChapter: Wearing silk for a valid excuse; Hadīth no. 4056.Jāmi' At-TirmidhiBook of Clothing as reported from the Messenger of Allah (PBUH)Chapter: What is reported on the concession to wear silk in battle; Hadīth no. 1722.Sunan An-Nasā'iBook of AdornmentChapter: The concession to wear silk; Hadīth no. 5310.Sunan Ibn MājahBook of ClothingChapter: Who is given concession to wear silk; Hadīth no. 3592.

Sahīh Al-Bukhāri

Book of Jihād and Military Expeditions

Chapter: Wearing silk in battle; Hadīth no. 2919.

Sahīh Muslim

Book of Dress and Adornment

Chapter: Permissibility of wearing silk for a man who suffers itchy skin or the like; Hadīth no. 2076.

Sunan Abu Dāwud

Book of Clothing

Chapter: Wearing silk for a valid excuse; Hadīth no. 4056.

Jāmi' At-Tirmidhī

Book of Clothing as reported from the Messenger of Allah (PBUH)

Chapter: What is reported on the concession to wear silk in battle; Hadīth no. 1722.

Sunan An-Nasā'ī

Book of Adornment

Chapter: The concession to wear silk; Hadīth no. 5310.

Sunan Ibn Mājah

Book of Clothing

Chapter: Who is given concession to wear silk; Hadīth no. 3592.

Chapter: Prohibition of dragging one's garment out of pride and stating the extent to which it is allowed to reach down, and what is recommended in this regard.

'Abdullāh ibn 'Umar (may Allah be pleased with him) reported that the Prophet (may Allah's peace and blessings be upon him) said: "Whoever drags his garment (behind him) out of conceit, Allah will not look at him on the Day of Resurrection." Abu Bakr (may Allah be pleased with him) said: "O Messenger of Allah, one side of my Izār (waist sheet) keeps sliding down if I do not take care of it." The Prophet (may Allah's peace and blessings be upon him) said: "You are not of those who do it out of conceit."

Sahīh Al-BukhāriBook of ClothingChapter: One who drags his Izār without conceit; Hadīth no. 5784.Sahīh MuslimBook of Dress and AdornmentChapter: Prohibition of dragging one's garment out of conceit and stating the extent to which it is allowed to reach down, and what is recommended in this regard; Hadīth no. 2085.Sunan Abu DāwudBook of ClothingChapter: What is reported on letting the Izār reach below the ankles; Hadīth no. 4085.Jāmi' At-TirmidhiBook of Clothing as reported from the Messenger of Allah (PBUH)Chapter: What is reported on the dislike of dragging one's Izār (behind him); Hadīth no. 1730.Sunan An-Nasā'iBook of AdornmentChapter: The strict warning against dragging the Izār; Hadīth no. 5327.Sunan Ibn MājahBook of ClothingChapter: Whoever drags his garment out of conceit; Hadīth no. 3569.

Book of Clothing

Chapter: One who drags his Izār without conceit; Hadīth no. 5784.

Sahīh Muslim

Book of Dress and Adornment

Chapter: Prohibition of dragging one's garment out of conceit and stating the extent to which it is allowed to reach down, and what is recommended in this regard; Hadīth no. 2085.

Sunan Abu Dāwud

Book of Clothing

Chapter: What is reported on letting the Izār reach below the ankles; Hadīth no. 4085.

Jāmi' At-Tirmidhi

Book of Clothing as reported from the Messenger of Allah (PBUH)

Chapter: What is reported on the dislike of dragging one's Izār (behind him); Hadīth no. 1730.

Sunan An-Nasā'i

Book of Adornment

Chapter: The strict warning against dragging the Izār; Hadīth no. 5327.

Sunan Ibn Mājah

Book of Clothing

Chapter: Whoever drags his garment out of conceit; Hadīth no. 3569.

Chapter: Throwing away the gold ring.

Ibn 'Umar (may Allah be pleased with him) reported that the Messenger of Allah (may Allah's peace and blessings be upon him) wore a ring made of gold or silver with its stone towards the palm of his hand. He had the words "Muhammad the Messenger of Allah" engraved on it. So the people started wearing rings like him. When he saw them doing that, he threw it away and said: "I will never wear it again." He then wore a silver (signet) ring, whereupon the people too started wearing silver rings. Ibn 'Umar added: "After the Prophet (may Allah's peace and blessings be upon him), Abu Bakr wore the ring then 'Umar then 'Uthmān wore it till it fell from 'Uthmān in the Arīs well."

Sahīh Al-BukhāriBook of ClothingChapter: Silver rings; Hadīth no. 5866.Sahīh MuslimBook of Dress and AdornmentChapter: Throwing away the gold ring; Hadīth no. 2091.Sunan Abu DāwudBook of RingsChapter: What is reported on having a (signet) ring; Hadīth no. 4218.Jāmi' At-TirmidhiBook of Clothing as reported from the Messenger of Allah (PBUH)Chapter: What is reported on wearing a ring on the right hand; Hadīth no. 1741.Sunan An-Nasā'iBook of AdornmentChapter: Gold rings; Hadīth no. 5164.Sunan Ibn MājahBook of ClothingChapter: Having something engraved on the ring; Hadīth no. 3639.

Book of Clothing

Chapter: Silver rings; Hadīth no. 5866.

Sahīh Muslim

Book of Dress and Adornment

Chapter: Throwing away the gold ring; Hadīth no. 2091.

Sunan Abu Dāwud

Book of Rings

Chapter: What is reported on having a (signet) ring; Hadīth no. 4218.

Jāmi' At-Tirmidhi

Book of Clothing as reported from the Messenger of Allah (PBUH)

Chapter: What is reported on wearing a ring on the right hand; Hadīth no. 1741.

Sunan An-Nasā'i

Book of Adornment

Chapter: Gold rings; Hadīth no. 5164.

Sunan Ibn Mājah

Book of Clothing

Chapter: Having something engraved on the ring; Hadīth no. 3639.

Chapter: The Prophet (PBUH) having a signet ring that he used in stamping the letters he sent to non-Arabs.

Anas ibn Mālik (may Allah be pleased with him) reported: "When the Prophet (may Allah's peace and blessings be upon him) wanted to write to the Romans, he was told that they would not read his letter unless it was stamped (with his name). So he had a signet ring made of silver with his name "Muhammad the Messenger of Allah" engraved on it. It is as if I am looking (now) at its brightness on his hand."

Sahīh Al-BukhāriBook of ClothingChapter: Using a signet ring for stamping something or signing the messages sent to the People of the Book or others; Hadīth no. 5875.Sahīh MuslimBook of Dress and AdornmentChapter: The Prophet (PBUH) having an engraved ring that he used in stamping the letters he sent to non-Arabs; Hadīth no. 2092.Sunan Abu DāwudBook of Rings.Chapter: What is reported on having a signet ring; Hadīth no. 4214.Jāmi' At-TirmidhiBook of Seeking Permission and Good Manners as reported from the Messenger of Allah (PBUH)Chapter: What is reported on stamping letters; Hadīth no. 2718.Sunan An-Nasā'iBook of AdornmentChapter: Description of the ring of the Prophet (PBUH); Hadīth no. 5201.Sunan Ibn MājahBook of ClothingChapter: Having something engraved on the ring; Hadīth no. 3640.

Book of Clothing

Chapter: Using a signet ring for stamping something or signing the messages sent to the People of the Book or others; Hadīth no. 5875.

Sahīh Muslim

Book of Dress and Adornment

Chapter: The Prophet (PBUH) having an engraved ring that he used in stamping the letters he sent to non-Arabs; Hadīth no. 2092.

Sunan Abu Dāwud

Book of Rings.

Chapter: What is reported on having a signet ring; Hadīth no. 4214.

Jāmi' At-Tirmidhi

Book of Seeking Permission and Good Manners as reported from the Messenger of Allah (PBUH)

Chapter: What is reported on stamping letters; Hadīth no. 2718.

Sunan An-Nasā'i

Book of Adornment

Chapter: Description of the ring of the Prophet (PBUH); Hadīth no. 5201.

Sunan Ibn Mājah

Book of Clothing

Chapter: Having something engraved on the ring; Hadīth no. 3640.

Chapter: Throwing away rings.

Anas ibn Mālik (may Allah be pleased with him) reported that he saw a silver ring in the hand of Allah's Messenger (may Allah's peace and blessings be upon him) for one day only. The people had silver rings made for themselves and wore them. Thereupon, the Messenger of Allah (may Allah's peace and blessings be upon him) threw away his ring, and so did the people.

Sahīh Al-BukhāriBook of ClothingChapter: Hadīth no. 5868.Sahīh MuslimBook of Dress and AdornmentChapter: Throwing away rings; Hadīth no. 2093.Sunan Abu DāwudChapter: Rings.Chapter: What is reported on giving up wearing a ring; Hadīth no. 4221.Jāmi' At-TirmidhiBook of Clothing as reported from the Messenger of Allah (PBUH)Chapter: What is reported on silver rings; Hadīth no. 1739.Sunan An-Nasā'iBook of AdornmentChapter: Throwing away the ring and giving up wearing it; Hadīth no. 5291.Sunan Ibn MājahBook of ClothingChapter: Having something engraved on the ring; Hadīth no. 3641.

Book of Clothing

Chapter: Hadīth no. 5868.

Sahīh Muslim

Book of Dress and Adornment

Chapter: Throwing away rings; Hadīth no. 2093.

Sunan Abu Dāwud

Chapter: Rings.

Chapter: What is reported on giving up wearing a ring; Hadīth no. 4221.

Jāmi' At-Tirmidhi

Book of Clothing as reported from the Messenger of Allah (PBUH)

Chapter: What is reported on silver rings; Hadīth no. 1739.

Sunan An-Nasā'i

Book of Adornment

Chapter: Throwing away the ring and giving up wearing it; Hadīth no. 5291.

Sunan Ibn Mājah

Book of Clothing

Chapter: Having something engraved on the ring; Hadīth no. 3641.

Chapter:: "Angels do not enter a house where there is a dog or an image."

Abu Talhah (may Allah be pleased with him) reported that the Prophet (may Allah's peace and blessings be upon him) said: "Angels do not enter a house where there is a dog or an image."

Sahīh Al-BukhāriBook of the Beginning of CreationChapter: If a fly falls into the drink of any of you, he should dip it (in the drink) then remove it, for in one of its wings there is a disease and in the other there is cure; Hadīth no. 3322.Sahīh MuslimBook of Dress and AdornmentChapter: "Angels do not enter a house where there is a dog or an image."; Hadīth no. 2106.Sunan Abu DāwudBook of ClothingChapter: Regarding images; Hadīth no. 4153.Jāmi' At-TirmidhiBook of Good Manners as reported from the Messenger of Allah (PBUH)Chapter: What is reported on: Angels do not enter a house where there is an image or a dog; Hadīth no. 2804.Sunan An-Nasā'iBook of Hunting and SlaughteringChapter: Angels refrain from entering a house where there is a dog; Hadīth no. 4282.Sunan Ibn MājahBook of ClothingChapter: Images in the house; Hadīth no. 3649.

Book of the Beginning of Creation

Chapter: If a fly falls into the drink of any of you, he should dip it (in the drink) then remove it, for in one of its wings there is a disease and in the other there is cure; Hadīth no. 3322.

Sahīh Muslim

Book of Dress and Adornment

Chapter: "Angels do not enter a house where there is a dog or an image."; Hadīth no. 2106.

Sunan Abu Dāwud

Book of Clothing

Chapter: Regarding images; Hadīth no. 4153.

Jāmi' At-Tirmidhi

Book of Good Manners as reported from the Messenger of Allah (PBUH)

Chapter: What is reported on: Angels do not enter a house where there is an image or a dog; Hadīth no. 2804.

Sunan An-Nasā'i

Book of Hunting and Slaughtering

Chapter: Angels refrain from entering a house where there is a dog; Hadīth no. 4282.

Sunan Ibn Mājah

Book of Clothing

Chapter: Images in the house; Hadīth no. 3649.

Chapter: Prohibition of the practice of a woman who lengthens hair artificially and the one who gets her hair lengthened, she who practices tattooing and the one who gets it done for herself, she who trims the eyebrows and the one who has her eyebrows trimmed, and the women who make spaces between their teeth and change thereby Allah's creation.

Ibn 'Umar (may Allah be pleased with him) said: "The Prophet (may Allah's peace and blessings be upon him) cursed the woman who lengthens hair artificially and the one who gets her hair lengthened, and the woman who practices tattooing and the one who gets it done for herself."

Sahīh Al-BukhāriBook of ClothingChapter: The woman who lengthens hair artificially; Hadīth no. 5940.Sahīh MuslimBook of Dress and AdornmentChapter: Prohibition of the practice of a woman who lengthens hair artificially and the one who gets her hair lengthened, she who practices tattooing and the one who gets it done for herself, she who trims the eyebrows and the one who has her eyebrows trimmed, and the women who make spaces between their teeth and change thereby Allah's creation; Hadīth no. 2124.Sunan Abu DāwudBook of Hair CombingChapter: Regarding lengthening the hair artificially; Hadīth no. 4168.Jāmi' At-TirmidhiBook of Clothing as reported from the Messenger of Allah (PBUH)Chapter: What is reported on lengthening the hair artificially; Hadīth no. 1759.Sunan An-Nasā'iBook of AdornmentChapter: The woman who lengthens hair artificially; Hadīth no. 5095.Sunan Ibn MājahBook of MarriageChapter: The woman who lengthens hair artificially and the woman who practices tattooing; Hadīth no. 1987.

Book of Clothing

Chapter: The woman who lengthens hair artificially; Hadīth no. 5940.

Sahīh Muslim

Book of Dress and Adornment

Chapter: Prohibition of the practice of a woman who lengthens hair artificially and the one who gets her hair lengthened, she who practices tattooing and the one who gets it done for herself, she who trims the eyebrows and the one who has her eyebrows trimmed, and the women who make spaces between their teeth and change thereby Allah's creation; Hadīth no. 2124.

Sunan Abu Dāwud

Book of Hair Combing

Chapter: Regarding lengthening the hair artificially; Hadīth no. 4168.

Jāmi' At-Tirmidhi

Book of Clothing as reported from the Messenger of Allah (PBUH)

Chapter: What is reported on lengthening the hair artificially; Hadīth no. 1759.

Sunan An-Nasā'i

Book of Adornment

Chapter: The woman who lengthens hair artificially; Hadīth no. 5095.

Sunan Ibn Mājah

Book of Marriage

Chapter: The woman who lengthens hair artificially and the woman who practices tattooing; Hadīth no. 1987.

'Abdullāh ibn Mas'ūd (may Allah be pleased with him) reported: "May Allah curse those women who practice tattooing and those who get themselves tattooed, and those women who remove the hair from their eyebrows, and those who make artificial spaces between their teeth in order to look more beautiful whereby they change Allah's creation." His words reached a woman from Bani Asad called Umm Ya'qūb who came (to 'Abdullah) and said: "I learned that you cursed such-and-such (women)?" He replied: "Why should I not curse those whom Allah's Messenger (may Allah's peace and blessings be upon him) had cursed and who are (cursed) in Allah's Book!" Umm Ya'qūb said: "I have read the whole Qur'an, but I did not find in it what you say." He said: "Verily, if you had read it, you would have found it. Did you not read: {And whatever the Messenger gives you take it, and whatever he forbids you, abstain from it}?" She replied: "Yes, I did." He said: "Verily, Allah's Messenger (may Allah's peace and blessings be upon him) forbade such things." She said: "But I see your wife doing these things?" He said: "Go and watch her." She went and watched her but could not see anything in support of her claim. Upon that, he said: "If my wife was as you thought, I would not keep her in my company."

Sahīh Al-BukhāriBook of the (Prophetic) Commentary on the QuranSurat Al-Hashr (The Gathering)Chapter: {And whatever the Messenger gives you take it, and whatever he forbids you, abstain from it}; Hadīth no. 4886.Sahīh MuslimBook of Dress and AdornmentChapter: Prohibition of the practice of a woman who lengthens hair artificially and the one who gets her hair lengthened, she who practices tattooing and the one who gets it done for herself, she who trims the eyebrows and the one who has her eyebrows trimmed, and the women who make spaces between their teeth and change thereby Allah's creation; Hadīth no. 2125.Sunan Abu DāwudBook of Hair CombingChapter: Regarding lengthening the hair artificially; Hadīth no. 4169.Jāmi' At-TirmidhiBook of Good Manners as reported from the Messenger of Allah (PBUH)Chapter: What is reported on a woman who lengthens hair artificially and the one who gets her hair lengthened, she who practices tattooing and the one who gets it done for herself; Hadīth no. 2782.Sunan An-Nasā'iBook of DivorceChapter: Making a thrice-divorced woman lawful for her ex-husband, and the strict warning against such practice; Hadīth no. 3416.Sunan Ibn MājahBook of MarriageChapter: The woman who lengthens hair artificially and the woman who practices tattooing; Hadīth no. 1989.

Book of the (Prophetic) Commentary on the Quran

Surat Al-Hashr (The Gathering)

Chapter: {And whatever the Messenger gives you take it, and whatever he forbids you, abstain from it}; Hadīth no. 4886.

Sahīh Muslim

Book of Dress and Adornment

Chapter: Prohibition of the practice of a woman who lengthens hair artificially and the one who gets her hair lengthened, she who practices tattooing and the one who gets it done for herself, she who trims the eyebrows and the one who has her eyebrows trimmed, and the women who make spaces between their teeth and change thereby Allah's creation; Hadīth no. 2125.

Sunan Abu Dāwud

Book of Hair Combing

Chapter: Regarding lengthening the hair artificially; Hadīth no. 4169.

Jāmi' At-Tirmidhi

Book of Good Manners as reported from the Messenger of Allah (PBUH)

Chapter: What is reported on a woman who lengthens hair artificially and the one who gets her hair lengthened, she who practices tattooing and the one who gets it done for herself; Hadīth no. 2782.

Sunan An-Nasā'i

Book of Divorce

Chapter: Making a thrice-divorced woman lawful for her ex-husband, and the strict warning against such practice; Hadīth no. 3416.

Sunan Ibn Mājah

Book of Marriage

Chapter: The woman who lengthens hair artificially and the woman who practices tattooing; Hadīth no. 1989.

Book of Salām (Greeting of Peace)

Chapter: Among the Muslim's rights over his fellow Muslim is returning his greeting of peace.

Abu Hurayrah (may Allah be pleased with him) reported that the Prophet (may Allah's peace and blessings be upon him) said: "A Muslim owes another Muslim five rights: returning the greeting of peace, visiting the sick, following the funerals, accepting the invitation, and responding to the sneezing person (saying to him: May Allah show you mercy)."

Sahīh Al-BukhāriBook of FuneralsChapter: The command to follow funerals; Hadīth no. 1240.Sahīh MuslimBook of Salām (Greeting of Peace)Chapter: Among the Muslim's rights over his fellow Muslim is returning his greeting of peace; Hadīth no. 2162.Sunan Abu DāwudBook of Good MannersChapter: Regarding sneezing; Hadīth no. 5030.Jāmi' At-TirmidhiBook of Good Manners as reported from the Messenger of Allah (PBUH)Chapter: What is reported on responding to one who sneezes; Hadīth no. 2737.Sunan An-Nasā'iBook of FuneralsChapter: Forbiddance of cursing the dead; Hadīth no. 1938.Sunan Ibn MājahBook of FuneralsChapter: What is reported on visiting the sick; Hadīth no. 1435.

Book of Funerals

Chapter: The command to follow funerals; Hadīth no. 1240.

Sahīh Muslim

Book of Salām (Greeting of Peace)

Chapter: Among the Muslim's rights over his fellow Muslim is returning his greeting of peace; Hadīth no. 2162.

Sunan Abu Dāwud

Book of Good Manners

Chapter: Regarding sneezing; Hadīth no. 5030.

Jāmi' At-Tirmidhi

Book of Good Manners as reported from the Messenger of Allah (PBUH)

Chapter: What is reported on responding to one who sneezes; Hadīth no. 2737.

Sunan An-Nasā'i

Book of Funerals

Chapter: Forbiddance of cursing the dead; Hadīth no. 1938.

Sunan Ibn Mājah

Book of Funerals

Chapter: What is reported on visiting the sick; Hadīth no. 1435.

Chapter: Tiyarah (drawing evil omen from birds) and good omens, and where ill fortune may lie.

'Abdullāh ibn 'Umar (may Allah be pleased with him) reported that Allah's Messenger (may Allah's peace and blessings be upon him) said: "There is neither 'Adwa (no contagious disease is conveyed to others without Allah's permission) nor Tiyarah (drawing bad omens from birds), and ill fortune may be found in three: a woman, a house, or a riding animal."

Sahīh Al-BukhāriBook of MedicineChapter: Tiyarah; Hadīth no. 5753.Sahīh MuslimBook of Greeting of PeaceChapter: Tiyarah (drawing evil omen from birds) and good omens, and where ill fortune may lie; Hadīth no. 2225.Sunan Abu DāwudBook of MedicineChapter: Regarding Tiyarah; Hadīth no. 3922.Jāmi' At-TirmidhiBook of Good Manners as reported from the Messenger of Allah (PBUH)Chapter: What is reported on ill fortune; Hadīth no. 2824.Sunan An-Nasā'iBook of HorsesChapter: Ill fortune drawn from horses; Hadīth no. 3569.Sunan Ibn MājahBook of MarriageChapter: Where do good fortune and ill fortune lie; Hadīth no. 1995.

Book of Medicine

Chapter: Tiyarah; Hadīth no. 5753.

Sahīh Muslim

Book of Greeting of Peace

Chapter: Tiyarah (drawing evil omen from birds) and good omens, and where ill fortune may lie; Hadīth no. 2225.

Sunan Abu Dāwud

Book of Medicine

Chapter: Regarding Tiyarah; Hadīth no. 3922.

Jāmi' At-Tirmidhi

Book of Good Manners as reported from the Messenger of Allah (PBUH)

Chapter: What is reported on ill fortune; Hadīth no. 2824.

Sunan An-Nasā'i

Book of Horses

Chapter: Ill fortune drawn from horses; Hadīth no. 3569.

Sunan Ibn Mājah

Book of Marriage

Chapter: Where do good fortune and ill fortune lie; Hadīth no. 1995.

Book of Merits

Chapter: The physical description of the Prophet (PBUH) and that he had the most handsome face among the people.

Al-Barā' ibn 'Āzib (may Allah be pleased with him) reported: "The Prophet (may Allah's peace and blessings be upon him) was of a medium stature, with shoulders wide apart. His hair reached down to his ear lobes. When I saw him wearing a red suit, I have never seen anything more beautiful than he was."

Sahīh Al-BukhāriBook of MeritsChapter: The physical description of the Prophet (PBUH); Hadīth no. 3551.Sahīh MuslimBook of MeritsChapter: The physical description of the Prophet (PBUH) and that he had the most handsome face among the people; Hadīth no. 2337.Sunan Abu DāwudBook of ClothingChapter: Regarding the concession in this regard; Hadīth no. 4072.Jāmi' At-TirmidhiBook of Clothing as reported from the Messenger of Allah (PBUH)Chapter: What is reported on the concession for men to wear red clothes; Hadīth no. 1724.Sunan An-Nasā'iBook of AdornmentChapter: Keeping one's hair uncut; Hadīth no. 5062.Sunan Ibn MājahBook of ClothingChapter: Men wearing red clothes; Hadīth no. 3599.

Book of Merits

Chapter: The physical description of the Prophet (PBUH); Hadīth no. 3551.

Sahīh Muslim

Book of Merits

Chapter: The physical description of the Prophet (PBUH) and that he had the most handsome face among the people; Hadīth no. 2337.

Sunan Abu Dāwud

Book of Clothing

Chapter: Regarding the concession in this regard; Hadīth no. 4072.

Jāmi' At-Tirmidhi

Book of Clothing as reported from the Messenger of Allah (PBUH)

Chapter: What is reported on the concession for men to wear red clothes; Hadīth no. 1724.

Sunan An-Nasā'i

Book of Adornment

Chapter: Keeping one's hair uncut; Hadīth no. 5062.

Sunan Ibn Mājah

Book of Clothing

Chapter: Men wearing red clothes; Hadīth no. 3599.

Chapter: The obligation to follow the way of the Prophet (PBUH)

'Abdullāh ibn az-Zubayr (may Allah be pleased with him) reported that a man from the Ansār disputed with Az-Zubayr about water streamlets in the lava plain which they used in irrigating the palm trees. The Ansāri man said: "Release the water and let it run." But Az-Zubayr refused. They raised their case to the Prophet (may Allah's peace and blessings be upon him) who said to Az-Zubayr: "Water your land, O Zubayr, then let the water run to your neighbour." The Ansāri man became angry and said: "O Messenger of Allah! It is because he is your cousin!" Thereupon, the face of the Messenger of Allah (may Allah's peace and blessings be upon him) changed in color and said: "Water your land, O Zubayr, then keep back the water till it returns to the embankment." Az-Zubayr said: "By Allah, I think the following verse was revealed about that incident: {But no, by your Lord! they can have no true faith until they make you judge of what is in dispute among them...}"

Sahīh Al-Bukhāri Book of Musāqāh Chapter: Dams on rivers; Hadīth no. 2359, 2360. Sahīh Muslim Book of Merits Chapter: The obligation to follow the way of the Prophet (PBUH); Hadīth no. 2357. Sunan Abu Dāwud Book of Legal Judgments Chapter: Judicial matters; Hadīth no. 3637. Jāmi' At-Tirmidhi Book of Rulings as reported from the Messenger of Allah (PBUH) Chapter: What is reported on the case of two men when the land of one of them is located in a place lower than the other with regard to water flow; Hadīth no. 1363. Sunan An-Nasā'i Book of the Code of Conduct of Judges Chapter: The judge inducing lenience; Hadīth no. 5416. Sunan Ibn Mājah Introduction of Ibn Mājah Chapter: Revering the Prophet's speech and the stern warning to those who oppose it; Hadīth no. 15.

Book of Musāqāh

Chapter: Dams on rivers; Hadīth no. 2359, 2360.

Sahīh Muslim

Book of Merits

Chapter: The obligation to follow the way of the Prophet (PBUH); Hadīth no. 2357.

Sunan Abu Dāwud

Book of Legal Judgments

Chapter: Judicial matters; Hadīth no. 3637.

Jāmi' At-Tirmidhi

Book of Rulings as reported from the Messenger of Allah (PBUH)

Chapter: What is reported on the case of two men when the land of one of them is located in a place lower than the other with regard to water flow; Hadīth no. 1363.

Sunan An-Nasā'i

Book of the Code of Conduct of Judges

Chapter: The judge inducing lenience; Hadīth no. 5416.

Sunan Ibn Mājah

Introduction of Ibn Mājah

Chapter: Revering the Prophet's speech and the stern warning to those who oppose it; Hadīth no. 15.

Book of the Virtues of the Companions

Chapter: Tthe virtue of 'Ā'ishah (may Allah be pleased with her).

'Ā'ishah (may Allah be pleased with her) reported that the Prophet (may Allah's peace and blessings be upon him) said to her: "O 'Ā'ishah, this is Jibrīl sending you the greeting of peace." She said: "May Allah's peace, mercy, and blessings be upon him. Indeed, you see what I do not see," referring to the Prophet (may Allah's peace and blessings be upon him).

Sahīh Al-Bukhāri Book of the Beginning of Creation Chapter: Mentioning the angels; Hadīth no. 3217. Sahīh Muslim Book of the Virtues of the Companions Chapter: The virtue of 'Ā'ishah (may Allah be pleased with her); Hadīth no. 2447. Sunan Abu Dāwud Book of Good Manners. Chapters on Salām (The Greeting of Peace) Chapter: A man saying: "So-and-so sends Salām to you"; Hadīth no. 5232. Jāmi' At-Tirmidhi Book of Virtues as reported from the Messenger of Allah (PBUH) Chapter: The virtue of 'Ā'ishah (may Allah be pleased with her); Hadīth no. 3881. Sunan An-Nasā'i Book of the Treatment of Women Chapter: A man loving some of his wives more than the others; Hadīth no. 3953. Sunan Ibn Mājah Book of Good Manners Chapter: Returning the greeting of peace; Hadīth no. 3696.

Book of the Beginning of Creation

Chapter: Mentioning the angels; Hadīth no. 3217.

Sahīh Muslim

Book of the Virtues of the Companions

Chapter: The virtue of 'Ā'ishah (may Allah be pleased with her); Hadīth no. 2447.

Sunan Abu Dāwud

Book of Good Manners. Chapters on Salām (The Greeting of Peace)

Chapter: A man saying: "So-and-so sends Salām to you"; Hadīth no. 5232.

Jāmi' At-Tirmidhī

Book of Virtues as reported from the Messenger of Allah (PBUH)

Chapter: The virtue of 'Ā'ishah (may Allah be pleased with her); Hadīth no. 3881.

Sunan An-Nasā'i

Book of the Treatment of Women

Chapter: A man loving some of his wives more than the others; Hadīth no. 3953.

Sunan Ibn Mājah

Book of Good Manners

Chapter: Returning the greeting of peace; Hadīth no. 3696.

Book of Dutifulness, Maintaining Ties, and Good Manners

Chapter: Dutifulness to the parents and that they are the most deserving of it.

'Abdullāh ibn 'Amr (may Allah be pleased with him) reported: "A man came to the Prophet (PBUH) and asked his permission to go strive in Allah's cause. The Prophet (PBUH) asked him: 'Are your parents alive?' He said: 'Yes.' So the Prophet (PBUH) said: 'Go strive in looking after them.'"

Sahīh Al-BukhāriBook of Jihād and Military ExpeditionsChapter: Performing Jihād with the parents' permission; Hadīth no. 3004.Sahīh MuslimBook of Dutifulness, Maintaining Ties, and Good MannersChapter: Dutifulness to the parents and that they are the most deserving of it; Hadīth no. 2549.Sunan Abu DāwudBook of JihādChapter: A man who goes to battle while his parents are not pleased with his action; Hadīth no. 2529.Jāmi' At-TirmidhiBook of Jihad as reported from the Messenger of Allah (PBUH)Chapter: The one who goes out for battle and leaves his parents; Hadīth no. 2529.Sunan An-Nasā'iBook of JihādChapter: Concession of not joining the battle for a man whose parents are alive; Hadīth no. 3103.Sunan Ibn MājahBook of JihādChapter: A man whose parents are alive and he joins a battle; Hadīth no. 2782.

Book of Jihād and Military Expeditions

Chapter: Performing Jihād with the parents' permission; Hadīth no. 3004.

Sahīh Muslim

Book of Dutifulness, Maintaining Ties, and Good Manners

Chapter: Dutifulness to the parents and that they are the most deserving of it; Hadīth no. 2549.

Sunan Abu Dāwud

Book of Jihād

Chapter: A man who goes to battle while his parents are not pleased with his action; Hadīth no. 2529.

Jāmi' At-Tirmidhī

Book of Jihād as reported from the Messenger of Allah (PBUH)

Chapter: The one who goes out for battle and leaves his parents; Hadīth no. 2529.

Sunan An-Nasā'ī

Book of Jihād

Chapter: Concession of not joining the battle for a man whose parents are alive; Hadīth no. 3103.

Sunan Ibn Mājah

Book of Jihād

Chapter: A man whose parents are alive and he joins a battle; Hadīth no. 2782.

Book of Dhikr, Invocation, Repentance, and Seeking Allah's forgiveness

Chapter: Dislike of wishing for death due to affliction.

Anas (may Allah be pleased with him) reported that the Messenger of Allah (may Allah's peace and blessings be upon him) said: "None of you should wish for death because of a calamity that has befallen him, and if he cannot but wish for death, then he should say, 'O Allah! Let me live as long as life is better for me, and cause me to die if death is better for me.'"

Sahīh Al-BukhāriBook of InvocationsChapter: Invoking Allah for life and for death; Hadīth no. 6351.Sahīh MuslimBook of Dhikr, Invocation, Repentance, and Seeking Allah's forgivenessChapter: Dislike of wishing for death due to affliction; Hadīth no. 2680.Sunan Abu DāwudBook of FuneralsChapter: Dislike of wishing for death; Hadīth no. 3108.Jāmi' At-TirmidhīBook of FuneralsChapter: What is reported on the forbiddance of wishing for death; Hadīth no. 971.Sunan An-Nasā'īBook of FuneralsChapter: Wishing for death; Hadīth no. 1820.Sunan Ibn MājahBook of AscetismChapter: Remembering death and preparing oneself for it; Hadīth no. 4265.

Book of Invocations

Chapter: Invoking Allah for life and for death; Hadīth no. 6351.

Sahīh Muslim

Book of Dhikr, Invocation, Repentance, and Seeking Allah's forgiveness

Chapter: Dislike of wishing for death due to affliction; Hadīth no. 2680.

Sunan Abu Dāwud

Book of Funerals

Chapter: Dislike of wishing for death; Hadīth no. 3108.

Jāmi' At-Tirmidhī

Book of Funerals

Chapter: What is reported on the forbiddance of wishing for death; Hadīth no. 971.

Sunan An-Nasā'i

Book of Funerals

Chapter: Wishing for death; Hadīth no. 1820.

Sunan Ibn Mājah

Book of Ascetism

Chapter: Remembering death and preparing oneself for it; Hadīth no. 4265.

Chapter: Seeking refuge with Allah from tribulations and otherwise.

'Ā'ishah (may Allah be pleased with her) reported that the Prophet (may Allah's peace and blessings be upon him) used to say: "O Allah, I seek refuge with You from laziness, senility, indebtness, and committing sins. O Allah, I seek refuge with You from the punishment of the Fire, the trial of the Fire, the trial of the grave, the punishment of the grave, the evil of the trial of richness, the evil of the trial of poverty, and the evil of the trial of the Anti-Christ. O Allah, wash me with the water of snow and hail, purify my heart from sins just as the white dress is purified from filth, and distance me from my sins just as You have distanced the East from the West."

Sahīh Al-BukhāriBook of InvocationsChapter: Seeking refuge with Allah from senility, from the trial of the worldly life, and from the trial of the Fire; Hadīth no. 6375.Sahīh MuslimBook of Dhikr, Invocation, Repentance, and Seeking Allah's forgivenessChapter: Seeking refuge with Allah from the evil of tribulations and otherwise; Hadīth no. 589.Sunan Abu DāwudBook of PrayerChapter: Regarding seeking refuge with Allah; Hadīth no. 1543.Jāmi' At-TirmidhiBook of InvocationsChapter: Hadīth no. 3495.Sunan An-Nasā'iBook of Seeking Refuge with AllahChapter: Seeking refuge with Allah from the evil of the trial of the grave; Hadīth no. 5466.Sunan Ibn MājahBook of InvocationsChapter: What the Messenger of Allah (PBUH) sought Allah's refuge from; Hadīth no. 3838.

Book of Invocations

Chapter: Seeking refuge with Allah from senility, from the trial of the worldly life, and from the trial of the Fire; Hadīth no. 6375.

Sahīh Muslim

Book of Dhikr, Invocation, Repentance, and Seeking Allah's forgiveness

Chapter: Seeking refuge with Allah from the evil of tribulations and otherwise; Hadīth no. 589.

Sunan Abu Dāwud

Book of Prayer

Chapter: Regarding seeking refuge with Allah; Hadīth no. 1543.

Jāmi' At-Tirmidhi

Book of Invocations

Chapter: Hadīth no. 3495.

Sunan An-Nasā'i

Book of Seeking Refuge with Allah

Chapter: Seeking refuge with Allah from the evil of the trial of the grave; Hadīth no. 5466.

Sunan Ibn Mājah

Book of Invocations

Chapter: What the Messenger of Allah (PBUH) sought Allah's refuge from; Hadīth no. 3838.

Book of Repentance

Chapter: Hadīth on the repentance of Ka'b ibn Mālik and his two companions.

'Abdur-Rahman ibn 'Abdullah ibn Ka'b ibn Mālik reported that (his father) 'Abdullah ibn Ka'b ibn Mālik, who was Ka'b's guide from among his sons when Ka'b turned blind, said: I heard Ka'b ibn Mālik relating his Hadīth in which he mentioned his story when he remained behind after the departure of the Messenger of Allah (PBUH) for the Battle of Tabūk. Ka'b said: "I did not miss any battle with the Messenger of Allah (PBUH) except the Battle of Tabūk. In fact, I did not take part in the Battle of Badr, but none who failed to take part in it was blamed, for Allah's Messenger (PBUH) had gone out to meet the caravans of the Quraysh. But Allah caused the Muslims to meet their enemy unexpectedly (without prior planning). I witnessed the night of the 'Aqabah pledge of allegiance with the Prophet (PBUH) when we jointly agreed to support Islam with all our efforts. It would not please me to have attended the Battle of Badr instead of the 'Aqabah pledge, although Badr is more notable than it among the people. As for my state at the time when I remained behind after the Messenger of Allah (PBUH) I had never been stronger nor wealthier than I was at the time when I remained behind in that battle. By Allah, I had never been in possession of two she-camels until the time of the battle. The Messenger of Allah (PBUH) used to conceal his intention to embark upon a battle by making reference to other battles, until that battle (Tabūk). The Messenger of Allah (PBUH) conducted that battle during a season of extreme heat, undertaking a lengthy journey through desert terrain. In addition, the enemy was great in number. Thus, the Prophet (PBUH) clarified the matter to the Muslims, in order that they would prepare themselves properly for the battle, and he informed them of the intended destination. The Messenger of Allah (PBUH) was accompanied by a considerable number of Muslims, whose names could not be recorded in a register." Ka'b continued: "Any individual who wished to remain behind would assume that his absence would pass unnoticed, unless it was revealed by Allah by means of divine revelation. The Messenger of Allah (PBUH) undertook that battle during a season wherein the fruit had ripened and the shade had become pleasant. The Messenger of Allah (PBUH) and the Muslims equipped themselves with the necessary provisions. I too went out in the morning in order to prepare myself; however, I returned without accomplishing anything and said to myself I am capable of it. In this manner, I continued to postpone my preparations until the departure of the Messenger of Allah (PBUH) and the Muslims with him while I had not prepared what I needed to join them. I said to myself I would prepare myself a day or two after his departure then catch up with them. Again, I did not accomplish anything until they hurried and departed. I intended to depart and catch up with them, and I wish I did, but I was not destined for it. I would go out amongst the people after the departure of the Messenger of Allah (PBUH) and it would make me sad to see no men around except one who was suspected of being a hypocrite, or a weak man whom Allah had excused from participation in battle. The Messenger of Allah (PBUH) did not mentioned me until he reached Tabūk. He was sitting amongst his people in Tabūk and asked: 'What happened to Ka'b ibn Mālik?' A man from the tribe of Bani Salimah responded: 'O Messenger of Allah, he was prevented by his preoccupation with his fine clothes and his self-admiration.' Mu'ādh ibn Jabal said: 'What an evil statement you have made! By Allah, O Messenger of Allah, we do not know about him save what is good.' The Messenger of Allah (PBUH) remained silent." Ka'b ibn Mālik continues: "When I learned that the Messenger of Allah (PBUH) had started his journey back from Tabūk, I was overwhelmed by distress, and thought, therefore, of inventing lies. I asked myself: With what can I avoid his anger tomorrow? I sought assistance from every individual of sound mind and judgment from my family. When it was mentioned that the arrival of the Messenger of Allah (PBUH) was imminent, the false excuses vanished from my mind. I knew that I could not pass safely from this situation by whatever lie I can come up with. I, therefore, resolved upon speaking the truth. The Messenger of Allah (PBUH) arrived the following morning. It was his practice when he returned from a journey that he would proceed towards the mosque and perform a two Rak'ah prayer therein and then sit amongst the people. After those matters had taken place, those who lagged behind approached him. They started to present their excuses and take oaths to that effect. There were some and eighty men in number. The Messenger of Allah (PBUH) accepted their apparent attitude and their pledge of allegiance, sought forgiveness for them, and he entrusted to Allah their secret affairs.

Thereafter, I approached him, and when I greeted him, he smiled like one who is angry. Then he said: 'Come forward.' I approached him walking until I was sitting before him. Then he said: 'What prevented you from accompanying us? Had you not purchased a riding animal?' I responded: 'Yes, I did. By Allah, if I were in the presence of any other man from amongst the inhabitants of this world, I am sure that I would avoid His wrath by presenting an excuse, for I have been granted the ability to speak in an eloquently persuasive manner. However, I am aware that if I utter a lie today in order to seek your pleasure, certainly Allah will cause you to become angry with me in the future. Alternatively, if I tell you the truth, thereby causing you to become angry, I may hope for a good consequence from Allah, Exalted and Glorified. No, By Allah I have no excuse to present. By Allah, I had never before been stronger nor wealthier than the time I failed to accompany you.' The Messenger of Allah (PBUH) said: 'As for this man, he has spoken the truth. So, stand up (and leave) until Allah gives a judgment concerning you.' I stood up, and a group of men from the tribe of Bani Salimah came along and followed me. They addressed me: 'By Allah! We have not known you to commit a misdeed before that. Verily you did wrong when you failed to find an excuse for yourself before the Messenger of Allah (PBUH) like the other absentees who excused themselves. It would have sufficed you against your sin that the Messenger of Allah would seek forgiveness for you.' They continued to reprimand me until I desired to return to the Messenger of Allah (PBUH) and speak contrary to what I had said to him before. Then I asked them: 'Is there any other individual in a similar position?' They responded: 'Yes, there are two men who uttered the same statement as you, and both received the same directive as you did. 'I asked: 'Who are these two men?' They answered: 'Murārah ibn ar-Rabī' and Hilāl ibn Umayyah al-Wāqifi.' They mentioned two virtuous men who had participated in the Battle of Badr and were good examples to be followed. After they had mentioned these two men, I remained steadfast upon my original statement. Thereafter, the Messenger of Allah (PBUH) prohibited Muslims from speaking to us - namely the three individuals from amongst the Muslims who failed to join him for the battle. So, the people avoided us and changed the way they treated us, until the land wherein I lived seemed strange; not one which I was familiar with. We remained in that state for fifty nights. As for my two companions, they committed themselves to their houses and stayed therein, weeping. However, I was the youngest and most enduring of the three, I would therefore leave my house to perform prayer with the Muslims. I would wander around the markets, yet no one would speak to me. I would approach the Messenger of Allah (PBUH) and offer the greeting of peace to him whilst he was sitting amidst his gathering after having performed the prayer. I would ask myself: Did his lips move with returning the greeting or not? Thereafter, I would perform the prayer close by him and look at him stealthily. When I was engaged with the prayer, he would turn towards me. However, when I looked in his direction, he would turn his face away from me. When this period of estrangement became too long, I set out to walk until I climbed over the wall of Abu Qatādah's garden. He was my cousin and the most beloved person to me. I offered the greeting of peace to him, and, by Allah, he did not return the greeting to me. Hence, I said: 'O Abu Qatādah: I adjure you by Allah, do you not know that I love Allah and His Messenger?' He remained silent. I appealed to him by Allah a second time, but he remained silent. Then in the third time he replied: 'Allah and His Messenger know best.' Thereupon, tears flowed from my eyes. I turned away and climbed over the wall." He continued: "While I was walking in the market of Madinah, I saw a Christian farmer from amongst the farmers of Sham (Greater Syria), who had traveled to Madinah to sell their produce. He said: 'Who shall direct me to Ka'b ibn Mālik?' The people pointed towards me, so he approached me and handed me a letter from the King of Ghassān. As I was a scribe, I could read the letter in which it was written: 'It has come to our knowledge that your companion has forsaken you. Verily, God has not rendered this world for you as a dwelling of disgrace and degradation, nor one of loss and destitution. So join us and we shall bestow upon you comfort and consolation.' Upon reading the letter I said to myself: This too is a trial. I went toward the oven and burnt it therein. When a period of forty out of fifty nights had passed, the messenger of the Messenger of Allah (PBUH) approached me and said: 'The Messenger of Allah (PBUH) commands you to stay away from your wife.' I said: 'Should I divorce her, or what should I do?' He responded: 'No, just stay away from her and do not approach her.' He issued a similar directive concerning my two companions. Hence, I said to my wife: 'Go to your parents and remain with them until Allah passes judgment on this matter.' The wife of Hilāl ibn Umayyah came to the Messenger of Allah (PBUH) and said: 'O Messenger of Allah, verily Hilāl ibn Umayyah is an old man who is incapable of taking care of himself, and he does not have a servant. Would you object if I serve him?' He replied: 'No, but he must not approach you.' She said: 'By Allah, he has no desire for any matter. By Allah, he has not ceased to weep from the day this matter started until this time now.' Some of my family members asked me: 'Why don't you seek permission from the Messenger of Allah (PBUH) concerning your wife, as he has granted permission for the wife of Hilāl ibn Umayyah to serve him?' I said: 'By Allah, I shall not seek permission from the Messenger of Allah (PBUH) concerning her. I do not know what the Messenger of Allah (PBUH) would say if I sought his permission in relation to her while I am still a young man.' I remained in that state for an additional ten nights, until fifty nights had passed from the time the Prophet (PBUH) had prohibited the people from speaking to us. On the morning of the fiftieth night, I performed Fajr prayer on the roof of one of our houses. While I was in the state that Allah described in His Book: feeling that my soul had become contracted, and the earth had contracted for me despite its vastness, all of a sudden, I heard a loud voice coming from the direction of Mount Sal'. Somebody shouted at the top of his voice: 'O Ka'b ibn Mālik, Rejoice!' I prostrated myself upon the ground, realizing that relief from this trial had finally arrived. The Messenger of Allah (PBUH) told the people that Allah accepted our repentance. After Fajr prayer, the people proceeded forth to congratulate us, and carriers of the good news rushed toward my two companions. A horseman raced towards me in order to congratulate me and a messenger from the tribe of Aslam raced towards the mountain and got over it in order to make the announcement. I heard his voice before that of the horseman. When the man whose voice I had heard approached me to convey the glad tidings, I took off my two garments and clothed him in them. By Allah, on that day I was not in possession of any other garments, so I borrowed two garments and put them on then I headed to the Messenger of Allah (PBUH). People started receiving me in groups, congratulating me for the acceptance of my repentance. They said: 'We congratulate you for Allah's acceptance of your repentance.' When I entered the mosque, the Messenger of Allah (PBUH) was sitting surrounded by people. Talhah ibn 'Ubaydillah hastened towards me. He shook my hand and congratulated me. By Allah, no one from amongst the Muhajirūn (Emigrants) stood in order to greet me save him. I never forgot that gesture from Talhah. When I greeted the Messenger of Allah (PBUH) his face was shining with happiness and he said: 'Rejoice for the best day you have witnessed since your mother gave birth to you.' I asked: 'Is this from you or from Allah?' He said: 'It is from Allah.' Whenever the Messenger of Allah (PBUH) was delighted, his face would become bright as if it were a piece of the moon. We recognized that as characteristic of him. When I sat before him, I said: 'O Messenger of Allah, part of my repentance is that I should give up my entire wealth as charity for the sake of Allah and His Messenger.' The Messenger of Allah (PBUH) said: 'Keep a portion of your wealth, for it is better for you to do so.' I said: 'I shall keep my share in Khaybar. O Messenger of Allah, verily Allah has delivered me from this trial because I spoke the truth. My repentance therefore dictates that I shall speak only the truth as long as I live.' By Allah, I am not aware of any Muslim whom Allah has blessed for speaking the truth more than myself, from the time I mentioned those words of truth to the Messenger of Allah (PBUH). By Allah, I have never intended to utter a word of falsehood from the time when I mentioned those words to the Messenger of Allah (PBUH) to the present day. I hope that Allah will protect me from uttering falsehood in the remaining part of my life. Allah revealed the following verse to His Messenger (PBUH): {Allah has forgiven the Prophet, the Muhajirūn, and the Ansar who followed him in the hour of difficulty after the hearts of a party of them had almost inclined [to doubt], and then He forgave them. Indeed, He was to them Kind and Merciful. And [He also forgave] the three who were left behind to the point that the earth became contracted on them despite its vastness and their souls confined them and they were certain that there is no refuge from Allah except in Him. Then He turned to them so they could repent. Indeed, Allah is the Accepting of repentance, the Merciful. O you who believe, fear Allah and be with those who are truthful.} [Surat At-Tawbah :117-119] By Allah, after guiding me to Islam, Allah has not bestowed upon me a favor greater in my sight than my statement of truth to the Messenger of Allah (PBUH) and my action of not uttering a lie to him, for I would have been ruined, as those who uttered lies were ruined. Allah ascribed to those who had uttered falsehood the most evil description he Had ever ascribed to anyone else when He revealed His statement: {They will swear by Allah to you when you return to them that you would leave them alone. So leave them alone; indeed they are evil; and their refuge is Hell as recompense for what they had been earning. They swear to you so that you might be satisfied with them. But if you should be satisfied with them - indeed, Allah is not satisfied with a defiantly disobedient people} [Surat At-Tawbah: 95-96] Ka'b continued: "We, the three who lagged behind, differed from those whose excuses were accepted by the Messenger of Allah (PBUH) when they swore to him to that effect. He accepted their pledge of allegiance and sought forgiveness for them and he deferred our case until Allah passed judgment in relation to it. In reference to that, Allah Almighty said: {He also forgave the three who remained behind ... } [Surat At-Tawbah:118] In this Verse, Allah did not refer to our remaining behind the military expedition. Rather, He refers to the deferment of passing judgment on us, in contrast to those who took an oath before the Messenger of Allah (PBUH) and excused themselves and he accepted their excuses."

Sahīh Al-Bukhāri Book of Military Expeditions Chapter: Hadīth of Ka'b ibn Mālik, and Allah's statement: {And the three who were left behind ...}; Hadīth no. 4418. Sahīh Muslim Book of Repentance Chapter: Hadīth on the repentance of Ka'b ibn Mālik and his two companions; Hadīth no. 2769. Sunan Abu Dāwud Book of Divorce Chapter: Statements that imply divorce, and intentions; Hadīth no. 2202. Jāmi' At-Tirmidhi Book of Interpretation of the Qur'an as reported from the Messenger of Allah (PBUH) Chapter: From Sūrat At-Tawbah; Hadīth no. 3102. Sunan An-Nasā'i Book of Divorce Chapter: A man saying to his wife: "Join your family."; Hadīth no. 3422. Sunan Ibn Mājah Book of Performance of Prayer and its Sunnah Chapter: What is reported on offering prayer and prostration for showing gratitude; Hadīth no. 1393.

Book of Military Expeditions

Chapter: Hadīth of Ka'b ibn Mālik, and Allah's statement: {And the three who were left behind ...}; Hadīth no. 4418.

Sahīh Muslim

Book of Repentance

Chapter: Hadīth on the repentance of Ka'b ibn Mālik and his two companions; Hadīth no. 2769.

Sunan Abu Dāwud

Book of Divorce

Chapter: Statements that imply divorce, and intentions; Hadīth no. 2202.

Jāmi' At-Tirmidhi

Book of Interpretation of the Qur'an as reported from the Messenger of Allah (PBUH)

Chapter: From Sūrat At-Tawbah; Hadīth no. 3102.

Sunan An-Nasā'i

Book of Divorce

Chapter: A man saying to his wife: "Join your family."; Hadīth no. 3422.

Sunan Ibn Mājah

Book of Performance of Prayer and its Sunnah

Chapter: What is reported on offering prayer and prostration for showing gratitude; Hadīth no. 1393.

Book of the Description of Paradise, Its Bliss, and Its People

Chapter: Showing the deceased his place in Paradise or Hell

and the affirmation of the punishment of the grave and seeking refuge with Allah from it.

Al-Barā' ibn 'Āzib (may Allah be pleased with him) reported that the Prophet (may Allah's peace and blessings be upon him) said: "When a believer is made to sit in his grave, the angels come to him and he testifies that none is truly worthy of worship but Allah and that Muhammad is Allah's Messenger.

This is what Allah refers to in His statement: {Allah will keep firm those who believe with the word that stands firm...}."

Saḥīḥ Al-BukhāriBook of the Prophetic Commentary on the Qur'an. Surat IbrāhīmChapter:: {Allah will keep firm those who believe with the word that stands firm...}; Hadīth no. 4699.Saḥīḥ MuslimBook of the Description of Paradise, Its Bliss, and Its PeopleChapter: Showing the deceased his place in Paradise or Hell and the affirmation of the punishment of the grave and seeking refuge with Allah from it; Hadīth no. 2871.Sunan Abu DāwudBook of SunnahChapter: Regarding the questioning in the grave and punishment in the grave; Hadīth no. 4750.Jāmi' At-TirmidhiBook of Interpretation of the Qur'an as reported from the Messenger of Allah (PBUH)Chapter: From Surat Ibrāhīm (peace be upon him); Hadīth no. 3120.Sunan An-Nasā'iBook of FuneralsChapter: Punishment of the grave; Hadīth no. 2056.Sunan Ibn MājahBook of AsceticismChapter: Mentioning the grave and decay of the body; Hadīth no. 4269.

Book of the Prophetic Commentary on the Qur'an. Surat Ibrāhīm

Chapter:: {Allah will keep firm those who believe with the word that stands firm...}; Hadīth no. 4699.

Saḥīḥ Muslim

Book of the Description of Paradise, Its Bliss, and Its People

Chapter: Showing the deceased his place in Paradise or Hell and the affirmation of the punishment of the grave and seeking refuge with Allah from it; Hadīth no. 2871.

Sunan Abu Dāwud

Book of Sunnah

Chapter: Regarding the questioning in the grave and punishment in the grave; Hadīth no. 4750.

Jāmi' At-Tirmidhi

Book of Interpretation of the Qur'an as reported from the Messenger of Allah (PBUH)

Chapter: From Surat Ibrāhīm (peace be upon him); Hadīth no. 3120.

Sunan An-Nasā'i

Book of Funerals

Chapter: Punishment of the grave; Hadīth no. 2056.

Sunan Ibn Mājah

Book of Asceticism

Chapter: Mentioning the grave and decay of the body; Hadīth no. 4269.

Book of Tribulations and Portents of the Hour

Chapter: The Hour will not come until a man passes by the grave of another

and wishes he were in his place due to affliction

Abu Hurayrah (may Allah be pleased with him) reported that the Messenger of Allah (may Allah's peace and blessings be upon him) said: "The Hour will not come until you fight the Turks, who have small eyes, red faces, and flat noses. Their faces look like hammered shields. And the Hour will not come until you fight people wearing shoes made of hair."

Saḥīḥ Al-BukhāriBook of Jihād and Military ExpeditionsChapter: Fighting the Turks; Hadīth no. 2928.Saḥīḥ MuslimBook of Tribulations and Portents of the HourChapter: The Hour will not come until a man passes by the grave of another and wishes he were in his place due to affliction; Hadīth no. 2912.Sunan Abu DāwudBook of Fierce BattlesChapter: Regarding fighting the Turks; Hadīth no. 4304.Jāmi' At-TirmidhiBook of Tribulations as reported from the Messenger of Allah (PBUH)Chapter: What is reported on fighting the Turks; Hadīth no. 2215.Sunan An-Nasā'iBook of JihādChapter: Conquering the Turks and Abyssinia; Hadīth no. 3177.Sunan Ibn MājahBook of TribulationsChapter: The Turks; Hadīth no. 4097.

Book of Jihād and Military Expeditions

Chapter: Fighting the Turks; Hadīth no. 2928.

Sahīh Muslim

Book of Tribulations and Portents of the Hour

Chapter: The Hour will not come until a man passes by the grave of another and wishes he were in his place due to affliction; Hadīth no. 2912.

Sunan Abu Dāwud

Book of Fierce Battles

Chapter: Regarding fighting the Turks; Hadīth no. 4304.

Jāmi' At-Tirmidhi

Book of Tribulations as reported from the Messenger of Allah (PBUH)

Chapter: What is reported on fighting the Turks; Hadīth no. 2215.

Sunan An-Nasā'i

Book of Jihād

Chapter: Conquering the Turks and Abyssinia; Hadīth no. 3177.

Sunan Ibn Mājah

Book of Tribulations

Chapter: The Turks; Hadīth no. 4097.

- Book of Faith 4
  - Chapter: The call to the two testimonies and Islamic teachings 4
  - Chapter: The branches of faith 5
  - Chapter: Clarifying that faith decreases by sin and that a sinner is deemed lacking in faith, meaning that his faith is incomplete 6
  - Chapter: Pointing out the strictness of the prohibition of letting the clothing hang below the ankles, reminding others of the favors one did to them, and promoting goods by swearing; and clarifying the three types of people whom Allah will not speak to on the Day of Judgment, nor will He look at them or purify them, and for them will be a painful punishment. 6
  - Chapter: The strict prohibition of killing oneself, and that whoever kills himself with something will be punished with it in Hell-fire, and that only Muslims will enter Paradise 6
- Book of Purification 8
  - Chapter: Ablution of the Prophet (PBUH) 8
  - Chapter: The tooth-stick 8
  - Chapter: The characteristics of Fitrah 8
  - Book: Cleaning after relieving oneself 8
  - Chapter: The prohibition of using the right hand in cleaning oneself after answering the call of nature 9
  - Chapter: Starting with the right side in ablution and other things 9
  - Chapter: Wiping over leather socks 10
  - Chapter: The ruling on dogs drinking from people's vessels 11
  - Chapter: The prohibition of urinating in still water 11
  - Chapter: The ruling on infant's urine and how to wash it 11
  - Chapter: The ruling on semen 11
  - Chapter: Impurity of blood and how to wash it 12
  - Chapter: Proof of the impurity of urine and the obligation to shield oneself from it 12
- Book of Menstruation 12
  - Chapter: Foreplay with a menstruating woman above the waist-wrapper. 12
  - Chapter: The recommended amount of water in ritual bath 13
  - and man and wife taking ritual bath together from the same vessel while in the same state and with one using water left by the other 13
  - Chapter: Menstruating woman may wash her husband's hair and comb it; her leftover water is pure; and he can recline in her lap and recite Qur'an therein 13
  - Chapter on pre-seminal fluid 13
  - Chapter: Ritually impure person may sleep and is recommended to make ablution and wash his private parts if he wants to eat, drink, sleep, or copulate 14
  - Chapter: Description of ritual bath 14
  - Chapter: Woman in Istihādah and her ritual bath and prayer 14

- Chapter: Woman in Istihādah is required to make up for missed fasting, but not missed prayer 15
- Chapter: A person taking a bath should screen himself with a cloth or the like 15
- Chapter: Abrogation of making ablution after eating something touched by fire 16
- Chapter: Hide of dead animals is rendered pure by tanning 16
- Chapter: Dry ablution 16
- Chapter: The proof that a Muslim does not become impure 17
- Chapter: What to say before entering the bathroom 17

Book of Prayer 17

- Chapter: The command to recite wording of Adhān twice and wording of Iqāmah once 17
- Chapter: The obligation of reciting Al-Fātihah in each Rak'ah, and if one cannot recite it properly or learn it, he may recite other verses that are easy for him; Hadīth no. 723. 18
- Chapter: Tashahhud in prayer 19
- Chapter: Invoking Allah's peace and blessings upon the Prophet after Tashahhud. 19
- Chapter: Saying "Allah hears whoever praises Him", "Praise be to You, our Lord", and "Amen". ... 20
- Chapter: Those led in prayer follow the Imām 20
- Chapter: The prohibition to get ahead of the Imām in Rukū', prostration, and the like 20
- Chapter: Straightening the rows and the merit of the first one and then the next and the next; competing over the first row; and letting virtuous people be in the front and close to the Imām. 21
- Chapter: Recitation in Fajr prayer 21
- Chapter: The recitation in 'Ishā' prayer 22
- Chapter: Being straight in prostration, placing the palms on the ground, lifting the elbows away from the sides, and keeping the abdomen away from the thighs in prostration. 22
- Chapter: The Sutrah (shield) of a praying person 23
- Chapter: Preventing one who passes in front of a praying person 23
- Chapter: Praying in one garment and how to wear it 24
- Chapter: The prohibition of talking during prayer and abrogation of the former permissibility 24
- Chapter: The dislike of wiping pebbles and leveling soil during prayer. 24
- Chapter: Forgetfulness during prayer and the prostration for it 25
- Chapter: He who catches up with one Rak'ah of a prayer has indeed caught up with that prayer ... 27
- Chapter: The times of the five prayers. 27
- Chapter: The desirability of offering Zhuhr prayer at its earliest time if there is no intense heat. ... 28
- Chapter: Stressing the sinfulness of missing 'Asr prayer. 28
- Chapter: Who is more worthy of being Imām 30
- Chapter: Making up for the missed prayer and the desirability of doing this promptly 30

Book of Prayer by Travelers and Shortening it 30

- Chapter: Prayer by Travelers and Shortening it 30

Chapter: The desirability of greeting the mosque by offering two Rak'ahs, the dislike of sitting before performing them, and the permissibility of this prayer at all times 31

Chapter: The permissibility of offering supererogatory prayers standing or sitting 32

and performing part of the Rak'ah standing and part of it sitting. 32

Chapter: The night prayer and the number of the Prophet's Rak'ahs in the night, ... 32

that Witr is one Rak'ah, and that one Rak'ah is a valid prayer. 32

Chapter: The night prayer offered in sets of two Rak'ahs 33

and Witr is one Rak'ah in the later part of the night. 33

Chapter: Encouragement of offering Ramadan night prayer known as Tarāwih. 33

Chapter: Supplication in the night prayer 33

Chapter: The merit of the Qur'an memorizer. 35

Chapter: The times during which prayer is forbidden. 35

Chapter: There is a prayer between every two Adhāns. 35

Chapter: The Fear Prayer. 35

Book of Friday 36

Chapter: Perfume and the tooth-stick on Fridays. 36

Chapter: Listening attentively during Friday sermon. 36

Chapter: Mention of the two sermons before prayer and the sitting between them. 37

Chapter: Giving a greeting while the Imām is delivering the sermon. 37

Book on the Prayer of the Two Eids 37

Chapter: Mention of the permissibility for women to go out in the two Eids 37

to the praying place and to attend the sermon, separately from men. 37

Book of the Prayer for Rain 38

Book of Eclipses 38

Chapter: Eclipse prayer. 38

Book of Funerals 38

Chapter: Patience over affliction at the first shock. 38

Chapter: The deceased suffers punishment due to his family weeping over him. 39

Chapter: Washing the dead. 39

Chapter: Shrouding the dead. 39

Chapter: Hastening the funeral 40

Chapter: The merit of joining the funeral prayer and procession. 40

Chapter: Making Takbīr over funeral (i.e. offering funeral prayer). 40

Chapter: Prayer at the grave. 40

Chapter: Standing for a funeral procession. 41

Chapter: Where the Imām stands in relation to the deceased during the funeral prayer. 41

Book of Zakah 41

Chapter: A Muslim is not required to pay Zakah on his slave or horse. 41

Chapter: Zakat al-Fitr on Muslims in the form of dates and barley. 42

Chapter: Reward of the honest storekeeper and the woman who gives charity from her husband's house, without being extravagant, and with his explicit or customary approval. 42

Book of Fasting 43

Chapter: Do not fast the day or two days before Ramadan. 43

Chapter: Validity of fasting of someone in a state of ritual impurity as dawn rises. 43

Chapter: Giving the option to fast or not to fast during travel. 43

Chapter: Making up for the missed days of Ramadan during Shaʻbān. 44

Chapter: The merit of fasting. 44

Chapter: Fasting of the Prophet (PBUH) outside Ramadan 44

and the desirability not to keep a month free from fasting. 44

Chapter: The prohibition of observing continuous fast, if the fasting person suffers harm because of it, ... 44

or neglects some duty because of it, or does not break the fast during Eids and the Days of Tashrīq 45

and showing the desirability of fasting on alternate days. 45

Book of Iʻtikāf (Retreat in Ramadhan) 45

Chapter: When should a person who wants to observe Iʻtikāf enter his place of Iʻtikāf. 45

Book of Hajj 45

Chapter: What is permissible and what is impermissible for a pilgrim for Hajj or ʻUmrah and pointing out the prohibition of using perfume by him. 46

Chapter: The Mīqāt (place where Muhrim assumes Ihrām) for Hajj and ʻUmrah. 46

Chapter: Talbiyah and its description and time. 46

Chapter: Assuming Ihrām from where the journey begins 47

Chapter: A Muhrim wearing perfume when entering Ihrām. 47

Chapter: Prohibition of hunting for a Muhrim. 47

Chapter: Permissibility of shaving a Muhrim's head if it has some ailment, the obligation of paying a ransom for shaving his head, and stating how much it is. 48

Chapter: Permissibility of cupping during Ihrām. 48

Chapter: What to do with a Muhrim who dies. 48

Chapter: Standing at ʻArafah and the verse: 49

{Then depart from the place from where the people depart}. 49

Chapter: Desirability of Ramal during Tawāf, ... 49

ʻUmrah, and the first Tawāf in Hajj. 49

Chapter: Permissibility of circumambulating around the Ka'bah on a camel or the like 49

and touching the Black Stone with a stick or the like for a rider. 49

Chapter: Clarifying that Sa'i between Safa and Marwah is a pillar necessary for the validity of Hajj. 50

Chapter: It is recommended that a pilgrim keeps making Talbiyah 50

until he begins throwing Jamrat al-'Aqabah on the Day of Nahr. 50

Chapter: Desirability of letting the weak among women and others to depart from Muzdalifah to Mina late at night ahead of the people to avoid the crowd, and the desirability for other than them to spend the night in Muzdalifah until they offer the Fajr prayer there. 51

Chapter: Stoning Jamrat Al-'Aqabah from the bottom of the valley 52

with Makkah being to the left of the pilgrim and reciting Takbīr while throwing each pebble. 52

Chapter: Desirability of sending sacrificial animals to the holy precincts in Makkah if one does not intend to go himself, and the desirability of garlanding them and plaiting the garlands, and that the one who sends the sacrificial animals is not considered in a state of Ihrām thereby, and nothing becomes prohibited for him. 52

Chapter: Obligation of the Farewell Tawāf and exempting women in a state of menstruation from it. 53

Chapter: Desirability of entering the Ka'bah for pilgrims and others, ... 54

praying therein, and offering supplications in all its sides. 54

Chapter: Demolishing the Ka'bah and rebuilding it. 55

Chapter: Performing Hajj on behalf of someone who is incapable of doing it because of chronic illness, ... 56

old age, or death. 56

Chapter: Permissibility of staying in Makkah for those who emigrated from it 57

for no more than three days after Hajj and 'Umrah are over. 57

Chapter: The sanctity of Makkah and the sanctity of its game, grasses, trees 58

and lost property, except for the one who announces it, is forever. 58

Chapter: Permissibility of entering Makkah without Ihrām. 59

Chapter: Merit of Madinah and the invocation of the Prophet (PBUH) that Allah bless it, stating its sanctity and the inviolability of its game and trees, and marking the borders of its sanctuary. 60

Book of Marriage 61

Chapter: Desirability of marriage for whoever longs for it and can afford it, and the desirability of fasting for whoever cannot afford it. 61

Chapter: Prohibition of taking a woman 62

and her paternal or maternal aunt as co-wives. 62

Chapter: Prohibition of getting married and dislike of proposing marriage for Muhrim (one in state of Ihrām). 63

Chapter: Prohibition of proposing to a woman whom 64

a fellow Muslim has proposed to until the latter gives permission or withdraws his proposal. 64

Chapter: Prohibition of Shighār marriage and its invalidity. 64

Chapter: Fulfilling the conditions in marriage. 65

Chapter: Seeking the permission of a previously-married woman for marriage 66

by her verbal consent and that of a virgin by her remaining silent. 66

Chapter: Dowry and the permissibility of it being in the form of teaching the Qur'an or a ring 67

made of iron or other things whether much or little, and the desirability 67

of it being five hundred dirhams if not causing harm to the suitor. 67

Chapter: Merit of freeing one's slave-girl then marrying her. 69

Chapter: A woman divorced thrice is not lawful for her ex-husband in marriage until she marries .. 70

another man who has sexual intercourse with her, then he leaves her (by divorce or death) and her waiting period is over. 70

Chapter: Ruling on coitus interruptus. 71

Book of Breastfeeding 72

Chapter: Unlawfulness of marriage due to kinship by birth is same in case of milk kinship. 72

Chapter: Unlawfulness to marry milk siblings is related to Mā' al-Fahl (wet nurse husband's semen). 73

Chapter: Detecting lineage of an infant from physical features. 74

Chapter: Desirability of marrying a virgin. 75

Book of Divorce 76

Chapter: Prohibition of divorcing a woman during her menses against her will and that 76

the divorce in this case is effective, and the husband is commanded to take her back. 76

Chapter: Obligation of paying expiation on one who said his wife is unlawful for him without intending divorce thereby. 77

Chapter: Clarifying that giving the choice to one's wife 78

is not considered divorce unless he intends it. 78

Chapter: Obligation of mourning during the post-death waiting period and its prohibition beyond that except for the period of three days. 79

Book of Li'ān (Oaths of Condemnation) 80

Book of Manumission of Slaves 82

Chapter: Walā' (Allegiance) is for the one who manumits. 82

Chapter: Forbiddance of selling Walā' or giving it as a gift. 83

Book of Sales 84

Chapter: Prohibition of selling Habal al-Habalah (the offspring of the offspring of a pregnant animal). 84

Chapter: Prohibition of making an offer in a sale of a fellow Muslim that is in progress, and of haggling 85

to compete with a fellow Muslim's haggling, and the prohibition of Najsh and leaving the animals unmilked (for sometime for the purpose of accumulation of milk to deceive the buyer). 85

Chapter: Invalidity of selling an item before it being in the seller's possession. 86

Chapter: Affirming that both parties of a sale transaction have the option (to rescind it) before they part company. 87

Chapter: Forbiddance of selling fruits before they are evidently 88

in a good state without the condition of them being cut. 88

Chapter: Prohibition of selling fresh dates in exchange for dry dates except in the case of 'Arāya. 89

Chapter: The one who sells date-palms bearing fruits. 90

Chapter: Forbiddance of Muhāqalah, Muzābanah, Mukhābarah, selling fruits before they are evidently in a good state, and Mu'āwamah sale which means to sell for many years ahead. 91

Chapter: Land lending. 92

Book of Musāqāh (Irrigation of land for a specific return) 93

Chapter: Musāqāh and contracting to utilize the land in return for a share of the fruits and crops... 93

Chapter: Whoever finds an item he sold with the buyer 94

who went bankrupt is entitled to rescind the sale. 94

Chapter: Prohibition of procrastination in paying off debts by a rich man and the validity of Hawālah (transference of debts) 95

and the desirability of accepting it if the debts are transferred to a rich man. 95

Chapter: Prohibition of a dog's price, the fees given to a soothsayer, and the earnings of a prostitute, and the forbiddance of selling a cat. 96

Chapter: The command to kill dogs and its abrogation and the prohibition of keeping them except for the purposes of hunting or guarding land or cattle and the like. 96

Chapter: Prohibition of selling alcohol, dead animals, swine and idols. 97

Chapter: Doing what is lawful and refraining from what is doubtful. 98

Chapter: Selling a camel and stipulating riding it. 99

Chapter: Salam sale (a sale in which a price is paid for goods to be delivered later). 100

Chapter: Pre-emption. 101

Book of the Law of Inheritance 101

Chapter: Inheritance of one who leaves behind neither ascendants nor descendants as heirs. 102

Chapter : Whoever leaves behind a property, then it is for his heirs. 102

Book of Gifts 103

Chapter: The dislike for a person to buy 103

what he has given as charity from the one to whom he gave it. 103

Chapter: Prohibition of taking back the charity and gift 104

after they have been received, except what one gives to his children down to all levels. 104

Chapter: Dislike of favoring some children over the others in gifts. 105

Chapter: 'Umra (gift without condition, where property is transferred to beneficiary following death of donor). 106

Book of Wills and Testaments ... 107

- Chapter: Making a will for one third (of the estate). ... 107
- Chapter: Waqf (endowment). ... 108

Book of Vows ... 109

- Chapter: The command to fulfill vows. ... 109
- Chapter: The forbiddance of making a vow and that it repels nothing. ... 110

Book of Oaths ... 111

- Chapter: Forbiddance to swear by other than Allah Almighty. ... 111
- Chapter: The one who swears by Al-Lāt. ... 112
- and Al-'Uzza should say: La ilāha illa-Allah (There is no true god except Allah). ... 112
- Chapter: It is recommended for one who takes an oath (to do something) then finds another ... 113 choice to be better, to go for the better choice and expiate his (first) oath. ... 113
- Chapter: The vow of a disbeliever and what he should do regarding it if he embraces Islam. ... 114
- Chapter: Permissibility of selling a Mudabbar (a slave who is promised to be manumitted after his master's death). ... 114

Book of Qasāmah (Compurgation), Muhāribīn (Rebels), Qasās (Retribution), and Diyyah (blood money) ... 115

- Chapter: Qasāmah ... 115
- Chapter: Ruling concerning Rebels and Apostates. ... 116
- Chapter: Confirmation of retribution in the case of killing with a stone or other sharp or heavy objects, and killing a man in retaliation for a woman. ... 117
- Chapter: What makes killing a Muslim lawful. ... 118
- Chapter: Blood money of a fetus, the obligation to pay blood money in case of manslaughter ... 119 and semi-intentional murder is on the perpetrator's male relatives. ... 119

Book of Prescribed Punishments ... 121

- Chapter: Prescribed punishment for theft and the amount that makes it due. ... 121
- Chapter: Amputating the hand of a thief of noble descent or otherwise ... 122 and forbiddance of interceding to waive a prescribed punishment. ... 122
- Chapter: The one who admits committing Zina (unlawful sexual intercourse) ... 123
- Chapter: No compensation is due for an injury caused by an animal, mine, or well. ... 124

Book of Legal Judgments ... 125

- Chapter: The oath is due on the defendant. ... 125
- Chapter: Issuing a judgment based on what is apparent and the plaintiff's eloquent presentation of his case. ... 126
- Chapter: Dislike of issuing verdict by judge when he is angry. ... 127

Book of Rulership ... 128

Chapter: Obligation to obey rulers in whatever does not involve sin, and prohibition to obey them in whatever involves sin. 128

Chapter: Pledging after the Conquest of Makkah to adhere to Islam, engage in Jihād, and do good; and explaining the meaning of: No Hijrah (emigration) is due after the Conquest. 129

Chapter: Defining the age of puberty. 130

Chapter: Horse racing and making them lean (for that purpose). 131

Chapter: Merit of Jihād and Ribāt. 131

Chapter: Merit of supplying the one who fights in the cause of Allah with a riding mount or anything else and taking good care of his family in his absence. 132

Chapter: The one who fights so that Allah's word be superior, then his fight is in the cause of Allah. 133

Chapter: The statement of Allah's Messenger (PBUH): "Indeed, deeds are judged based on the intention" and that fighting in Allah's cause and other deeds are included in it. 134

Chapter: Merit of military campaigning by sea. 135

Book of Hunting and Slaughtering, and Animals that are Lawful to Eat 136

Chapter: Hunting by trained hounds. 136

Chapter: The prohibition of eating beasts of prey with fangs and birds with talons. 138

Chapter: The permissibility of eating dead animals of the sea. 139

Chapter: Regarding eating horse meat. 139

Chapter: The permissibility of eating rabbits. 140

Book of Udhiyahs (Sacrifices) 141

Chapter: It is recommended to offer Udhiyah, and slaughter it directly without delegation, and it is recommended to mention Allah's name on it and recite Takbīr 141

Chapter: The permissibility of slaughtering by any tool that causes blood to flow except for a tooth, nail, and all other bones. 142

Book of Fara' and 'Atīrah (Sacrificial animals dedicated to idols) 143

Book of Drinks 144

Chapter: The dislike of soaking dates and raisins together. 144

Chapter: Stating that every intoxicant is an alcoholic drink and every alcoholic drink is unlawful. . 144

Book of Dress and Adornment 146

Chapter: The prohibition of using utensils made of gold and silver for both men and woman, the prohibition of wearing a gold ring or silk clothes for men and their permissibility for women, and the permissibility for a man to wear clothes that have silk strips as long as they do not exceed the width of four fingers. 146

Chapter: Permissibility of wearing silk for a man 148

who suffers itchy skin or the like. 148

Chapter: Prohibition of dragging one's garment out of pride and stating the extent to which it is allowed to reach down, and what is recommended in this regard. 149

Chapter: Throwing away the gold ring. 149

Chapter: The Prophet (PBUH) having a signet ring that he used in stamping the letters he sent to non-Arabs. 150

Chapter: Throwing away rings. 151

Chapter:: "Angels do not enter a house where there is a dog or an image." 152

Chapter: Prohibition of the practice of a woman who lengthens hair artificially and the one who gets her hair lengthened, she who practices tattooing and the one who gets it done for herself, she who trims the eyebrows and the one who has her eyebrows trimmed, and the women who make spaces between their teeth and change thereby Allah's creation. 153

Book of Salām (Greeting of Peace) 155

Chapter: Among the Muslim's rights over his fellow Muslim is returning his greeting of peace. 155

Chapter: Tiyarah (drawing evil omen from birds) and good omens, and where ill fortune may lie. 156

Book of Merits 156

Chapter: The physical description of the Prophet (PBUH) and that he had the most handsome face among the people. 156

Chapter: The obligation to follow the way of the Prophet (PBUH) 157

Book of the Virtues of the Companions 158

Chapter: Tthe virtue of 'Ā'ishah (may Allah be pleased with her). 158

Book of Dutifulness, Maintaining Ties, and Good Manners 159

Chapter: Dutifulness to the parents and that they are the most deserving of it. 159

Book of Dhikr, Invocation, Repentance, and Seeking Allah's forgiveness 160

Chapter: Dislike of wishing for death due to affliction. 160

Chapter: Seeking refuge with Allah from tribulations and otherwise. 161

Book of Repentance 162

Chapter: Hadīth on the repentance of Ka'b ibn Mālik and his two companions. 162

Book of the Description of Paradise, Its Bliss, and Its People 165

Chapter: Showing the deceased his place in Paradise or Hell 165

and the affirmation of the punishment of the grave and seeking refuge with Allah from it. 165

Book of Tribulations and Portents of the Hour 166

Chapter: The Hour will not come until a man passes by the grave of another 166

and wishes he were in his place due to affliction 166

www.ingramcontent.com/pod-product-compliance
Lightning Source LLC
LaVergne TN
LVHW021047100526
838202LV00079B/4736